ANDREA ROBINSON'S

2010 WINE BUYING GUIDE

THE 1000 WINES THAT MATTER

for Everyone

WINE CAN BE COMPLICATED.

WINE GLASSES DON'T HAVE TO BE.

THE ONE

by Andrea Robinson

THE PERFECT SHAPE

—

DISHWASHER SAFE

—

BREAK RESISTANT

—

SIMPLIFIES WINE SERVING

Stemware doesn't have to be complicated to be good.

After more than two years testing the best glass designs and prototypes with every grape, style, age and quality level of wines, Master Sommelier Andrea Robinson has developed *The One,* just one glass for all reds and one for all whites. These are the only glasses you will ever need to optimize the aroma and taste of any wine—even when compared to varietal specific stems.

For videos and more information on *The One* please visit **www.andreawine.com.**

ANDREA ROBINSON'S

2010 WINE BUYING GUIDE

THE 1000 WINES THAT MATTER

for Everyone

Andrea Robinson

JGR Productions, LLC

PUBLISHED BY JGR PRODUCTIONS, LLC

www.Andreawine.com

First edition published 2002

Previously published in the United States by Broadway Books, an imprint of The Doubleday Broadway Publishing Group, a division of Random House, Inc., New York

The Library of Congress has cataloged the first edition as follows:
Immer, Andrea
[Wine buying guide for everyone]
Andrea Immer's wine buying guide for everyone /
Andrea Immer; edited by Anthony Giglio.—1st ed.
p. cm.
Includes index.
1. Wine and wine making. I. Title: Wine buying guide
for everyone. II. Giglio, Anthony. III. Title.

   TP548 .I4624 2002
   641.2'2—dc21   2002023077

ISBN-13: 978-0-9771032-5-6
ISBN-10: 0-9771032-5-0

PRINTED IN THE UNITED STATES OF AMERICA

10 9 8 7 6 5 4 3 2 1

CONTENTS

ANDREA ROBINSON'S

2010 WINE BUYING GUIDE

THE 1000 WINES THAT MATTER

for Everyone

INTRODUCTION

Although enjoying a good glass of wine is easy, all the types and confusing labels can make *shopping* for a bottle pretty hard. For the typical wine consumer, critics' scores and elaborate tasting reports of rare and exclusive bottlings aren't much help. That is why I wrote *Andrea Robinson's Wine Buying Guide for Everyone*. It is your road map to the real world of wine buying. Here is what you'll find inside.

The 1000 Wines that Matter

This guide showcases the 1000 wines that are, in my view, the most relevant and worthy for any real-world wine lover. These wines fall into three main categories:

Broadly Available, Benchmarks, & Emerging Labels

My thumbnail reviews showcase more than 800 of the most popular and available wines on the market. That includes everything from the very best of the supermarket stalwarts to selected high-end boutique brands found mostly in restaurants and upscale wine shops. In choosing what brands to include, I focus above all on **taste**, with a heavy bias toward **quality for the price**, and **track record** (quality consistency). Why? There are literally thousands of wines on the market; and even the 100 or so labels in a warehouse store, or the 30 bottles on a casual restaurant wine list, can seem overwhelming. By culling it down to the wines that really deliver on these criteria - the benchmarks of wine - this guide greatly simplifies the task of finding a great bottle without overpaying.

I also spotlight an exciting array of "new kids on the block" that show real promise. The constant emergence of new talent, whether in music, sports, or wine, is part of the fun. As much as sommeliers love to praise the prowess of the longtime leaders in wine quality, we also love to turn our guests (and readers) on to new discoveries. This book includes those I've found in the last year or so that are really worth seeking out.

> THE WINE STRATOSPHERE: Some of the world's benchmark wines occupy such an elite tier of rarity and price that only high-rollers and big-time collectors can afford them. Even professional sommeliers like me only encounter these labels in the context of getting to serve them in the finest restaurants, or at special tastings hosted by a collector or the winery itself. They still "matter" to you and me in the sense that they represent the ultimate example of their style, grape, or region. They are the Picassos, the Gretzkys, the Pavarottis of their genre, inspiring universal admiration and, often, imitation. At the back of the book I've included a "bucket list" of the unassailable "great ones" to get you started stocking the dream cellar. (On that note, if after winning the lottery or solving the clean energy conundrum, you decide to sink your fortune into great wines, here's one sommelier who's available to help ensure they are served and paired to perfection!)

Price, Personal Preference & Quality

As you use this book to try new wines, keep in mind three things:

It doesn't have to be expensive to be good. I've preached this mantra for a long time, and I think the average wine consumer has now bought in to the idea. While it is true that you can pay more and get a better wine, it is also true that a higher price doesn't guarantee the wine will be better, or that *you* will like it more. Obviously, pricey wines should really deliver, but I also hold value wines to a high standard. They are the intro to wine for most people, and you know what they say about first impressions!

Personal preference counts as much as quality. If you like a wine, then by definition it "matters." So don't fret if your favorite wine is not included in this guide. All that means is that in my judgment, the wine's availability isn't sufficiently broad or, I have found other wines in the same category to perform better on my three dimensions (taste, price/quality and consistent track record). Since the wine market changes constantly, my hope is that the winners in my extensive tastings will bring you new options to supplement your own "short list" of favorites.

Quality comes from the vineyard. As any pro will tell you, it takes great grapes to make great wine, and where each type of grape is planted (soil, sun, slope, etc.) is critical to its ultimate quality potential. In other words, Chardonnay in an average vineyard site will taste like average white wine, while Chardonnay in an ideally-suited site can taste sublime, achieving the highest expression of true "Chardonnay-ness." As such, the best vineyards command top prices for their grape crops, and that drives up the price of the wines made from them. That is the connection between quality and price.

In conclusion: The Wines That Matter, for the purposes of this book, are those that offer the best expression of quality and character in their price and style category. Whether it is a $8 Aussie Chardonnay for everyday drinking, or a splurge Cabernet to tuck away in honor of your child's birth, you deserve no less.

My Scores and Reviews

Each wine entry includes my tasting notes and score for the wine. In addition, if I have discovered a great-tasting dish or cheese to pair with the wine, I share it.

I keep the rating criteria simple, with taste scores listed on a 100-point scale, a well-established industry standard. Here is how the scores are defined:

0–69 Poor (not included)
70-79 Fair (not included)
80-86 **Very good** - A good-quality, well-made wine that is pleasant to drink
87-94 **Excellent** - A wine that is delicious to drink, and is exemplary in its category and the world of wine
95-100 **Amazing** - A wine that rocks your world and seizes your senses with its utterly exciting complexity and expressiveness.

Note that for this buying guide, I only include wines rated as top quality (80 points or higher). With limited space in this book and time on your hands, I prefer to use it telling you what you *should* buy, rather than what to avoid.

Andrea's Favorites

I give my personal favorite wines a medal, and you will notice that my medals aren't simply next to all of the top-scoring wines. Rather, medals go to wines whose *style* I particularly love. The same type of wine or grape can vary, based on the winemaking technique, vineyard source, etc. in the same way that barbecue can vary from one pitmaster to the next, or fried chicken from one mom to the next. If as you try the recommended wines in this book you notice that your palate preferences and mine are on the same wavelength, targeting the wines with medals is likely to give you extra bang for the buck. On that note...

Match Your Palate

You know your taste, and it may not always synch with that of the uber-critics. It happens to me all the time. The "experts" often disagree because our individual palates are different. A wine that you love might not get a high rating from an expert and, if that's the case, you are certainly not "wrong." In fact, you just may be lucky because often wines that get the super-scores are more expensive, and harder to find. See How the Guide is Organized for a key to the different "palate profile" categories that can help dial in your selection according to your taste and the buying occasion.

Kitchen Survivor™ Grades

"How long will a wine keep after it's opened?" Having heard this question more than any other from my restaurant customers and wine students, I decided several years ago that it was time to find out, so I started putting wines to the "kitchen survivor test." The resulting report card should help you make the most of the leftovers, by simply recorking and storing them in the fridge or on the counter, for enjoying later. Refer to How the Guide is Organized for a breakdown of how the grading works.

Your Notes

There's space in each listing for your notes so you can keep track of the wines you try, and you can also enter your ratings and reviews at my Web site, Andreawine. com. Set up a free profile, and then you can search by wine name, and add your review.

Other Helpful Buying Tools In the Guide

Throughout the *Guide,* I've included simple tools to address just about every major wine buying question I've ever been asked. They are:

Top Ten Lists—A quick reference to the best wines in each grape or style category (filtered by price: $50 and under "For Everyone," and budget - $15 and under).

Food & Wine Pairing Basics—The core techniques sommeliers use to expertly match wine and food.

Andrea's Best Bets—These are my top, quick-reference recommendations for every common wine occasion and buying dilemma, from Thanksgiving wines to restaurant wine list best bets, party-crowd pleasers, blue chip bottles to impress the client, and more.

Affordable Agers—My short-list of wines that will age well for ten years or longer in your cellar, while not costing an arm and a leg. Cheers to that!

Entertaining with Wine—Everyone loves a wine party, and serving the right wine can make even a casual gathering memorable. These are my tips on choosing, buying the right amount, serving and highlighting wine when you're having company.

Wine List Decoder—This handy cross-reference chart will help you crack the code of different wine list terms, so you can quickly and easily find the styles you like.

Andrea's Complete Wine Course "Mini-Course"— Mini-lessons covering wine styles, label terms, glassware, buying wine in stores and restaurants, and other housekeeping details to simplify buying and serving wine, so you can focus on enjoying it.

I had been in the restaurant wine business for more than a decade before I wrote my first book, *Great Wine Made Simple*. Having studied like crazy to pass the Master Sommelier exam (the hardest wine test you can imagine), I knew there were lots of great books out there. So why another? Because as I worked training waiters and budding sommeliers, I began to see that in practice those books weren't much help. Wine, like food, golf, the saxophone, and so many other sensory pursuits, is something you learn not by studying but by doing. So my books and my *Complete Wine Course* DVD teach wine not through memorization but the way I learned it—through tasting. It works, and it's fun, whether you are just a dabbler or a committed wine geek.

Similarly, I intend this guide to fill a gap. Most people around the country buy wine based on price and convenience. And whether it's people taking my wine classes, viewers of my TV shows, or visitors to my Web site, www.andreawine.com, they all have the same questions: What are the good, inexpensive wines? And if I'm going to splurge, which wines are really worth it? This is the only buying guide that answers those questions realistically, by featuring the best wines in the broad marketplace, along with plenty of shrewd pro advice to help you make the most of every wine purchase.

What's New in This Year's Guide

Up-to-date prices - For this *Guide* I have reviewed the most recent vintage available as of the book's publication date, and included the national average suggested retail prices for each wine. Although prices for the same wine vary widely by market (due to differences in local taxes and retailer discount practices), the national average retail price will give you some idea of what to expect when you are shopping.

Up-to-date vintages - This guide focuses heavily on top-selling wines in the market, and so, for the most part, the year available in stores and restaurants will be the vintage covered in the guide. But if you find a different vintage, don't worry. Part of the quality promise of the wineries included in the *Guide* is that they have good consistency from one year to the next. That said, prices can vary based on vintage, and there are certain wine categories for which vintage is a bigger consideration. If you find a different vintage from the one listed, here is a guideline:

White wines and reds under $20 - 1 year older or younger than the vintage in the *Guide* is a safe buy.

Reds over $20 - 2 years older or 1 year younger than the year in the *Guide* is safe to buy, but the price may differ if the vintage quality differed from the year reviewed.

Champagne/sparkling - most are non-vintage; for vintage-dated bottlings, the wine can be up to 5 years older or 1 year younger than the year in the *Guide*.

My Best Wine Advice "For Everyone" - After years of including in this guide popular ratings from users on my Web site, I have made a change. In this edition, the wine ratings are strictly my own. I have observed that as the wine market has grown exponentially, broad wine consumers have become too overwhelmed by the massive number of wine and wine information choices to feel confident rating lots of wines on their own. More than ever, they are looking for easy-to-use guidance from a trusted source, so they can save time and spend their money wisely. Critics are a solid bet for advice, because their opinions are based on extensive tasting experience. Having said that, the top critics' tasting reports are chock-a-block with many hundreds of wines per month. For most people it's too much to wade through to find the gems that are available and affordable (often a small fraction). That is why I have focused on my picks for the 1000 Wines That Matter. I am confident they will keep you happy for at least a year - until the next guide comes out! Please visit www.andreawine.com for updates and tasting videos, and email me at andrea@andreawine.com with your feedback. Cheers!

HOW THE GUIDE IS ORGANIZED

There are two ways to look up wines:

1. By Grape, Region, or Type
The wine reviews are grouped by major grape variety, region, or type, from white to red, and lightest to heaviest, as follows:

Within each section the wines are in alphabetical order by winery name.

2. By winery name

To find a specific winery's reviews, use the Winery Index at the back of the book.

Key to the Ratings and Symbols

This sample entry identifies the components of each wine listing.

1. **The Facts** - Name, vintage & where it is from
2. **The Price** - the national average retail price; Prices can vary a lot by market based on taxes and discount policies, but this will give you an idea of what to expect
3. **The Score** - on a 100-point scale; as with your grades in school, a 100 is perfect. (Yes, perfection in wine is subjective!)
4. **The Symbols** - There are two different kinds of symbols, as follows:

   Andrea's favorites
   ♀ Indicates an Andrea personal favorite wine

   Palate matchers
   ✹ A food-friendly wine that pairs well with diverse dishes and food flavors.
   🍎 A fruit-forward, "new world" style wine.
   ⚱ An "old world" style wine, with an earthy or mineral scent and flavor and subtle fruit
   ☺ A "crowd-pleaser" wine that will satisfy a lot of palates; generally big, lush wines
   👍 A wine-geek favorite - perfect for your connoisseur or wine aficionado friends.

5. **The Reviews** - My review, tasting notes and pairings for each wine.
6. **My Kitchen Survivor™** Grade
7. **Your notes** - Space for your wine notes.

---

❶ **Chateau Andrea Rose 2008**　　　　　❷ $　❸ Pts
New York　　　　　　　　　　　　　　22　88
❹ ✹　Wine lovers marvel at this wine's amazing
❺ quality for a bag-in-the-box. I find it every bit as good as the finest Cold Duck ... and sometimes better!
❻ *Kitchen Survivor™ Grade: A*
❼ Your notes: _____

Kitchen Survivor™ Grades

Since "How long will it keep after I open it?" is one of the most common wine questions I'm asked, I decided it was time to give some solid answers.

And thus were born the Kitchen Survivor™ experiments. To test wines' open-bottle longevity, I handle them as follows:

Whites—Recorked with the original cork (whether natural or synthetic). Placed in the fridge.

Reds—Recorked with the original cork. Placed on the kitchen counter.

Sparkling wines—Opened carefully without popping (popping depletes carbonation faster). Closed with a "clamshell" stopper designed for sparkling wines—sold in housewares departments and sometimes wine stores. Placed in the fridge.

The same process is repeated after each daily retaste, until the wine's taste declines noticeably.

I do this for every wine I taste that's a candidate for inclusion in the guide. The great news is that far more often than you'd think, the good wines stay that way for days. Even more interesting, some wines that seem initially under whelming actually come around and start tasting better after being open for awhile (in the same way that some cheeses need to sit out at room temperature to show their best flavor or a pot of chili can taste better after a day or two in the fridge). Based on these taste tests, I grade each wine as follows:

C = a "one-day wine," which tastes noticeably less fresh the next day. This doesn't mean the wine is less worthy, just less sturdy—so plan to finish it with tonight's dinner.

B = holds its freshness for 2–3 days after opening

B+ = holds *and gets better* over 2–3 days after opening

A = has a 3- to 4-day "freshness window"

A+ = holds *and gets better* over 3–4 days

I hope these grades will give you the confidence to enjoy wine more often with your everyday meals, knowing that in most cases the bottle won't go "bad" if you don't finish it right away.

Your Notes

The best way to learn about wine is to keep tasting, and keep notes. Whether you're at home or in a restaurant, the *Guide* is a handy place to keep track of what you drank, what you paid, what food you had with it, and what you thought. Don't you hate it when you've enjoyed a wine, then can't remember the name when you want to buy it again?

Andrea's Top Wines for Everyone*

Best of the Big Six Grapes ($50 and under)

Name	Score	Price
Top 10 Rieslings		
Selbach-Oster Zeltinger Schlossberg Mosel, Germany 2007	94	30
Nigl Kremsleiten, Austria 2007	92	36
Eroica, Columbia Valley, Washington 2008	90	22
Schloss Johannisberger, Rheingau, Germany 2007	90	33
Saint M, Mosel, Germany 2008	89	12
Beringer Dry, Napa Valley, California 2008	89	14
Trimbach, Alsace, France 2006	89	18
Leitz Dragonstone, Rheingau, Germany 2008	89	18
Darting Durkheimer Kabinett, Nahe, Germany 2008	89	19
Dashe Dry, Potter Valley, California 2007	89	20
Top 10 Sauvignon/Fume Blancs		
Silverado Miller Ranch, Napa, California 2008	94	17
Chalk Hill, Chalk Hill, California 2007	94	28
Concha y Toro Terrunyo, Casablanca, Chile 1008	93	22
Robert Mondavi Fume Blanc Reserve, To-Ka-Lon Vineyard, Napa 2007	93	40
Matanzas Creek, Sonoma 2007	92	24
Robert Mondavi Fume Blanc, Napa 2007	91	20
St. Supery, Napa 2008	90	23
Morgan, Monterey, California 2008	89	16
Chateau Coucheroy, Graves, France 2007	89	17

*Only wines $50 and under are ranked here. See the back of the book for the best-of-the-budget wines rankings, and listings of the benchmark wines including all wines regardless of price. The wine ranking in each style category reflects the wine's numerical taste score, and its relative value for the money. Among multiple wines with the same rating, the less expensive wines are pushed higher in the ranking. To find the complete tasting notes for each wine, refer to the Winery Index in the back of the book. Also visit Andreawine. com for wine tasting videos and more information on wines, grapes and regions.

Drylands, Marlborough,
New Zealand 2008   89   17

Top 10 Chardonnays

Chalk Hill Estate, Chalk Hill-Sonoma 2006	97	40
Antinori Cervaro della Sala, Italy 2007	95	50
Kali Hart, Monterey 2008	94	19
Talbott Sleepy Hollow Vineyard, Santa Lucia Highlands, Monterey, California 2006	94	40
Mer Soleil, Monterey 2006	93	40
Calera Central Coast, California 2007	93	16
Chateau St. Jean Robert Young Vyd, Alexander Valley 2006	92	25
Sbragia Home Ranch, Dry Creek Valley, California 2007	92	26
Matanzas Creek, Sonoma Valley 2007	92	29
Chappellet Estate, Napa 2007	92	32

Top 10 Pinot Noirs

Williams-Selyem, Russian River 2007	93	45
Robert Mondavi Carneros 2007	92	27
Cristom Mt. Jefferson Cuvee, Willamette Valley 2006	92	30
Chateau St. Jean Sonoma County 2007	91	20
Sokol-Blosser Dundee Hills, Willamette Valley, Oregon 2007	91	38
Calera Central Coast, California 2007	90	24
Etude, Carneros, California 2007	90	40
Acacia, Carneros, California 2007	89	26
J Russian River Valley, California 2007	89	35
Ponzi, Willamette Valley, Oregon 2006	89	35

Top 10 Merlots

Grgich Hills Estate, Napa 2005	94	42
Northstar, Columbia Valley, Washington	92	40
St. Clement, Napa Valley 2006	91	36
Sebastiani, Sonoma 2006	90	17
Chateau Ste. Michelle Indian Wells, Columbia Valley, Washington 2006	90	18
Raymond Reserve, Napa 2005	90	24
Matanzas Creek, Bennett Valley Sonoma 2006	90	35

Chateau St. Jean, Sonoma 2006	89	25
Chateau Ste. Michelle Canoe Ridge Estate, Columbia Valley 2006	89	25
Stag's Leap Wine Cellars, Napa 2006	89	45

Top 10 Cabernet Sauvignons and Blends

Penfolds Bin 389, Australia 2006	94	37
Trefethen Estate, Oak Knoll, Napa 2005	94	50
Beringer Knights Valley, Sonoma 2007	93	27
Heitz Cellars, Napa 2005	92	42
Frank Family Vineyards, Napa 2005	91	45
Souverain, Alexander Valley, Sonoma 2006	90	20
Chateau St. Jean, Sonoma 2006	90	27
Sequoia Grove, Napa 2006	90	34
St. Clement, Napa 2006	90	35
Mt. Veeder, Napa 2006	90	40

Top 10 Shiraz/Syrahs and Rhone-Style Reds

Morgan Double L Syrah, Santa Lucia Highlands, Monterey, California 2007	93	40
Morgan, Monterey 2007	90	18
Penfolds St. Henri, South Eastern Australia 2005	90	26
Chapoutier Cotes du Rhone Rouge Belleruche, Rhone 2007	89	13
Wolf-Blass Yellow Label, Australia 2007	89	13
D'Arenberg The Footbolt Shiraz, Australia 2007	89	20
Jade Mountain Napa Syrah, California 2005	89	26
Penfolds Kalimna Bin 28 Shiraz, Australia 2006	89	26
Jaboulet Parallele 45 Cotes du Rhone, Rhone, France 2007	88	17
Brokenwood McLaren Vale, Australia 2007	88	27

Best of the Rest

Name	Score	Price
Top 10 Champagnes and Sparkling Wines		
Piper-Heidsieck Brut Rose Sauvage, Champagne NV	97	50
Chartogne-Taillet Brut, Champagne NV	93	44
Taittinger Brut La Francaise, Champagne NV	91	45
Pol Roger Brut, Champagne NV	90	45
P. Gimonnet 1er Cru, Champagne NV	90	50
Piper-Sonoma, Sonoma, California NV	89	16
Chandon Brut, California NV	89	16
Roederer Estate, Anderson Valley, CA NV	89	22
Schramsberg Blanc de Noirs, California NV	89	40
A. Margaine 1er Cru, Champagne NV	89	46
Top 10 Pinot Gris/Grigios		
Bollini Trentino, Italy 2008	89	18
Pighin Friuli Grave, Italy 2007	89	16
Lageder, Italy 2008	88	18
Flora Springs, Napa 2008	87	14
Maso Canali, Italy 2008	87	23
Danzante, Italy 2008	86	8
Castello di Gabbiano, Italy 2008	86	10
Robert Mondavi Private Selection, California 2008	86	11
Erath, Oregon 2008	86	14
Clos du Bois, California 2008	86	15
Top 10 Italian and Spanish Reds		
Baron de Ley Rioja Gran Reserva, Spain 1998	92	24
Castello di Gabbiano Alleanza, Tuscany, Italy 2006	92	35
La Rioja Alta Vina Ardanza Reserva, Rioja, Spain 2000	92	35
Pesquera Crianza, Ribera del Duero 2006	91	35
Lopez de Heredia Vina Bosconia Rioja Reserva, Rioja, Spain 2001	91	37
Abadia Retuerta Seleccion Especial, Sardon de Duero, Spain 2006	90	20
Val di Suga Rosso di Montalcino, Tuscany, Italy 2006	90	26
Muga Rioja Reserva, Spain 2005	90	30
Tenuta Sette Ponti Crognolo, Tuscany 2007	90	35
Falesco Vitiano, Umbria, Italy 2007	89	12

Top 10 Red Zinfandels

Frank Family, Napa 2007	93	35
DeLoach, Russian River Valley 2007	92	18
Grgich Hills Estate, Napa 2006	92	28
Deloach Heritage, California 2007	90	12
Inspiration, Alexander Valley 2007	90	23
Quivira Anderson Ranch, Dry Creek Valley 2006	90	34
Ravenswood Old Vines, Sonoma County 2007	89	15
Di Arie, Shenandoah Valley 2007	89	22
Girard Old Vine, California 2007	89	24
Frog's Leap, Napa 2007	89	27

Top 15 "Other Whites"

Qupe Marsanne, California 2008	94	18
Miner Family Viognier Simpson Vineyard, California 2007	94	20
Heidi Schrock Ried Vogelsang, Austria 2007	92	16
Guado al Tasso Vermentino, Italy 2008	91	25
Inama Vin Soave, Italy 2008	90	17
Tablas Creek Cotes de Tablas Blanc, California 2008	90	25
Crios Torrontes, Argentina 2008	89	14
Bastianich Tocai Friulano, Italy 2008	89	15
Hidalgo Manzanilla Sherry, Spain NV	89	16
Hirsch Gruner-Veltliner #1, Austria 2007	89	16
Rocca delle Macie Vermentino, Italy 2008	89	17
Anselmi Soave, Veneto, Italy 2007	88	17
Ca' del Solo Muscat, California 2008	88	18
Brundlmayer Gruner-Veltliner, Austria 2007	88	19
Schloss Gobelsburg Gruner-Veltliner Steinsetz, Austria 2007	88	29

Budget Wines and Benchmark Bottles

My Best Budget Wines - the Top 20 whites and reds priced at $15 and under - begin on page 215. Following that is the listing of what are considered the benchmarks of the fine wine world - the standard-bearers against which all other wines are judged.

THE REVIEWS

WHITE WINES
Champagne/Sparkling

Style Profile: Although all the world's bubblies are modeled on Champagne, only the genuine article from the Champagne *region* of France is properly called *Champagne. Sparkling wine* is the proper term for the other bubblies, some of which can be just as good as the real thing. Limited supply and high demand—plus a labor-intensive production process—make Champagne expensive compared to other sparklers but still an affordable luxury in comparison to other world-class wine categories, like top French Burgundy or California Cabernet estates. The other sparklers, especially Cava from Spain and Italian Prosecco, are affordable for everyday drinking. *Brut* (rhymes with *root*) on the label means the wine is utterly dry, with no perceptible sweetness. But that *doesn't* mean they all taste the same. In fact, each French Champagne house is known for a signature style, which can range from delicate and elegant to rich, full, and toasty—meaning there's something for every taste and food partner.

Serve: Well chilled; young and fresh (only the rare luxury French Champagnes improve with age). Open with utmost care: flying corks can be dangerous.

When: Anytime! Bubbly not just for special occasions, and it's great with meals.

With: Anything and anyone, but especially sushi, shellfish, fried foods and popcorn.

In: A narrow tulip- or flute-type glass; the narrow opening preserves the bubbles.

Kitchen Survivor™ Tip for Bubbly Wine: Kitchen-ware shops and wine stores often sell "clamshell" stoppers specially designed to close Champagnes and sparkling wines if you don't finish the bottle. I've found that if you open the bottle carefully in the first place (avoid "popping" the cork, which is also the safest technique), a stoppered sparkling wine will keep its fizz for at least three days in the fridge, often longer. Having a hard time thinking of something else to toast? How about, "Here's to [insert day of week]." That's usually good enough for me!

| **A. Margaine Cuvee Traditionelle Brut** | **$** | **Pts** |
| **1er Cru, Champagne, France NV** | **46** | **89** |

A grower Champagne that's worth the search. Elegant and lacy, with charged-up acidity and crisp citrus and pear notes plus a hint of mushroomy savoriness.
Kitchen Survivor™ Grade: A
Your notes: _____

| **Bollinger (*BOLL-en-jur*) Brut Special** | **$** | **Pts** |
| **Cuvee Champagne, France NV** | **60** | **88** |

Expensive for a Brut NV, but the wine's nutty-toasty, brioche scents and flavors are unique in the category.
Kitchen Survivor™ Grade: A
Your notes: _____

| **Bouvet (*boo-VAY*) Brut Sparkling,** | **$** | **Pts** |
| **Loire Valley, France NV** | **16** | **84** |

☺ Classy and affordable, with a complex scent of chamomile blossoms and sweet hay, a crisp apple-quince flavor, and creamy texture.
Kitchen Survivor™ Grade: B+
Your notes: _____

| **Chandon (*shahn-DOHN*) Brut** | **$** | **Pts** |
| **Rose Sparkling, California NV** | **18** | **88** |

One of the best California roses on the market right now, with delicious spiced cherry fruit and a long finish. Pair it with blackened chicken.
Kitchen Survivor™ Grade: B
Your notes: _____

Chandon Brut Classic $ Pts
Sparkling, California NV   16   89

"Another notch!" as Emeril would say, and that's after
last year's impressive quality leap. This uber-popular,
very well-priced bubbly earns its fans, with apple cobbler scents and flavors and wonderful texture.
Kitchen Survivor™ Grade: B+
Your notes: _____

Charles Heidsieck (*HIDE-sick*) Brut $ Pts
Reserve Champagne, France NV   55   90

♀ Full-bodied with toasted hazelnut and apple
streusel scents and flavors, and a long toffee finish.
Kitchen Survivor™ Grade: A
Your notes: _____

Chartogne-Taillet Cuvee Ste. Anne Brut, $ Pts
Champagne, France NV   44   93

♀ A smokin' value for the quality, and clear proof
that sommeliers' love for small-grower Champagne is
well-founded. This is toasty, nutty, luxuriant!
Kitchen Survivor™ Grade: A
Your notes: _____

Codorniu Cava Rose, Penedes $ Pts
Spain NV   14   87

A rare Pinot Noir-based cava, and worth seeking out!
Creamy bubble, dried cherry fruit, soft spicy finish
that pairs deliciously with BBQ chicken.
Kitchen Survivor™ Grade: A
Your notes: _____

Domaine Carneros Brut Sparkling, $ Pts
California 2005   25   87

One of the most elegant California bubblies, biscuity,
floral and lively. Great with smoked eel sushi.
Kitchen Survivor™ Grade: B
Your notes: _____

Domaine Carneros Le Reve Blanc de $ Pts
Blancs Sparkling, California 2003   75   88

☝ This is one of California's best bubblies, with a
firm core of ripe pear fruit, potpourri and granola
scents, and long finish. Pair with St. Andre or Brie.
Kitchen Survivor™ Grade: A+
Your notes: _____

Domaine Ste. Michelle Brut	$	Pts
Sparkling, Washington NV	12	84

☺ You can't beat the price and consistency of this nicely balanced, crisp, and appley sparkler.

Kitchen Survivor™ Grade: B

Your notes: _____

Dom Perignon Champagne Brut,	$	Pts
France 2002	165	87

People buy it for the bragging rights, but the quality is there, too. Apple compote, bread dough and fresh hay scents are the signature, with a pure core of pear and anise and a long finish.

Kitchen Survivor™ Grade: B

Your notes: _____

Freixenet (*fresh-uh-NETT*) Brut	$	Pts
de Noirs, Cava Rose, Spain NV	10	86

A juicy taste of tangy strawberries that's great with spicy tuna sushi, barbecue, and anything else with a kick. An amazing deal that's worth the search.

Kitchen Survivor™ Grade: A+

Your notes: _____

Gaston Chiquet Brut Tradition,	$	Pts
Champagne, France NV	48	89

A favorite of sommeliers for its laser purity and expression of red fruit: currants, snappy red cherry. A "foodie's" bubbly at its best with duck confit or quail.

Kitchen Survivor™ Grade: A

Your notes: _____

G.H. Mumm Cordon Rouge Brut,	$	Pts
Champagne, France NV	35	86

Medium-bodied, with a pretty floral and hay scent with granola-apple compote flavors. A deal!

Kitchen Survivor™ Grade: A

Your notes: _____

Gloria Ferrer Sonoma Brut,	$	Pts
California NV	20	85

Crisp Anjou pear with a mushroomey note. Nice acidity that refreshes with spicy dishes, garlicky fare, and briny shellfish such as chilled oysters & clams.

Kitchen Survivor™ Grade: A

Your notes: _____

Henriot (*ahn-ree-OH*) Brut Souverain, Champagne, France NV $ 40   Pts 87

Pure elegance, with a creamy texture, pear-streusel scents and flavors and a subtle almond-anise finish.
Kitchen Survivor™ Grade: A
Your notes: _____

Iron Horse Classic Vintage Brut, Green Valley (of RRV), California 2004 $ 33   Pts 88

You may fall for the Wedding Cuvee (see next), but this became my true love from Iron Horse, for its toastiness, baked apple dumpling flavors, and length.
Kitchen Survivor™ Grade: B
Your notes: _____

Iron Horse Wedding Cuvee Brut Sparkling, California 2006 $ 38   Pts 85

☺ Everyone loves the name, the apples-and-cream flavors and the crisp bubble. Ideal with fried foods.
Kitchen Survivor™ Grade: B
Your notes: _____

J Cuvee 20 Brut Sparkling, Sonoma, California NV $ 32   Pts 86

The singular flavor profile - quince paste and lemon-grass - showcases the cool climate Russian River grapes, and the let-the-fruit show winemaking.
Kitchen Survivor™ Grade: A
Your notes: _____

Krug Grande Cuvee Multivintage Champagne, France $ 165   Pts 89

☝👍 I love this wine. Krug's truly unique, full, nutty, baked-brioche style is big enough to pair with roasted meats and game birds, or truffled risotto.
Kitchen Survivor™ Grade: A
Your notes: _____

Mionetto DOC Prosecco Brut, Veneto, Italy NV, $ 16   Pts 86

☺ Dry, refreshing, and sophisticated but also affordable (add peach puree to make the Bellini cocktail). Great with savory antipasti (sausage, cheese, olives).
Kitchen Survivor™ Grade: B
Your notes: _____

Moët & Chandon (*MWETT eh*   **$**   **Pts**
***shahn-DOHN*) Brut Imperial**   **40**   **87**
Champagne, France NV

Wildly popular, with quality to match. It's medium-bodied and completely harmonious, with biscuit and chamomile scents and spiced apple dumpling flavors.

Kitchen Survivor™ Grade: B

Your notes: _____

Moët & Chandon White Star   **$**   **Pts**
Champagne, France NV   **40**   **85**

☺ With just a whisper of sweetness, plus quince and candied ginger notes, this is great with spicy sushi.

Kitchen Survivor™ Grade: A

Your notes: _____

Mumm Napa Brut Cuvee   **$**   **Pts**
Sparkling, California NV   **18**   **87**

☺ An encore of last year's quality jump. The toasty baked apple flavor and finesse are the best-ever.

Kitchen Survivor™ Grade: B

Your notes: _____

Mumm Napa Brut Rose   **$**   **Pts**
Sparkling, California NV   **22**   **87**

🍷 Maybe I just love Roses? Nah, this is the real deal, with loads of red fruit, structure, firmness, and yet lovely harmony and length. Great to drink as a bubbly, and to pair as a red wine. Get some!

Kitchen Survivor™ Grade: B

Your notes: _____

Perrier-Jouët (*PEAR-ee-ay JHWETT*)   **$**   **Pts**
Fleur de Champagne Brut, France 2000   **139**   **94**

Elegant notes of white flowers, ladyfingers and apple tart dance delicately on the palate, and linger with an apple compote and crusty bread note in the finish.

Kitchen Survivor™ Grade: A

Your notes: _____

Perrier-Jouët Grand Brut   **$**   **Pts**
Champagne, France NV   **45**   **85**

This one is crisp and light, with snappy apple and cornsilk scents, and soft citrusy flavors on the palate.

Kitchen Survivor™ Grade: B

Your notes: _____

Pierre Gimonnet 1er Cru Brut   **$**   **Pts**
Champagne, France NV   50   90

Like lemon mousse minus the fat and sugar! Lacy and vivacious on the palate, with ginger and green tea notes. Sleek, long, the perfect pairing with eggs Benedict.

Kitchen Survivor™ Grade: A+

Your notes: _____

Piper-Heidsieck (*HIDE-sick*) Brut   **$**   **Pts**
Rose Sauvage Champagne, France NV   50   97

This is without a doubt the best rose Champagne on the market. It smells and tastes like snappy, savory and smoky red Burgundy, but with the refreshment of bubbles and a chill. You will love the red cherry and Asian spice notes that simply sing out of the glass, and bring you back again and again. Pair it with teriyaki, spicy sushi or spicy-chocolatey mole sauce.

Kitchen Survivor™ Grade: A+

Your notes: _____

Piper-Heidsieck (*HIDE-sick*) Cuvee   **$**   **Pts**
Brut Champagne, France NV   42   88

Major toastiness in the scent, followed by a frisky acidity and white pepper spiciness on the palate, make this great for food - from sushi to fried chicken.

Kitchen Survivor™ Grade: A

Your notes: _____

Piper-Heidsieck (*HIDE-sick*) Cuvee Brut   **$**   **Pts**
2002 Champagne, France NV   65   94

A fantastic example of a vintage Champagne, showing brioche, toffee and marzipan scents and flavors. Pair it with trout (or other fish) amandine, duck confit or even smoked pork.

Kitchen Survivor™ Grade: A

Your notes: _____

Piper-Sonoma Brut Sparkling, Sonoma,   **$**   **Pts**
California NV   16   89

This California outpost of the French Champagne Piper-Heidsieck yields one of California's best bubblies - especially for the price. It's got a toastiness that makes it rich enough to pair with pork or even duck.

Kitchen Survivor™ Grade: A+

Your notes: _____

Pol Roger Brut Reserve
Champagne, France NV

	$	Pts
	45	90

👍 One of the top brut Champagnes in the delicate style with fragrant talcum, buttercream and ripe pear notes, perfectly proportioned and full of finesse.
Kitchen Survivor™ Grade: A+
Your notes: _____

Roederer Estate Brut Sparkling,
California NV

	$	Pts
	22	89

☺ A full, toasty style that tastes like apple cobbler on the palate (but no sugar!). Great with roast turkey.
Kitchen Survivor™ Grade: A
Your notes: _____

Schramsberg Blanc de Noirs,
North Coast, California 2006

	$	Pts
	40	89

🍴 A classic California bubbly that earns its fan club with pumped-up yeasty potpourri and dried cherry flavors and a spicy note that pairs great with BBQ.
Kitchen Survivor™ Grade: A
Your notes: _____

Segura Viudas (*seh-GUHR-uh*
***vee-YOU-duss*) Aria Estate Cava**
Brut, Spain NV

	$	Pts
	12	85

🍴 ☺ For the $, one of the best on the market, with vibrant pear fruit and a creamy texture. Yummy!
Kitchen Survivor™ Grade: A
Your notes: _____

Segura Viudas Reserva Heredad
Estate Cava Brut, Spain NV

	$	Pts
	20	87

👍 Both the handsome metal-clad bottle and the earthy, mushroomy scent and flavor are quite commanding. Definitely a bubbly for a meal of seafood stew laced with fennel and Pernod.
Kitchen Survivor™ Grade: A
Your notes: _____

Taittinger (*TATE-in-jur*) Brut La
Française Champagne, France NV

	$	Pts
	45	91

🍴 One of my favorites for its bewitching notes of fresh fennel and Asian pear, and positively sleek texture. Pair it with satiny scallops or oyster bisque.
Kitchen Survivor™ Grade: A
Your notes: _____

Taittinger Comtes de Champagne Blanc $ Pts
de Blancs Champagne, France 1998   190   92

👍 🍷 My favorite of the big-name luxury bubblies for its elegance, toasty brioche & caramelized pear flavors, and a finish that lasts for days. Blow out the decadence and pair it with truffle risotto, lobster or halibut. You can tighten your belt tomorrow!

Kitchen Survivor™ Grade: A

Your notes: _____

Pinot Gris/Pinot Grigio

Grape Profile: Pinot Gris (*pee-no GREE*) is the French and Grigio (*GREE-jee-oh*) the Italian spelling for this white grape with a split personality. The French and American versions tend toward the luscious style. The Italian versions (and a few American imitators) are more mineral and crisp - mostly everyday drinking wines, although a few producers' bottlings stand above the pack and make truly special versions. In France, Pinot Gris is a signature in the Alsace region, and Oregon vintners in particular have made this style a calling card. The California bottlings tend to be labeled according to the style they are mimicking - Pinot Gris if it's the exotic French style, Pinot Grigio if it's the crisp and minerally Italian style. To many it's the quintessential quaffing wine and an easy by the glass choice in restaurants. Happily, it remains true that you need not pay a lot for tasty Pinot Grigio/Gris. The choice is yours!

Serve: Well chilled; young and fresh (as one of my wine buying buddies says to the waiters *she* teaches: "The best vintage for Pinot Grigio? As close to yesterday as possible!").

When: Anytime, but ideal with cocktails, outdoor occasions, lunch, big gatherings (a crowd pleaser).

With: Very versatile, but perfect with hors d'oeuvres, salads, salty foods, and fried foods.

In: The One™ glass for white, or an all-purpose wineglass.

Adelshiem Vineyard Pinot Gris, $ Pts
Willamette Valley, Oregon 2007   18   85

👍 This Oregon classic winery's signature is elegance. The mineral, gingery scents and pear fruit are subtle. A great match for Cobb salad or tabbouleh.

Kitchen Survivor™ Grade: B

Your notes: _____

Alois Lageder (ah-lo-EEZ *la-GAY-der*) $ Pts
Pinot Grigio, Alto Adige, Italy 2008   18   88

👍 🍾 One of the benchmark PGs. The pear fruit, floral scent, and smoky finish add up to complexity that's rare in Pinot Grigio. Pair with clam pasta or salumi.

Kitchen Survivor™ Grade: B

Your notes: _____

Bollini Pinot Grigio Trentino, $ Pts
Italy 2008   18   89

⏳ 👍 🏆 This is Pinot Grigio on a whole different level: creme anglaise, Jordan almond, Fuji apple flavors, juicy texture, great length. Pair with salumi.

Kitchen Survivor™ Grade: A+

Your notes: _____

Castello di Gabbiano Pinot Grigio, $ Pts
Delle Venezia, Italy 2008   10   86

🍾 It's far too easy to pay a lot more and get a lot less in Pinot Grigio, but why? Sweet hay scent and pure sliced cantaloupe on the palate. Just add prosciutto!

Kitchen Survivor™ Grade: C

Your notes: _____

Cavit (*CAV-it;* rhymes with $ Pts
"have it") Pinot Grigio, Italy 2008   10   84

So lean and crisp it actually tasted better the day after opening, and really blossomed with food (a tangy goat cheese). It would pair well with lemony sauces, too.

Kitchen Survivor™ Grade: B+

Your notes: _____

Clos du Bois Pinot Grigio, $ Pts
California 2008   15   86

☺ This is tops in CA PG with laser-pure ripe pear fruit, and a hint of mineral. Great with summer salads.

Kitchen Survivor™ Grade: A

Your notes: _____

Danzante Pinot Grigio, Delle Venezie   **$**   **Pts**
Italy 2008   8   86

Compared to a lot of the better-known Italian PGs this is twice the wine at half the price. It's subtle, with ripe and crisp peach flavors that pair with anything salty or fatty - can you say fried chicken?

Kitchen Survivor™ Grade: B

Your notes: _____

Ecco Domani (*ECK-oh dough-*   **$**   **Pts**
***MAH-nee*) Pinot Grigio, Italy 2007**   10   82

☺ Tastes clean and refreshing, with fresh almond, mineral and citrus notes.

Kitchen Survivor™ Grade: B

Your notes: _____

Erath Pinot Gris,   **$**   **Pts**
Oregon 2008   14   86

One of Oregon's best PGs for the price, with crisp pear and mineral notes. Great with summer salads.

Kitchen Survivor™ Grade: B

Your notes: _____

Estancia Pinot Grigio,   **$**   **Pts**
California 2007   12   85

This wine's subtle chalkiness and snappy grapefruit flavors scream for goat cheese or a Greek salad.

Kitchen Survivor™ Grade: B

Your notes: _____

Flora Springs Pinot Grigio,   **$**   **Pts**
California 2007   14   87

I think this is the best California Pinot Grigio on the market. Its vibrant peach, kiwi and key lime flavors are fantastic with ceviche and smoked salmon.

Kitchen Survivor™ Grade: B

Your notes: _____

Gallo Family Vineyards Sonoma Reserve   **$**   **Pts**
Pinot Gris, California 2007   15   86

As winemaker Gina Gallo says, this wine is "all about the fruit: peach, fig, and mandarin orange." Yum!

Kitchen Survivor™ Grade: C

Your notes: _____

J Pinot Gris, Russian River Valley, $ Pts
Sonoma, California 2008   16   86

A class act, balancing hay, floral and mineral scents with ripe melon and tangerine fruit, and fresh acidity.
Kitchen Survivor™ Grade: B

Your notes: _____

King Estate Pinot Gris, $ Pts
Oregon 2007   17   86

This winery's best Pinot Gris yet, with bright tutti-frutti, pineapple, quince and Asian pear flavors.
Kitchen Survivor™ Grade: B

Your notes: _____

Livio Felluga (*LIV-ee-oh fuh-LOO-* $ Pts
***guh*) Map Label Pinot Grigio, Italy 2007**   18   86

🍴 👍 *Lean, stylish,* and *exciting* are words pros use to describe this standout Pinot Grigio. I like the pretty floral nose, white pepper, and ripe apricot flavors.
Kitchen Survivor™ Grade: B

Your notes: _____

MacMurray Ranch Pinot Gris, Sonoma $ Pts
Coast, California 2008   20   85

Wet stone minerality and honeyed pear fruit. Tender and juicy, it's a perfect pair with sweetcorn & shrimp.
Kitchen Survivor™ Grade: B

Your notes: _____

Maso Canali Pinot Grigio, $ Pts
Italy 2008   23   87

🔑 🍴 Expensive for PG, but it also delivers much more than you expect. It is sleek, minerally, citrusy, appley, layered and long. Pair it with shellfish pasta.
Kitchen Survivor™ Grade: A

Your notes: _____

Pighin Pinot Grigio Grave, $ Pts
Italy 2007   16   89

🍴 🔑 This continues to be one of the top PGs. White flowers, grapefruit, minerals, ginger and fresh pears. It's got wonderful acidity, and a subtle anise note that cries out for seafood stew such as cioppino.
Kitchen Survivor™ Grade: A

Your notes: _____

Ponzi Pinot Gris,   **$**   **Pts**
Oregon 2007   **17**   **86**

♟ This wine's mineral and ripe pear character is like classic Alsace Pinot Gris, but without the heaviness. Delicious with seafood salads and fresh crab.
Kitchen Survivor™ Grade: A

Your notes: _____

Robert Mondavi Private Selection   **$**   **Pts**
Pinot Grigio, California 2008   **11**   **86**

☺ Still one of the best budget Pinot Grigios from California, with crisp minerality, lemony freshness and great food affinity. Linguine with clams, anyone?
Kitchen Survivor™ Grade: B+

Your notes: _____

Ruffino Lumina Pinot Grigio, Venezia-   **$**   **Pts**
Giulia, Italy 2007   **13**   **84**

♟ More to it than the usual Italian Pinot Grigio; pear flavor and mineral with scents of flowers and hay. Great with tomato-sauced pastas or sausages.
Kitchen Survivor™ Grade: C

Your notes: _____

Santa Margherita Pinot Grigio,   **$**   **Pts**
Italy 2008   **18**   **82**

A solid but pricey offering in the crowded PG category, with clean citrus and green apple flavors.
Kitchen Survivor™ Grade: B

Your notes: _____

WillaKenzie Pinot Gris,   **$**   **Pts**
Oregon 2007   **17**   **85**

🍎 Asian pears and vanilla with a subtle fennel note. A great bet to pear with spicy Thai or Indian fare.
Kitchen Survivor™ Grade: C

Your notes: _____

Willamette Valley Vineyard Pinot   **$**   **Pts**
Gris, Oregon 2007   **15**   **86**

🍴 In the super-ripe Alsace style, with an apricot and juicy pear flavor that's perfect with creamy curries.
Kitchen Survivor™ Grade: C

Your notes: _____

Woodbridge (Robert Mondavi)	$	Pts
Pinot Grigio, California 2008	8	85

I had given up for awhile on Woodbridge. I'm back on the fan list. This Pinot Grigio is crisp and chalky, with zippy lemon notes and an amazingly long finish. Sip it solo, or pair with pizza bianca or garlicky pastas.
Kitchen Survivor™ Grade: B

Your notes: _____

Riesling

Grape Profile: I am thrilled to say that after many years of steering clear, consumers have finally embraced Riesling, one of my very favorite grapes. There's lots to love, including the price/quality ratio, and high Kitchen Survivor™ grades - thanks to their tangy, crisp acidity, Riesling wines really hold up in the fridge. That makes them ideal for lots of everyday dining situations, e.g., you want a glass of white with your takeout sushi, but your dinner mate wants red with the beef teriyaki. Or maybe you want to start with a glass of white wine while you're cooking dinner and then switch to red with the meal. It's nice to know that with many Rieslings you can go back to the wine over several days, and every glass will taste as good as the first one.

Germany, the traditional source of great Rieslings, continues to grow its presence in the *Guide*. And that's great, because no other region offers so many *world class* wines for under $30. Look for German Rieslings from the Mosel, Rheingau, Pfalz, and Nahe regions. Other go-to Riesling regions are Washington State, Australia, New Zealand, and Alsace, France.

Prepare to be impressed. Rieslings are generally light bodied but loaded with stunning fruit flavor, balanced with tangy acidity. Take note of the value bottlings for delicious crowd-pleasing drinking. The classic producers listed here (from Alsace, Germany, Austria and the United States) set the standard for Riesling, and are worshipped by sommeliers for how their wines pair and age. If you can't find the particular bottling I've noted here, you can be confident buying any Riesling they make. They are specialists with the utmost pedigree.

Serve: Lightly chilled is fine (the aromas really shine when it's not ice cold); it's good young and fresh, but the French and German versions can evolve nicely for up to 5 years.

When: Every day (okay, my personal taste there); classy enough for "important" meals and occasions.

With: Outstanding with shellfish and ethnic foods with a "kick" (think Asian, Thai, Indian, Mexican). There's also an awesome rule-breaker match: braised meats and BBQ!

In: The One™ glass for white, or an all-purpose wine-glass.

	$	Pts
Beringer Napa Valley Dry Riesling, California 2007	14	89

A top Napa Riesling, with snappy white flowers, citrus peel and flint on the nose. The lively, totally dry palate delivers petrol, peaches and melons, and an almost creamy finish. Bring on the bivalves!
Kitchen Survivor™ Grade: A
Your notes: _____

	$	Pts
Blue Fish Original Riesling, Pfalz, Germany 2008	11	84

Whether you find the blue bottle catchy or kitschy, you have to laud the real-deal Riesling character of this wine: creamy apple fruit with a touch of petrol minerality in the scent. Perfect with raw shellfish.
Kitchen Survivor™ Grade: B+
Your notes: _____

	$	Pts
Brundlmayer Riesling Kamptaler Terrassen, Kamptal, Austria 2008	23	87

You have arrived at Riesling geekdom when you delve into Austria's vivid, bone-dry Rieslings. This one is savory, with herb tea, lemon and white pepper notes that make it a great match with oysters mignonette.
Kitchen Survivor™ Grade: B+
Your notes: _____

Chateau Ste. Michelle Columbia Valley   **$**   **Pts**
Dry Riesling, Washington 2008   **10**   **86**
☺ "Tender" is the fruit of this juicy apple, peach and mandarin orange wine; perfect for Asian or spicy foods.
Kitchen Survivor™ Grade: A
Your notes: _____

Clean Slate Riesling, Mosel,   **$**   **Pts**
Germany 2008   **11**   **85**
Tasty white peach/petrol/apple scents and flavors, great price.   A nice partner for fried chicken or ribs.
Kitchen Survivor™ Grade: A
Your notes: _____

Columbia Crest Grand Estates Riesling,   **$**   **Pts**
Columbia Valley, Washington 2007   **8**   **83**
☺ Lipsmacking apple pie-filling flavors, with a hint of sweetness offset by zingy acidity, so it's not heavy.
Kitchen Survivor™ Grade: B
Your notes: _____

Darting Durkheimer Riesling Kabinett,   **$**   **Pts**
Pfalz, Germany 2008   **19**   **89**
👍 🍷 🌿 Seek this one out! The mineral and tangy-blossomy scents and tangerine-citrus core are German Riesling, defined. Pair with sushi or spicy ribs.
Kitchen Survivor™ Grade: A+
Your notes: _____

Dashe Dry Riesling, Potter Valley,   **$**   **Pts**
California 2007   **20**   **89**
🌿 Look out, Eroica (see below)! Here's a quality rival among American Rieslings. Pineapple sundae flavors and great acidity, super concentration, looong!
Kitchen Survivor™ Grade: B
Your notes: _____

"Dr. L" Loosen Brothers Riesling,   **$**   **Pts**
Mosel, Germany 2008   **12**   **86**
🌿 Textbook Mosel: peaches 'n' cream, slaty mineral-ity, a tender sense of sweetness like a ripe tangerine. Pair with clam and sausage pasta or spicy Tex Mex.
Kitchen Survivor™ Grade: A
Your notes: _____

Dr. Loosen Estate Riesling Kabinett Blue Slate, Mosel, Germany 2007

$ 20   Pts 87

Master Sommelier students: Here is your practice wine for Mosel Riesling. Study the spritzy-slaty, tangerine, cream and petrol scents and flavors of this wine and you could ace that blind tasting.

Kitchen Survivor™ Grade: A

Your notes: _____

Donnhoff Estate Riesling, Estate, Nahe, Germany 2008

$ 24   Pts 88

Laser-focused and pure, with notes of citrus, lapsang souchong tea, Asian pear, and a kiss of sweetness. Pair with creamy bisques or sweet shellfish.

Kitchen Survivor™ Grade: A

Your notes: _____

Eroica (*ee-ROY-cuh*) Riesling, Columbia Valley, Washington 2008

$ 22   Pts 90

As ever, this is my pick for best American Riesling. It's got the slaty petrol note that eludes most other American Rieslings, and a fantastic core of dense yet delicate tangerine, peach and Asian pear fruit, eddying out into the long, long finish. Pair with crab or lobster.

Kitchen Survivor™ Grade: A+

Your notes: _____

Fetzer Valley Oaks Johannisberg Riesling, California 2007

$ 12   Pts 84

They've lightened up on the sweetness of this wine, and the character is more delicate and floral - very nice. A delicious match with Chinese food.

Kitchen Survivor™ Grade: B+

Your notes: _____

Firestone Vineyard Riesling, California 2007

$ 10   Pts 83

☺ Riesling is Firestone's signature wine, and always a peachy, juicy, easy quaffer with a touch of sweetness that makes it a great match with Tex Mex.

Kitchen Survivor™ Grade: C

Your notes: _____

Gunderloch Riesling Estate,   **$**   **Pts**
Germany 2008   17   86

👍This wine exemplifies great German Riesling—so approachable, yet with amazing complexity: flowers, chamomile tea, fresh cream, white peach.

Kitchen Survivor™ Grade: A

Your notes: _____

Hogue Johannisberg Riesling,   **$**   **Pts**
Washington 2008   10   85

☺ Yummy and authentically Riesling, with a lot of fruit concentration and length for the price point. Zingy citrus and orange blossom scent, lush tangerine fruit on the palate and a long finish. Bravo!

Kitchen Survivor™ Grade: B

Your notes: _____

J.J. Prum Riesling Kabinett   **$**   **Pts**
Wehlener Sonnenuhr, Germany 2008   22   85

👍This is textbook Mosel Riesling—peaches-and-cream and petrol notes, with both delicacy and depth.

Kitchen Survivor™ Grade: A

Your notes: _____

J&HA Strub Niersteiner Paterberg Riesling,   **$**   **Pts**
Rheinhessen, Germany, 2008   25   88

♟ I have served this by-the-glass for years because the response from Riesling neophytes is such a "wow." It perfectly illustrates how a hint of sweetness, when balanced by acidity, yields perfect pitch on the palate, like biting into a fresh apricot. Fabulous with chilled crab or spicy curry with Thai basil.

Kitchen Survivor™ Grade: A+

Your notes: _____

J. Lohr Bay Mist Riesling, Monterey,   **$**   **Pts**
California 2008   8.50   84

The Golden Delicious apple scent doesn't prepare you for the seductively gamy, Asian duck sauce character on the palate. Bring on the Chinese takeout!

Kitchen Survivor™ Grade: C

Your notes: _____

Kendall-Jackson Vintner's Reserve   **$**   **Pts**
Riesling, Monterey, California 2008   12   86

☺ If you're new to Riesling, try this one for a blue

chip brand name & nice varietal character - honeysuckle & tangerine with a hint of slate and a whisper
of sweetness. A home run with Chinese takeout.
Kitchen Survivor™ Grade: A

Your notes: _____

Leitz Dragonstone Riesling,	$	Pts
Rheingau, Germany 2008	18	89

A neon wine: the intense mandarin orange, pineapple sage and lemon curd flavors dance across the palate on a taut wire of acidity. A perfect example of the
fully-loaded/finesse dichotomy of German Riesling.
Kitchen Survivor™ Grade: A

Your notes: _____

Marc Kreydenweiss Andlau Riesling,	$	Pts
Alsace, France 2007	30	87

Ripe peach, floral, fresh hay and stony scents lead to
a bone-dry, dense palate of citrus, quince and ripe
apple and more stony minerals in the finish.
Kitchen Survivor™ Grade: B

Your notes: _____

Maximin Grunhauser Abtsberg	$	Pts
Riesling Spatlese, Mosel, Germay 2007	31	87

♟ 👍 Behold classic Mosel Riesling: slate-y, peach,
honeysuckle & cream scents, a hint of sweetness and
a bewitching honeyed-mineral quality in the finish.
Kitchen Survivor™ Grade: A

Your notes: _____

Muller-Catoir Riesling Trocken,	$	Pts
Pfalz, Germany 2008	22	87

Muller-Catoir is the spice of Riesling life: ginger, apricot, lychee, allspice, with mandarin orange fruit and a
savory duck stock note. Awesome with Peking duck.
Kitchen Survivor™ Grade: A

Your notes: _____

Nigl Riesling Kremsleiten,	$	Pts
Kremstal, Austria 2007	36	92

Wildly complex and exotic: buttercream, rosehips,
mandarin orange and fresh ginger. The fat, honeyed
texture begs for seared scallops with cream sauce.
Kitchen Survivor™ Grade: A

Your notes: _____

Pacific Rim Dry Riesling,   **$**   **Pts**
USA/Germany 2008   14   85

☺ 🍴 This endures as one of the most popular
wines in my classes thanks to the come-hither appley
peachy style. *Pacific Rim* is the winery's shorthand
for "drink with Asian foods" like sushi or Chinese.

Kitchen Survivor™ Grade: A

Your notes: _____

Pierre Sparr Selection Riesling,   **$**   **Pts**
Alsace, France 2007   9   87

Beaucoup charm for the price. Tangerine, crisp apple
and just a touch of sweetness make it great for sipping
solo, or with spicy foods such as Thai or Indian. Bravo!

Kitchen Survivor™ Grade: A

Your notes: _____

Robert Mondavi Private Selection   **$**   **Pts**
Riesling, California 2007   11   86

☺ 🍴 How do they do it? The petrol and peach are
classic Riesling, but the yum factor and great price
are "house wine" material. Bravo!

Kitchen Survivor™ Grade: B+

Your notes: _____

Saint M Pfalz Riesling,   **$**   **Pts**
Germany 2008   12   89

🏆 Absolutely outstanding, and a gift at this price.
Loaded with peaches and cream, mandarin orange
and minerally-slatiness that just goes on and on.

Kitchen Survivor™ Grade: A+

Your notes: _____

Schloss Johannisberger Riesling,   **$**   **Pts**
Rheingau, Germany 2007   33   90

👍 🍴 Totally dry, so sweet-phobes should reach for
this amazing German benchmark. Green apple Jolly
Rancher, ginger-spicy minerality, loooong finish.

Kitchen Survivor™ Grade: A

Your notes: _____

Selbach-Oster Zeltinger Schlossberg   **$**   **Pts**
Riesling Spatlese, Mosel, Germany 2007   30   94

👍 Oh, marvelous mandarin! There's also minty-slaty
minerality and a creamy quince and honey flavor that
is bewitching with aged Gouda. Loooong!

Kitchen Survivor™ Grade: A+

Your notes: _____

Trefethen Estate Dry Riesling,   **$**   **Pts**
Napa 2008   22   88

♟ 👍 🍸 Trefethen's decades of commitment to this grape shows in the creamy, green apple and mineral complexity. The bone dry elegant style screams for a sophisticated seafood dish like Oysters Rockefeller.
Kitchen Survivor™ Grade: A

Your notes: _____

Trimbach Riesling,   **$**   **Pts**
Alsace, France 2006   18   89

🍸 ♟ Still worthy of its benchmark status after all these years: this wine is bone-dry, with scents of talcum powder, hay and flowers and amazing quince and limoncello fruit density, without a whisper of oak. An ideal match for trout with lemon-butter and capers.
Kitchen Survivor™ Grade: A+

Your notes: _____

Willi Schaefer Estate Riesling,   **$**   **Pts**
Mosel, Germany 2008   23   86

👍 Gulpable and juicy in a knock-it-back-with-appetizers sort of way. Guava-papaya-tangerine-yum!
Kitchen Survivor™ Grade: B

Your notes: _____

Sauvignon Blanc/Fume Blanc

Grape Profile: Sauvignon Blanc (*soh-veen-yoan BLAHNK*), one of my favorite white wine grapes, is on the rise, and for good reason: Truly great ones are still available for under $15—something you can't say about many wine categories these days. Depending on where it's grown (cool, moderate, or warm zones), the exotically pungent scent and taste range from zesty and herbal to tangy lime-grapefruit to juicy peach and melon, with vibrant acidity. The grape's home base is France's Loire Valley and Bordeaux regions. The Loire Valley versions are usually minerally, with elegance and great acidity; the Bordeaux versions are most often barrel-fermented and blended with the local Semillon grape, giving them a waxy, creamy richness. California and Washington State make excellent versions, often labeled Fume Blanc (*FOO-may BLAHNK*) - a tip-off that the wine is barrel-fermented and barrel-aged, and thus fuller in body. In the Southern Hemisphere, New Zealand Sauvignon Blancs continue to earn pro and consumer raves, South Africa produces some smokin' examples, and now Chile is coming on strong with great bottlings that scream character for a bargain price. Another of Sauvignon Blanc's major virtues is its food versatility: It goes so well with the foods many people eat regularly (especially those following a less-red-meat regimen), like chicken and turkey, salads, sushi, Mexican, and vegetarian.

> **THANKS, KIWIS**! Most New Zealand Sauvignon Blancs are now bottled with a screw cap for your convenience and to ensure you get fresh wine without "corkiness" (see "Buying Lingo" for a definition). Hooray!

Serve: Chilled but not ice cold.

When: An amazing food partner, but the tasting notes also spotlight styles that are good on their own, as an aperitif.

With: As noted, great with most everyday eats as well as popular ethnic tastes like Mexican food.

In: The One™ glass for white, or an all-purpose wineglass.

	$	Pts
Arboleda Sauvignon Blanc, California 2008	**17**	**86**

A super example of how Chile is making it happen with the SB grape. Truly impressive, with grassy and herbaceous, vivid green apple, pineapple and lime sorbet notes.

Kitchen Survivor™ Grade: A

Your notes: _____

Benziger Sauvignon Blanc,   **$**   **Pts**
Sonoma, California 2007   15   85

A solid, citrusy SB from with chalky lime flavors that are great with ceviche and goat cheese.

Kitchen Survivor™ Grade: B

Your notes: _____

Beringer Sauvignon Blanc, Napa,   **$**   **Pts**
California 2008   15   87

🍎 A lush potion of Granny Smith apple, lime, kiwi, melon. It's both juicy and crisp, to drink solo or pair with grilled shrimp, Tex Mex, or fried chicken.

Kitchen Survivor™ Grade: A

Your notes: _____

Bonterra Sauvignon Blanc,   **$**   **Pts**
Mendocino, California 2007   14   87

🍎 Bonterra is one of the largest wineries using all organically-grown grapes, and also one of the best. This SB drips with juicy melon and kiwi flavors.

Kitchen Survivor™ Grade: A

Your notes: _____

Brancott Sauvignon Blanc,   **$**   **Pts**
Marlborough, New Zealand 2008   11   87

☺ A perennial NZ SB favorite, with all the classic character: cut grass, gooseberry, grapefruit and passion fruit and a flinty finish. Bring on the guacamole!

Kitchen Survivor™ Grade: A

Your notes: _____

Cakebread Cellars Sauvignon Blanc,   **$**   **Pts**
Napa, California 2007   30   87

🍎 👍 Fans of Cakebread's Chard should try this. The zippy citrus aromas with a hint of fig and vanilla are tailor-made for fresh fennel and fig salad.

Kitchen Survivor™ Grade: C

Your notes: _____

Casa Lapostolle (*lah-poh-STOLE*)   **$**   **Pts**
Sauvignon Blanc, Casablanca, Chile 2008   10   85

☺ As always, a value star, with honeydew and kiwi flavors. Pair with ceviche or fresh tomato salad.

Kitchen Survivor™ Grade: C

Your notes: _____

Chalk Hill Winery Sauvignon Blanc,	$	Pts
Chalk Hill-Sonoma, California 2007	28	94

🍸 🍎 Still sumptuous without being over-the-top, with lavish oak, pure and dense fig and pineapple fruit, and a honeyed richness. Bring on the lobster!

Kitchen Survivor™ Grade: B

Your notes: _____

Chateau Coucheroy Bordeaux Blanc,	$	Pts
Graves, France 2007	17	89

🏆 Tasted blind, this rivaled great Bordeaux whites at 3x the price. Creamy, minerally, waxy lemon and almond flavors, with a really long finish. A steal!

Kitchen Survivor™ Grade: B+

Your notes: _____

Chateau Ste. Michelle Columbia Valley	$	Pts
Sauvignon Blanc, Washington 2008	10	88

☺ Three cheers: tasty, affordable, consistent. Okay, four—exotic: grapefruit and lemongrass scent, ginger flavor, creamy texture. Irresistible with sushi or crab.

Kitchen Survivor™ Grade: B

Your notes: _____

Chateau St. Jean Fume Blanc,	$	Pts
Sonoma, California 2007	12	86

A touch of barrel aging gives this wine a creamy scent, balanced by fruit flavors of ripe pear, melon, and fig, plus tangy acidity. Smokin' for the price.

Kitchen Survivor™ Grade: B+

Your notes: _____

Chimney Rock Fume Blanc,	$	Pts
Napa, California 2007	19	88

This wine leaps out of the glass with lively melon, cucumber, lime and floral-chalky notes. A great part-ner for sushi, avocado-crab salad, or goat cheese.

Kitchen Survivor™ Grade: A

Your notes: _____

Cloudy Bay Sauvignon Blanc,	$	Pts
Marlborough, New Zealand 2008	28	87

👍 This wine put the now-famous "grassy gooseberry" style of NZ SBs on the map in the 1980s. It is now hard to find and expensive but it remains a bench-mark. Perfect with fish in tarragon cream sauce.

Your notes: _____

Concha y Toro Terrunyo Sauvignon,   **$**   **Pts**
Blanc, Casablanca, Chile 2008   **22**   **93**
♟ The flinty notes and laser acidity might seem to be posing as Pouilly-Fume, but the exotic passion fruit flavor is all Chile. It's pricey but also OMG delish and unique. Pair with seafood in caper butter.
Kitchen Survivor™ *Grade:* A
Your notes: _____

Dancing Bull Sauvignon Blanc,   **$**   **Pts**
California 2008   **12**   **86**
Lively grassy, flint and lime peel notes - much more character than you expect from budget Sauvignon Blanc. A home run with salads and guacamole.
Kitchen Survivor™ *Grade:* A
Your notes: _____

Dry Creek Vineyard Fume Blanc,   **$**   **Pts**
Sonoma, California 2008   **12**   **86**
☺ The vivid tangerine and peach flavors, and the nice price, are great for porch-sippin' and picnics.
Kitchen Survivor™ *Grade:* A
Your notes: _____

Drylands Marlborough Sauvignon Blanc,   **$**   **Pts**
New Zealand 2008   **17**   **89**
This is the best release from Drylands yet: creamy and custardy, with zingy and exotic passion fruit flavors and acidity that screams for briny shellfish.
Kitchen Survivor™ *Grade:* A+
Your notes: _____

Duckhorn Sauvignon Blanc, Napa   **$**   **Pts**
California 2007   **23**   **89**
☝ ✋ You pay a premium for the famous Duckhorn name, but the tangerine-melon fruit and awesome length are worth it when you want to impress. Pair with sundried tomato and goat cheese pasta.
Kitchen Survivor™ *Grade:* A
Your notes: _____

Emiliana Natura Sauvignon Blanc,   **$**   **Pts**
Casablanca, Chile 2008   **10**   **85**

Delicious passion fruit, kiwi and starfruit flavors, plus organically grown grapes, recycled glass bottles, and a great price. A feel-good, real good wine.

Kitchen Survivor™ Grade: A

Your notes: _____

Ferrari-Carano Fume Blanc, Sonoma,   **$**   **Pts**
California 2007   **17**   **86**

☺ This is one of California's benchmark Fumes, balancing grapefruit and subtle herbaceousness with richness from the touch of oak and the exotic tropical-guava-mango fruit. Delish with crabcakes.

Kitchen Survivor™ Grade: B+

Your notes: _____

Flora Springs Soliloquy, Napa,   **$**   **Pts**
California 2008   **25**   **89**

I love the laser-pure key lime and kiwi fruit, steely minerality and tingly acidity of this vibrant wine that's tailor-made for fried green tomatoes.

Kitchen Survivor™ Grade: A+

Your notes: _____

Frei Brothers Reserve Sauvignon Blanc   **$**   **Pts**
Russian River Valley, California 2007   **20**   **87**

The price is edging up, but the fresh, vivid cling peach and passion fruit flavors and incredibly long finish really impress. Match it with coconut milk curries, or shellfish in a tarragon cream sauce.

Kitchen Survivor™ Grade: A

Your notes: _____

Frog's Leap Sauvignon Blanc,   **$**   **Pts**
Rutherford, Napa, California 2008   **18**   **87**

A wine list regular worth looking for. The 100% SB character of gooseberries and flinty, penetrating citrus is always utterly delicious (not just leap years!).

Kitchen Survivor™ Grade: A

Your notes: _____

Geyser Peak Sauvignon Blanc, Alexander Valley, California 2007	$	Pts
	14	85

This is a tasty, classic California Sauvignon Blanc, combining the crisp tang of citrus with the juicier taste of kiwi. Match it with bacon-arugula salad.

Kitchen Survivor™ Grade: B+

Your notes: _____

Girard Sauvignon Blanc, Napa, California 2008	$	Pts
	15	**

Honeydew & Asian pear flavor that always tastes like twice the price. Pair with goat cheese crostini. Full disclosure here: we sell our SB grapes to Girard, so I am biased. Thus, no score, but I recommend it!

Kitchen Survivor™ Grade: A+

Your notes: _____

Grgich (*GER-gich;* both are hard *g* as in *girl*) Hills Fume Blanc, Napa, California 2008	$	Pts
	30	89

Grgich's signature style is tangy and fresh, with grapefruit, melon, lemon curd and cut grass notes. Pair with Cioppino with aioli, or goat cheese.

Kitchen Survivor™ Grade: B+

Your notes: _____

Groth Sauvignon Blanc, Napa, California 2008	$	Pts
	18	86

Barrel aging gives this wine a creamy pineapple decadence, tempered by zesty acidity. Pair it with heirloom tomatoes, olive oil and crusty bread.

Kitchen Survivor™ Grade: A

Your notes: _____

Hall Sauvignon Blanc, Napa, California 2007	$	Pts
	20	84

A solid offering in the clean, citrusy-grapefruit style that's a perfect match for raw oysters or spicy wings.

Kitchen Survivor™ Grade: B

Your notes: _____

Hanna Sauvignon Blanc, Russian River Valley, California 2007 $ 18 Pts 85

🍐 The honeydew, fig and grapefruit notes are signatures for Russian River SB. A great match for spinach and feta crostini, or fennel foccacia with ricotta.
Kitchen Survivor™ Grade: B

Your notes: _____

Haras Estate Sauvignon Blanc, Maipo Valley, Chile 2008 $ 12 Pts 87

🗝 Another great Chilean Sauvignon Blanc offering so much character - gooseberry, kiwi and honeydew - for a great price. A perfect match for mu shoo pork.
Kitchen Survivor™ Grade: A

Your notes: _____

Hogue Fume Blanc, Columbia Valley, Washington 2008 $ 10 Pts 84

☺ Great varietal character and minerality - that's a triumph at this price. Lime peel, lemongrass, chalky notes and smoke in the finish. Pair with ceviche.
Kitchen Survivor™ Grade: B

Your notes: _____

Honig Sauvignon Blanc, Napa, California 2008 $ 16 Pts 84

Intriguing anise, lime and gunflint notes on the nose, pure melon fruit; a primo match for tarragon chicken.
Kitchen Survivor™ Grade: B+

Your notes: _____

Joel Gott Sauvignon Blanc, California 2008 $ 12 Pts 86

☺ A perennial bang-for-the-buck crowd-pleaser: it's like a big salad of juicy peaches and Mirabelle plums.
Kitchen Survivor™ Grade: A+

Your notes:: _____

Jolivet (Pascal) Sancerre, (*jhoe-lee-VAY sahn-SAIR*), Loire Valley, France 2007 $ 23 Pts 88

🏆 🗝 A major favorite of sommeliers, this creamy-chalky, citrusy, utterly alive wine shows buttermilk, crisp apple, fennel and green papaya notes. Pairs with anything, especially anything prepared *au gratin*.
Kitchen Survivor™ Grade: A+

Your notes: _____

Kendall-Jackson Vintner's Reserve $ Pts
Sauvignon Blanc, California 2008 12 87
🍎 ☺Ripe pear and peach sparked with a zing of key lime and flinty notes make this a tasty sipper, but paired with goat cheese, it'll buckle your knees!
Kitchen Survivor™ Grade: A
Your notes: _____

Kim Crawford Sauvignon Blanc, $ Pts
Marlborough, New Zealand 2008 19 86
As always, a laser-pure NZ SB with charged-up scents and flavors of gooseberry, passion fruit and key lime.
Kitchen Survivor™ Grade: B
Your notes: _____

Kunde Magnolia Lane Sauvignon Blanc, $ Pts
Sonoma, California 2007 16 86
Tasty and refreshing, with lively grapefruit and tangerine flavors and scents. Nice on its own, but also great with a Greek salad (feta, tomatoes, olives).
Kitchen Survivor™ Grade: C
Your notes: _____

Long Boat Sauvignon Blanc, Marlborough $ Pts
New Zealand 2008 16 88
🍷 🦪 This exuberant and juicy new label is a great intro to the NZ SB category: more passion fruit than grassiness, but still with a mineral undertone and tingling acidity. Delicious for solo sipping but a home run with goat cheese or sundried tomato crostini.
Kitchen Survivor™ Grade: A
Your notes: _____

Lucien Crochet (*loo-SYEN crow- SHAY*) $ Pts
Sancerre, Loire Valley, France 2007 23 88
🏆 👍 Definitive Sauvignon Blanc that you'll see on many a fine wine list. Scents of cream, chalk and lemon custard with a bone-dry, beeswax-y lemon and green apple flavor on the palate. Ideal with oysters.
Kitchen Survivor™ Grade: B+
Your notes: _____

Markham Vineyards Sauvignon Blanc, $ Pts
Napa, California 2008   15   86

☺ A nice go-to SB that's got allspice and fig, grilled pineapple and zesty citrus flavors, making for tasty solo sipping, and a fantastic match with steamed mussels, Caprese salad, or goat cheese crostini.

Kitchen Survivor™ Grade: B

Your notes: _____

Mason Sauvignon Blanc, Napa, $ Pts
California 2008   16   86

🍎 I love this kiwi and passion fruit–scented wine that's like New Zealand SB with less grassiness. Great for tangy tomato dishes, and nice value.

Kitchen Survivor™ Grade: B+

Your notes: _____

Matanzas Creek Sauvignon Blanc, $ Pts
Sonoma, California 2007   24   92

⏳ I have put this classy, blue chip SB on wine lists for years, and it always delivers great melon-peach fruit and creamy texture- like a Chard but with crisper acidity. A great match for lobster or scallops.

Kitchen Survivor™ Grade: A+

Your notes: _____

Matua Valley Sauvignon Blanc,, $ Pts
Marlborough, New Zealand 2008   16   85

Laser lime, flint and herb on the palate, passion fruit on the palate. Better invite some ceviche to dinner!

Kitchen Survivor™ Grade: B

Your notes: _____

Merryvale Starmont Sauvignon Blanc, $ Pts
Napa, California 2008   17   85

🍎 One of the best wines in Merryvale's lineup, with lush and lively kiwi, melon, and grapefruit flavors.

Kitchen Survivor™ Grade: B

Your notes: _____

Michel Redde Pouilly-Fume La Moynerie, $ Pts
Loire Valley, France 2007   30   82

Flinty and lean, with grapefruit and smoky notes.

Kitchen Survivor™ Grade: B

Your notes: _____

Monkey Bay Sauvignon Blanc, $ Pts
New Zealand 2008   11   87

☺ Amazing—this wine bested benchmark Cloudy
Bay *twice* in blind tastings with pro palates. Cut grass,
lime, grapefruit, long finish—cool label, too!

Kitchen Survivor™ Grade: A

Your notes: _____

Montes Limited Selection Sauvignon $ Pts
Blanc, Leyda Valley, Chile 2008   12   86

⚡ Wake-up, taste buds! Like so many Chilean SBs
these days, a lively zinger of a wine with snappy mineral, chalk, lime and passion fruit notes - just waiting
to be paired with exotic and hard-to-match foods.

Kitchen Survivor™ Grade: A+

Your notes: _____

Morgan Sauvignon Blanc, Monterey, $ Pts
California 2008   16   89

⚡ ○ One of my go-to wine list picks, because it's so
luscious —cling peach, pineapple and lime —and yet
pairs so well with anything from garlic to wasabi.

Kitchen Survivor™ Grade: A+

Your notes: _____

Murphy-Goode 'The Fume' Sauvignon , $ Pts
Blanc, North Coast, California 2008   12   87

🍎 The oak has been dialed down, and the fruit and
charm turned way up: it's got succulent honeydew
fruit balanced by a zingy tangerine quality. The
creamy texture and lush fruit beg for sweet crab.

Kitchen Survivor™ Grade: C

Your notes: _____

Nobilo Sauvignon Blanc, Marlborough $ Pts
New Zealand 2008   13   86

☺ This NZ SB is the Mojito of wines: muddled
mint and lime notes, with hints of chalk and celery. A
great match for oysters, mussels, sushi or ceviche.

Kitchen Survivor™ Grade: A+

Your notes: _____

Oberon Sauvignon Blanc, Napa Valley,   **$**   **Pts**
California 2007   **13**   **87**

Cantaloupe and honeydew-a-go-go! Just add pro-sciutto - this is delish.

Kitchen Survivor™ Grade: B

Your notes: _____

Provenance Vineyards Rutherford   **$**   **Pts**
Sauvignon Blanc, California 2008   **20**   **86**

🍎 More tangy and mineral-tinged than past vintages, with lively grapefruit and cut grass notes. A perfect pair for summer salads and grilled veggies.

Kitchen Survivor™ Grade: A+

Your notes: _____

Rancho Zabaco Sauvignon Blanc,   **$**   **Pts**
Russian River Valley, California 2008   **18**   **85**

Tropical kiwi and passion fruit notes, kissed with zingy gooseberry. The long chalky finish makes it a perfect match for briny oysters and clams.

Kitchen Survivor™ Grade: B

Your notes: _____

Robert Mondavi Napa Fume Blanc,   **$**   **Pts**
Napa, California 2007   **20**   **91**

🍷 ☺ Perennially one of Mondavi's best wines, this often wins in my blind tastings against pricier bottles. It's got fig fruit, ginger spice, and lemongrass, and a rich texture. A great match for cheddar-bacon paninis or fennel and parmesan gratin.

Kitchen Survivor™ Grade: B+

Your notes: _____

Robert Mondavi To-Ka-Lon Reserve   **$**   **Pts**
Fume Blanc, Napa, California 2007   **40**   **93**

🍷 🥄 Waxy, honeyed, rich and layered, with plenty of lemon pie acidity to balance. Caramelized leeks, or a Hollandaise dish, are blow-you-away pairings.

Kitchen Survivor™ Grade: B+

Your notes: _____

Rodney Strong Charlotte's Home   **$**   **Pts**
Sauvignon Blanc, Sonoma, California 2008   **14**   **86**

Yay! They dialed down the oak on this wine, and out

popped the zesty citrus, pear and lemon flavors, and a chalky minerality. Ideal with mussels or goat cheese.
Kitchen Survivor™ Grade: B
Your notes: _____

Souverain Sauvignon Blanc, Alexander   **$**   **Pts**
Valley, Sonoma, California 2007   **15**   **86**
Souverain's quality across the board is super for the price. There's lots of juicy melon, peach and citrus fruit with a whisper of herbaceousness that makes this a great match for seafood salads & sushi.
Kitchen Survivor™ Grade: A
Your notes: _____

St. Supery Sauvignon Blanc, Napa,   **$**   **Pts**
California 2008   **23**   **90**
♻ Perennially one of the best Cali SBs, with exotic fennel, fig and grilled pineapple notes balanced by a tangerine tanginess. I love it with creamy curries.
Kitchen Survivor™ Grade: A+
Your notes: _____

Silverado Miller Ranch Sauvignon Blanc,   **$**   **Pts**
Napa, California 2008   **17**   **94**
♟ Free of oak, and chock-full of laser-pure fruit: melon, apple, peach and passion fruit, all layered and lingering into the endless finish. One of the best Cali SBs, period. Pair with clams or steamed mussels.
Kitchen Survivor™ Grade: A
Your notes: _____

Simi Sauvignon Blanc, Sonoma,   **$**   **Pts**
California 2007   **15**   **85**
This wine's got a creamy roundness from oak, balanced with a clean melony tang. Great with ceviche.
Kitchen Survivor™ Grade: C
Your notes: _____

Sterling Vineyards Napa County   **$**   **Pts**
Sauvignon Blanc, California 2008   **15**   **84**
A stalwart SB with grapefruit, herb, lime and super-crisp green apple flavors. Great with summer salads.
Kitchen Survivor™ Grade: C
Your notes: _____

Veramonte Sauvignon Blanc,   **$**   **Pts**
Chile 2008   **12**   **88**

✻ Another superb bargain offering in Chilean SB, with exotic kiwi, honeydew, and passion fruit flavors.

Kitchen Survivor™ *Grade: B*

Your notes: _____

Voss Sauvignon Blanc,   **$**   **Pts**
California 2007   **16**   **87**

🍎 A super-lively Sauvignon Blanc—juicy with lips-macking kiwi, white peach, and grapefruit flavors.

Kitchen Survivor™ *Grade: B*

Your notes: _____

Wairau River Sauvignon Blanc,   **$**   **Pts**
Marlborough, New Zealand 2008   **17**   **86**

Textbook NZ SB style. Think the "3Gs": grapefruit, grass and gooseberry. Pair it with another "g," goat cheese, and the fruit comes bursting forth.

Kitchen Survivor™ *Grade: A+*

Your notes: _____

Woodbridge Sauvignon Blanc,   **$**   **Pts**
California 2008   **5.99**   **86**

You can't find better SB in this price point. Arguably you can't find better *white wine* at this price point. There's plenty of snappy, grassy-citrus varietal character, soft melon on the palate, and great food affinity for guacamole, ceviche, salads. Pick up a case!

Kitchen Survivor™ *Grade: B*

Your notes: _____

Chardonnay

Grape Profile: Chardonnay is the top-selling white varietal wine in this country and the fullest-bodied of the major white grapes. That rich body, along with Chardonnay's signature fruit intensity, could explain its extraordinary popularity with Americans, although in truth this grape's style is pretty chameleon-like. It can yield wines of legendary quality, ranging from crisp and austere to soft and juicy to utterly lush and exotic (and very often oaky), depending on whether it's grown in a cool, moderate, or warm climate. I am pleased to say that, based on the broad popularity of varying styles, including the growing "unoaked or "oak free" style, buyers find all of these styles worthy, perhaps offering some hope to pros who bemoan a noticeable "sameness" to many of the supermarket brand names. All Chardonnays are modeled on white Burgundy wines from France. The world-class versions are known for complexity, and often oakiness; the very best are age worthy. The rest, in the $20-and-under price tier, are pleasant styles meant for current drinking. California Chardonnays by far dominate store and restaurant sales, but the quality and value of both Washington State's and Australia's are just as good. Although no Oregon offerings made the survey due to limited production, they're worth seeking out. Outside of Australia, Chardonnay is not a particular calling card of the Southern Hemisphere; I have included the worthy examples in this listing.

Serve: Chilled; however, extreme cold mutes the complexity of the top bottlings. Pull them off the ice if they get too cold.

When: There's no occasion where Chardonnay *isn't* welcomed by the majority of wine lovers; the grape's abundant fruit makes it great on its own, as an aperitif or a cocktail alternative.

With: Some sommeliers carp that Chardonnay "doesn't go well with food," but I don't think most consumers agree. Maybe they have a point that it "overpowers" some delicate culinary creations in luxury restaurants, but for those of us doing most of our eating and drinking in less-rarefied circumstances, it's a great partner for all kinds of food. The decadent, oaky/buttery styles that are California's calling card can even handle steak. And my personal favorite matches are lobster when I'm splurging, and buttered popcorn or aged Gouda cheese when I'm not. Any of these 3 pairings will make you swoon.

In: The One™ glass for white, or an all-purpose wineglass.

A by Acacia Chardonnay,   **$**   **Pts**
California 2007   **11**   **84**

A value bottling from a Chardonnay and Pinot specialist. For this price point, surprisingly toasty, with stony minerality and sweet apple compote flavors.

Kitchen Survivor™ Grade: B

Your notes: _____

Acacia Chardonnay Carneros, Napa   **$**   **Pts**
California 2007   **22**   **89**

Intense sweet-sour lemon curd flavors, with some residual sweetness on the palate that would pair nicely with spicy curries or mango salsa.

Kitchen Survivor™ Grade: B

Your notes: _____

Alamos (Catena) Chardonnay,   **$**   **Pts**
Australia 2008   **12**   **85**

☺ Fully-loaded fruit flavors ranging from zippy lemon to exotic pineapple, at a great price. Pair with chicken Caesar salad or cheese tortellini.

Kitchen Survivor™ Grade: B+

Your notes: _____

Alexander Valley Vyds Estate Chardonnay,   **$**   **Pts**
Alexander Valley, California 2007   **15**   **84**

Nice affinity with clams and oysters, thanks to the cut of flinty minerality melded with the pure pear fruit.

Kitchen Survivor™ Grade: B

Your notes: _____

Alice White Chardonnay,   **$**   **Pts**
Australia 2008   **9**   **85**

☺ A lot of lip-smacking Golden Delicious apple fruit for not a lot of money. Great price & taste for parties.

Kitchen Survivor™ Grade: B+

Your notes: _____

Antinori Cervaro della Sala Chardonnay/   **$**   **Pts**
Grechetto, Umbria, Italy 2007   **50**   **95**

Are we in Puligny? I'd have guessed Burgundy, thanks to the minerality, depth of crisp apple and pure lemon fruit, and gentle stony, nutty toastiness and cinnamon from the light oak treatment. A real triumph coming from Italy. Pair with scallops.

Kitchen Survivor™ Grade: B

Your notes: _____

Arrowood Chardonnay, Sonoma,   **$**   **Pts**
California 2007   **30**   **84**

A Sonoma classic Chardonnay that strikes a subtle balance of toasty oak and plump peach and apple fruit.

Kitchen Survivor™ Grade: B+

Your notes: _____

Au Bon Climat Santa Barbara   **$**   **Pts**
Chardonnay, California 2007   **20**   **89**

Twice the wine at half the price compared to many big-name California Chardonnays. The oak is subtle, keeping the flamboyant tropical fruit - papaya, guava and banana - at center-stage. Pair with scallops or coconut-curried mussels, or just a warm sunny day.

Kitchen Survivor™ Grade: A

Your notes: _____

Benziger Family Chardonnay Los Carneros,   **$**   **Pts**
Sonoma, California 2007   **18**   **87**

Cool-climate Carneros fruit gives this crisp quince and cinnamon-apple flavors and juicy acidity.

Kitchen Survivor™ Grade: C

Your notes: _____

Beringer Founders' Estate   **$**   **Pts**
Chardonnay, California 2007   **11**   **83**

A solid, sippable budget Chard with soft melon and pear fruit and a smooth, round mouthfeel.

Kitchen Survivor™ Grade: C

Your notes: _____

Beringer Napa Chardonnay,   **$**   **Pts**
California 2007   **16**   **85**

☺ A benchmark Napa Valley Chardonnay that's clean and lively, showcasing Meyer lemon and Fuji apple flavors and only a whisper of soft oak. Great with grilled chicken Caesar

Kitchen Survivor™ Grade: C

Your notes: _____

Beringer Private Reserve Chardonnay,   **$**   **Pts**
California 2007   **35**   **86**

A cinnamon-apple tart in a bottle, with vanilla, baking spice, and sweet apple compote notes, all balanced by juicy acidity. Pair with grilled corn and shrimp.

Kitchen Survivor™ Grade: C

Your notes: _____

Blackstone Monterey Chardonnay,   **$**   **Pts**
California 2008   **12**   **84**
Super-tangy and tropical, like pineapple upside-down cake crossed with lemon meringue pie (less calories!). Consistent quality and you can't beat the price/value.
Kitchen Survivor™ Grade: C
Your notes: _____

Bonterra Chardonnay, Mendocino,   **$**   **Pts**
California 2007   **14**   **84**
Clean and crisp, with Golden Delicious apple and melon flavors. Made from organically grown grapes.
Kitchen Survivor™ Grade: B
Your notes: _____

Buena Vista Carneros Chardonnay,   **$**   **Pts**
California 2007   **19**   **84**
If you've always wanted to experience "buttery" Chardonnay, try this one. Lots of ripe tropical fruit, too.
Kitchen Survivor™ Grade: B+
Your notes: _____

Cakebread Cellars Napa Chardonnay,   **$**   **Pts**
California 2007   **45**   **86**
👍 This is a Napa classic in style - toasty, rich baked apple fruit, cinnamon spice, soft vanilla oak. Great concentration, and impress-the-boss pedigree.
Kitchen Survivor™ Grade: B
Your notes: _____

Calera Central Coast Chardonnay,   **$**   **Pts**
California 2007   **16**   **93**
I have not encountered a lovelier, more expressive Chardonnay at this price, and it beats many more expensive bottlings, too. Day 1 is decadent and tropical mangos with fantastic acid/fruit balance. Days 2-3 it became toasty, stony and cinnamon-appley, with a long finish. Pair it with butter-and-sage pasta.
Kitchen Survivor™ Grade: A+
Your notes: _____

Cambria Katherine's Vineyard Chardonnay, $ Pts
Santa Barbara, California 2007 19 86

The toasted marshmallow and apple dumpling scent make you expect a fruit bomb, but this is balanced and minerally, with a long cinnamon-apple finish.

Kitchen Survivor™ Grade: C

Your notes: _____

Casa Lapostolle Cuvee Alexandre $ Pts
Chardonnay, Casablanca, Chile 2007 14 89

🍎 A benchmark "oaky" Chardonnay with toasty brioche and tropical fruit flavors. Super-classy, and great quality for the price. Pair with sauteed mushrooms.

Kitchen Survivor™ Grade: B

Your notes: _____

Catena Alta Chardonnay, Mendoza, $ Pts
Argentina 2007 25 90

From the winery that put Argentine wine on the map; this signature Chardonnay is exotically tropical, with pineapple-mango-passion fruit flavors and world class quality. Pair with fish and mango salsa.

Kitchen Survivor™ Grade: B

Your notes: _____

Chalk Hill Estate Chardonnay, $ Pts
California 2006 40 97

Surprising subtlety, finesse and toasty minerality, overlaying a core of vivid stone fruit and deft cinnamon-toasty oak. The finish lasts for several minutes, and I am always impressed by its ageability . This is America's Puligny-Montrachet. Pair with lobster.

Kitchen Survivor™ Grade: B

Your notes: _____

Chalone Chardonnay Estate, Chalone, $ Pts
California 2007 25 87

One of the Chardonnays that showed California's potential with the grape, and still going strong. This one trades on minerality, subtle toastiness and concentrated Fuji apple-spice flavors. Ages well, too.

Kitchen Survivor™ Grade: B+

Your notes: _____

Chalone Monterey Chardonnay, $ Pts
California 2007   11   84

Pretty impressive for the price. The buttery-mango flavors are tasty solo, or paired with Cobb salad.

Kitchen Survivor™ Grade: B+

Your notes: _____

Chappellet Chardonnay, Napa Valley, $ Pts
California 2007   32   92

A classic Napa name that kicks some of the more trendy newbies' butts in terms of complexity and, I think, aging potential. Wonderfully fresh acidity gives a great foil to the coconutty-toasty, sumptuous tropical fruit. Family winemaking at its best!

Kitchen Survivor™ Grade: B+

Your notes: _____

Chateau Montelena Chardonnay, $ Pts
Napa, California 2007   42   90

The wine that launched CA Chardonnay to the world stage. Montelena's understated elegance, featuring flinty-citrus zest aromas; laser pure apple fruit; and a subtle, long finish, are class in the glass, with the structure and concentration to age beautifully! A great match for delicate fish in cream sauce.

Kitchen Survivor™ Grade: A

Your notes: _____

Chateau Ste. Michelle Canoe Ridge $ Pts
Estate Chardonnay, Washington 2007   22   90

This won our blind tasting against famous Chards at 2x the price. The creamy coconut and butter scent and lush mango and tangerine fruit make you think "expensive" but it's not. Fabulous with aged Gouda.

Kitchen Survivor™ Grade: B+

Your notes: _____

Chateau Ste. Michelle Columbia $ Pts
Valley Chardonnay, Washington 2008   13   85

As always, on-form with a butterscotch, cream and apple character that's big but balanced. Bravo!

Kitchen Survivor™ Grade: B

Your notes: _____

Chateau St. Jean Robert Young Chardonnay, Alexander Vly, California 2006 — $ 25 — Pts 92

🏅 🍷 A California classic with a Burgundy-like nuttiness vivid and ripe pear and apple fruit, soft cinnamon spice and great length. Serve with trout amandine to bring out the mineral-toastiness.

Kitchen Survivor™ Grade: B+

Your notes: ________________________________

Chateau St. Jean Chardonnay, Sonoma, California 2008 — $ 15 — Pts 87

☺ A woman's touch? Winemaker Margo Van Staaveren seems to make this classic better every year. The rich tropical and pear fruit and soft oak are in perfect balance for sipping, or pairing with scallops.

Kitchen Survivor™ Grade: B

Your notes: ________________________________

Clos du Bois Chardonnay, North Coast, California 2008 — $ 15 — Pts 86

☺ A huge seller, for good reason: lots of crisp apple and melon fruit with subtle buttered popcorn scent—at a good price. A great match with smoked chicken.

Kitchen Survivor™ Grade: B

Your notes: ________________________________

Clos du Bois Sonoma Reserve Chardonnay, Russian River Valley, California 2007 — $ 16.99 — Pts 89

Drinks like fancy Chard, without the fancy price! Buttery, toasted marshmallow scents, vanilla and apple compote on the palate with a creamy texture and long finish. Pair with lobster or Gouda cheese.

Kitchen Survivor™ Grade: B

Your notes: ________________________________

Columbia Crest Grand Estates Chardonnay, Washington 2008 — $ 11 — Pts 83

☺ For devotees of the buttery, tropical, slightly sweet style of Chardonnay, you can't beat this value.

Kitchen Survivor™ Grade: B+

Your notes: ________________________________

Cuvaison (*KOO-veh-sahn*) Carneros   **$**   **Pts**
Chardonnay, California 2007   22   86
🍎 This is deliciously lively, with a luscious tropical
richness and lavish-but-balanced oak. Delish with
grilled corn on the cob and steamed clams.
Fridge Survivor Grade: B
Your notes: _____

Domaine Leflaive Puligny-Montrachet,   **$**   **Pts**
Burgundy, France 2007   105   92
🍷 🥄A true benchmark white Burgundy, pricey
because there is so little made. Even in youth it
shows a multitude of pretty layers: toasted coconut,
wet stones, honey, lemon curd and pineapple.
Kitchen Survivor™ Grade: A
Your notes: _____

Estancia Pinnacles Ranches Chardonnay,   **$**   **Pts**
Monterey, California 2008   15   85
Very Monterey - meaning intensely tropical and juicy
with banana-mango fruit flavors. Great with polenta.
Kitchen Survivor™ Grade: B
Your notes: _____

Far Niente Estate Bottled Chardonnay,   **$**   **Pts**
California 2007   56   90
🍷 🥄 California fruit, French-style subtlety.
There's a spicy-nutty-stony minerality, very subtle
vanilla oak and a dense core of golden pineapple
fruit. It's structured for aging, but pairs well now
with seared halibut on a bed of caramelized leeks.
Kitchen Survivor™ Grade: A+
Your notes: _____

Ferrari-Carano Alexander Valley   **$**   **Pts**
Chardonnay, California 2007   25   87
🍎 This wine delivers an artful balance of toasty oak
and ripe tropical fruit, with a touch of subtle mineral-
ity that's more old world in style. One of California's
most food-friendly Chardonnays - crabcakes, anyone?
Kitchen Survivor™ Grade: B
Your notes: _____

Fetzer Valley Oaks Chardonnay,   **$**   **Pts**
California 2008   **9**   **84**

☺ Kudos for the sustainable farming, juicy, sippable style—and great price. Pair with Caesar salad.

Kitchen Survivor™ Grade: B

Your notes: _____

Flora Springs Barrel Fermented   **$**   **Pts**
Chardonnay, Napa, California 2007   **26**   **89**

♥ 🍎 This wine is decadence, with balance: lush tropical fruit, crème brûlée and buttered popcorn flavors and scents. Pair with risotto scented with truffle oil and parmesan; or, just popcorn & a movie!

Kitchen Survivor™ Grade: B+

Your notes: _____

Franciscan Oakville Chardonnay, Napa,   **$**   **Pts**
California 2007   **18**   **84**

Cinnamon-toast, vanilla, baked apple dumpling: that's Napa Chard, defined. Pair with duck or pork.

Kitchen Survivor™ Grade: C

Your notes: _____

Frank Family Chardonnay,   **$**   **Pts**
Napa, California 2007   **32.50**   **90**

Here's what a Hollywood fortune paired with a passion for wine can craft: the full spectrum of fruits from tangerine to Honeydew to mango, deftly layered with rich and sweet vanilla-scented oak. The juicy texture is irresistible. Pair with buttery mushrooms.

Kitchen Survivor™ Grade: B

Your notes: _____

Frei Brothers Chardonnay   **$**   **Pts**
Russian River Valley, California 2007   **20**   **86**

🍎 Nice RRV Chardonnay character for the price, with lush and juicy stone fruit flavors balanced with bright acidity, and kissed with soft vanilla oak.

Kitchen Survivor™ Grade: B

Your notes: _____

Gallo Family Vineyards Sonoma County   **$**   **Pts**
Chardonnay, California 2007   15   86

⚕ A perennial price/quality star, with a lovely scent and flavor of buttercream and fresh apples, and a soft and toasty finish. Pair with butter and sage pasta.

Kitchen Survivor™ Grade: B

Your notes: _____

Grgich (*GER-gich;* both are hard *g,* as in *girl*) Hills
Estate Chardonnay, Napa,   **$**   **Pts**
California 2007   42   92

⚕ 🏆 👌 The name has for decades meant blue-chip Napa Chard that's packed with rich fruit, yet elegant, subtle and with a long, pure mineral finish. It often wins our blind tastings against wines twice the price.

Kitchen Survivor™ Grade: A

Your notes: _____

Hess Select Chardonnay,   **$**   **Pts**
California 2007   10   86

☺ A great value for the money favorite in the market thanks to the lively fruit: pineapple, mango, pear, and lemon. Soft and easy-drinking, with food or solo.

Kitchen Survivor™ Grade: B

Your notes: _____

Inspiration Vineyards Chardonnay,   **$**   **Pts**
Russian River Valley, California 2007   22   90

⚕ In our tastings versus French Meursault, this boutique wine from gifted vintner Jon Phillips shines every time. The subtle stony-toastiness and laser-pure core of crisp Fuji apple fruit are complemented by a soft cinnamon note that lingers in the finish. Pair it with lobster, mushroom risotto or aged Gouda.

Kitchen Survivor™ Grade: A

Your notes: _____

Iron Horse Estate Chardonnay, Green Valley   **$**   **Pts**
of Russian River Valley, California 2007   22   89

Old world chamomile-and-minerals on the nose, new world pineapple and butterscotch on the palate. What a lovely combo! Pair with summer corn and shellfish, or winter squash bisque.

Kitchen Survivor™ Grade: A

Your notes: _____

Jacob's Creek Chardonnay,   **$**   **Pts**
Australia 2008   **10**   **84**

Tee up popcorn, a movie and a crowd if you're the social type, because he bright citrus flavor without oak heaviness will please them, and your budget

Kitchen Survivor™ Grade: C

Your notes: _____

Jacob's Creek Reserve Chardonnay,   **$**   **Pts**
Australia 2007   **12**   **86**

Worth the trade-up from the quite-tasty basic bottling (above): the tropical fruit, buttery-coconut scent and long finish deliver a lot of bang for the buck. Pair with shrimp scampi or seafood chowder.

Kitchen Survivor™ Grade: C

Your notes: _____

J. Lohr Estates Riverstone Chardonnay,   **$**   **Pts**
Arroyo Seco, California 2007   **14**   **88**

An extremely well-done version of the buttery, "big" style Chard, with lots of mango-peach palate richness. Pair with grilled corn on the cob or shrimp.

Kitchen Survivor™ Grade: B

Your notes: _____

Jordan Russian River Valley Chardonnay   **$**   **Pts**
California 2007   **30**   **85**

Buttery-coconut banana notes on the scent, and super-lively acidity and citrus fruit on the palate, make this a natural match for fish with lemon butter.

Kitchen Survivor™ Grade: B

Your notes: _____

Joseph Drouhin La Foret Bourgogne   **$**   **Pts**
Chardonnay, France 2007   **14.50**   **86**

♟ Honey and chamomile, lemon and apple; elegant, balanced, long finish. Tops in the basic Bourgogne category. Pair with chicken salad or chilled shellfish.

Kitchen Survivor™ Grade: B

Your notes: _____

Joseph Drouhin Macon-Villages　　　**$**　　**Pts**
France 2007　　　　　　　　　　　14.50　　86
♟ Splurge on great oysters, and save on this clean,
elegant, chamomile tea-scented, appley wine. Yum!
Kitchen Survivor™ Grade: A
Your notes: _____

Joseph Drouhin Pouilly-Fuisse　　　**$**　　**Pts**
(*poo-YEE fwee-SAY*), France 2007　29.50　　88
♟ A seductive creamy roundness on the palate sets
this P-F apart. The juicy apple and fresh almond
scents, steely dryness, and long finish are classic.
Kitchen Survivor™ Grade: A
Your notes: _____

Kali Hart Chardonnay, Monterey,　　**$**　　**Pts**
California 2008　　　　　　　　　　19　　94
♀ This is one of the most delicious Chardonnays I
have tasted this year, and luxuriantly Monterey. That
means explosive tropical fruit - mango, papaya, pineapple, with hints of tangerine and honeysuckle nectar. Pair it with sweet seafood like scallops or crab.
Kitchen Survivor™ Grade: B
Your notes: _____

Kendall-Jackson Vintner's Reserve　　**$**　　**Pts**
Chardonnay, California 2008　　　　14　　89
☺ Every year, a price/quality champ. That's because
of the incredible vineyard sources - a rarity for a wine
so widely available. Its luscious mango and pineapple fruit and soft oak are a triumph of balance and
juiciness that keeps you coming back to the glass.
Kitchen Survivor™ Grade: A
Your notes: _____

Kim Crawford Unoaked　　　　　**$**　　**Pts**
Chardonnay, New Zealand 2008　　17　　83
Less concentrated than in past vintages, with lean
and soft apple flavors and a touch of soft minerality.
Kitchen Survivor™ Grade: A
Your notes: _____

La Crema Chardonnay, Russian River　**$**　**Pts**
Valley, Sonoma, California 2007　　27　　88
🍎 Further proof that La Crema has nailed coastal

CA Chards and Pinots. It's got yummy baked apple/tropical fruit; toasty-sweet oak, soft cinnamon spice.
Kitchen Survivor™ Grade: B
Your notes: _____

	$	Pts
Landmark Vineyards Overlook Chardonnay, Sonoma, California 2007	27	84

🍎 If you like big-fruit/big-body in your Chardonnays, this is the ticket. Pair with grilled shrimp skewers.
Kitchen Survivor™ Grade: C
Your notes: _____

	$	Pts
Leeuwin (LEE-win) Estate Art Series Chardonnay, Margaret River, Australia 2005	89	94

♟ One of the world's best Chardonnays, in part for its unabashed uniqueness: old world Chard scents of beeswax, honey, chamomile and white blossoms; new world fruit intensity with flavors of lemon curd and pineapple; the longest finish of toast, cream and honey; excellent ageability. Seek it out.
Kitchen Survivor™ Grade: B+
Your notes: _____

	$	Pts
Lindemans Bin 65 Chardonnay, South Eastern Australia 2008	8	82

☺ Always a bargain fave for its easy-drinking, apple-pear fruit and bright acidity.
Kitchen Survivor™ Grade: B
Your notes: _____

	$	Pts
Louis Jadot Macon-Villages (*LOO-ee jhah-DOUGH mah-COHN vill-AHJH*) Chardonnay, France 2007	20	85

♟ Clean and classy, with refreshing green apple Jolly Rancher flavors and a pretty chamomile-floral scent.
Kitchen Survivor™ Grade: B+
Your notes: _____

	$	Pts
Louis Jadot Meursault (*mur-SOW*), Burgundy, France 2007	45	86

♟ Toasted nut and baked apple character, a la classic Meursault, but with a lovely creamy mouthfeel.
Kitchen Survivor™ Grade: B
Your notes: _____

Louis Jadot Pouilly-Fuisse,   **$**   **Pts**
France 2007   **28**   **86**

🍃 ⚱ A fresh-air scent of hay and lemon, and softly chalky minerality are the signatures of this classic. When I taste it I stack the deck and pair it with food and you should, too, to appreciate its true calling.

Kitchen Survivor™ Grade: A

Your notes: _____

Matanzas Creek Chardonnay, Sonoma   **$**   **Pts**
Valley, California 2007   **29**   **92**

👍 ✋ A classic that deserves its fan club for quality and style consistency: Meursault-like toastiness, minerality and finesse, with rich baked apple fruit.

Kitchen Survivor™ Grade: B

Your notes: _____

McWilliam's Hanwood Estate   **$**   **Pts**
Chardonnay, Australia 2007   **12**   **87**

👍 Sweet butter and juicy melon, long toasty finish. Amazing quality for the price. Buy it by the case and pair it with everything from grilled cheese to corn on the cob pasta to chicken Caesar salad.

Kitchen Survivor™ Grade: C

Your notes: _____

Merryvale Starmont Chardonnay,   **$**   **Pts**
Napa, California 2007   **20**   **84**

Always a solid offering with peach and baked apple flavors kissed by a touch of cinnamon and vanilla from the oak barrel aging. Nice with corn chowder.

Kitchen Survivor™ Grade: B

Your notes: _____

Mer Soleil (mare sew-*LAY*) Chardonnay,   **$**   **Pts**
Santa Lucia Highlands, California 2006   **40**   **93**

🍎 Yummy, and a jaw-dropper for its screaming tropical, passion fruit notes, spark plug acidity and long, toasty finish. Sweet crab, crawfish, scallops, anyone? (Also try the equally-delicious sister wine, Mer Soleil Silver unoaked Chardonnay. Delicious!)

Kitchen Survivor™ Grade: B+

Your notes: _____

Patz & Hall Chardonnay, Napa
Valley, California 2007

$	Pts
38	92

A word of advice for the here-and-now wine lover: decant this wine! We drank it the day after opening, and went from "ho hum" to "va va voom" in our notes. It is going to age well. That said, after aeration the cinnamon-baked apple dumpling flavors are irresistible. This is the perfect wine for seared scallops.

Kitchen Survivor™ Grade: B

Your notes: _____

Penfolds Koonunga Hill
Chardonnay, Australia 2007

$	Pts
12	84

Real character bang for the buck, with apple fruit, spice and butterscotch, all in balance.

Kitchen Survivor™ Grade: B

Your notes: _____

Robert Mondavi Napa Chardonnay,
California 2007

$	Pts
20	87

Better than ever, thanks to a new depth and concentration to the baked apple, toasted nut and honeyed notes that linger into the finish. Pair with risotto.

Kitchen Survivor™ Grade: B

Your notes: _____

Rodney Strong Sonoma
Chardonnay, California 2007

$	Pts
12	84

☺ Cleaner and less oaky than it used to be. The crisp apple fruit and soft drinkability make it a crowd-pleaser, an easy solo sipper, and versatile with food.

Kitchen Survivor™ Grade: B

Your notes: _____

Rosemount Diamond Label
Chardonnay, Australia 2007

$	Pts
10	83

☺ Always a crowd-pleaser for the price and crisp, easy-drinking apples-and-citrus style. Pair with Cobb salad.

Kitchen Survivor™ Grade: B+

Your notes: _____

Rosemount Roxburgh Chardonnay   **$**   **Pts**
Hunter Valley, Australia 2007   **25**   **89**
Honeyed mangos, with a mushroomey earthiness that echoes in the long finish. Pair with seared scallops.
Kitchen Survivor™ Grade: B
Your notes: _____

St. Francis Chardonnay, Sonoma,   **$**   **Pts**
California 2007   **17**   **84**
🍎 A benchmark in the ultra-ripe Sonoma Chardonnay style: pear, tropical fruit and buttery notes.
Kitchen Survivor™ Grade: B
Your notes: _____

Sbragia Family Home Ranch Chardonnay,   **$**   **Pts**
Dry Creek Valley, California 2007   **26**   **92**
🍎 For several vintages in a row, one of *the* top Cali Chards. If you like the fully-loaded, decadent style this honeyed mango, golden pineapple and marzipan-laden beauty will make you swoon. Pair with lobster.
Kitchen Survivor™ Grade: B+
Your notes: _____

Sebastiani Sonoma Chardonnay,   **$**   **Pts**
California 2007   **13**   **89**
🍎 An absolutely stunning value for the price, with full-blown exotic mango-pineapple fruit and a browned butter toastiness and subtle minerality. Enjoy it with mushroom pasta or seared scallops.
Kitchen Survivor™ Grade: A
Your notes: _____

Shafer Red Shoulder Ranch,   **$**   **Pts**
Chardonnnay, Carneros, California 2007   **48**   **94**
🍷 🍎 The best-ever of Shafer's Chardonnay bottling, and its a beaut! The usual baked apple ripeness is now balanced by a delicate minerality that lasers through the long finish. Surely a candidate for the cellar.
Kitchen Survivor™ Grade: A
Your notes: _____

Silverado Napa Valley Chardonnay, $ Pts
California 2007   20   86

Lots of crisp apple flavor in balance with soft oak, excellent structure and mineral notes on the long finish. A great match for subtle fish dishes and risottos.

Kitchen Survivor™ Grade: A

Your notes: _____

Simi Chardonnay, Sonoma, $ Pts
California 2008   20   87

Even better than the turning point '07 vintage, this has notched it up with concentrated cinnamon-baked apple flavors and plenty of food-friendly acidity. Rock on winemaker Steve Reeder! Sip on its own or pair with crabcakes or coconut milk curries.

Kitchen Survivor™ Grade: B

Your notes: _____

Sonoma Coast Vineyards Chardonnay, $ Pts
California 2007   45   92

Like buttercream frosting without the fat and sugar. If you love decadent Chardonnays this unctuous beauty is like silk PJs for your tongue. Slip into a glass, and pair with popcorn and a chick-flick. A boutique bottling that's worth the search.

Kitchen Survivor™ Grade: C

Your notes: _____

Sonoma-Cutrer Russian River $ Pts
Ranches Chardonnay, California 2007   23   86

This wine's enormous popularity proves the case that not all Cali Chard lovers go for huge oak and sweetness: it's got subtle oak, gentle apple and pear fruit and soft minerality that are built for food.

Kitchen Survivor™ Grade: B+

Your notes: _____

Souverain Chardonnnay, Alexander $ Pts
Valley, California 2008   17   90

Hello, honeydew! And cantaloupe, coconut and cream. The tender texture is almost nectar-like, without being heavy. Worthy of the silkiest scallops, lobster bisque or a fine Camembert.

Kitchen Survivor™ Grade: A

Your notes: _____

Staglin Family Estate Chardonnay,
Napa, California 2007

$	Pts
75	96

One of the best California Chardonnays, period, and also one of the most Burgundian, with a stony Meursault-like minerality, white flowers scent and a tight core of cinnamon-apple fruit. Will age 10 years, easy.
Kitchen Survivor™ Grade: A+
Your notes: _____

Stag's Leap Wine Cellars Karia Chardonnay,
Napa, California 2007

$	Pts
34	90

The Cabs are Stag's Leap's calling cards so this and their more expensive Arcadia Chardonnay caught me off-guard with their elegance and expressive detail. The backed-off oak lets the minerality, layered apple and floral notes with a hint of fresh fennel, shine through beautifully. Pair with panko-crusted fish.
Kitchen Survivor™ Grade: B+
Your notes: _____

Sterling Vineyards Napa
Chardonnay, California 2007

$	Pts
15	83

There's oak-a-go-go on this Napa stalwart. The buttered toastiness dominates the nose, but the ripe apple fruit comes through on the palate.
Kitchen Survivor™ Grade: A
Your notes: _____

Sterling Vintner's Collection Chardonnay,
Central Coast, California 2007

$	Pts
10	84

The trifecta: appley-crisp, easy-drinking, great value.
Kitchen Survivor™ Grade: B
Your notes: _____

Stonestreet Alexander Estate Chardonnay,
Alexander Valley California 2007

$	Pts
28	90

The best it's ever been. Creamy and almost honeyed in texture, with caramelized banana scents, grilled pineapple flavors, excellent balance and a long toasty finish. Pair with sesame-crusted, seared scallops.
Kitchen Survivor™ Grade: B
Your notes: _____

Stuhlmuller Reserve Chardonnay,   **$**   **Pts**
Alexander Valley, California 2006   **35**   **90**

🍷 Really worth seeking out, for its layers and complexity: subtle cinnamon, brioche and baked apple, with a Burgundy-like nuttiness in the finish.

Kitchen Survivor™ Grade: C

Your notes: _____

Talbott (Robert) Sleepy Hollow Chardonnay, **$**   **Pts**
Sta. Lucia Highlands, California 2006   **40**   **94**

🍎 👍 True to this wine's classic style, with succulent tropical mango-papaya-guava scents and flavors and an unctuous texture, with the right balance of lively acidity to make it lovely with hedonistic dishes like lobster and seared scallops.

Kitchen Survivor™ Grade: B

Your notes: _____

Taz Chardonnay, Santa Barbara   **$**   **Pts**
County, California 2007   **16**   **86**

🍎 A great example of the Santa Barbara Chard style: tropical mango and pineapple flavors with minimal oak - just enough to give a hint of toast to the finish.

Kitchen Survivor™ Grade: A

Your notes: _____

Toasted Head Chardonnay,   **$**   **Pts**
California 2008   **14**   **84**

☺ "Toasted Head" means more oakiness from toasting the end pieces of the barrels as well as the sides. It yields a rich butterscotch and caramelized banana character that's nice with cheesy ravioli or tortellini.

Kitchen Survivor™ Grade: C

Your notes: _____

Trefethen Estate Chardonnay,   **$**   **Pts**
California 2006   **30**   **89**

🍴 🍷 Trefethen's signature classy and subtle style, with pear and pineapple fruit and a touch of mineral. Perfect with trout in browned butter or crabcakes. Classic wine from some of Napa's nicest people.

Kitchen Survivor™ Grade: B

Your notes: _____

Wente Riva Ranch Chardonnay,   **$**   **Pts**
Livermore, California 2007   **22**   **87**

Embrace total decadence with this honeyed mango, butterscotch and caramel-scented wine. Pure yum.

Kitchen Survivor™ Grade: A

Your notes: _____

Wolf Blass Yellow Label   **$**   **Pts**
Chardonnay, Australia 2007   **13**   **86**

Such a cut above all the other big-brand Aussie Chards at a similar price. It's got lively apple-peach-melon fruit, creamy texture and classy toasty oak.

Kitchen Survivor™ Grade: B

Your notes: _____

Woodbridge Chardonnay,   **$**   **Pts**
California 2008   **7.99**   **85**

☺ A budget Chard that delivers: soft apple compote fruit and a creamy texture and toastiness from light oak. Sippable on its own, or with Caesar salad.

Kitchen Survivor™ Grade: C

Your notes: _____

Yellowtail Chardonnay,   **$**   **Pts**
Australia 2008   **8**   **83**

The phenom that launched the critter craze, going strong due to its lots-of-fruit-for-the-$ value prop.

Kitchen Survivor™ Grade: B

Your notes: _____

Uncommon White Grapes and Blends

Category Profile: Welcome to one of the funnest sections of the book! A label of "other" for wines that don't fit neatly into a major category means some may not get the respect they deserve. But trust me, here is where you will find the gems in terms of deliciousness and uniqueness for the price. The group includes a diverse collection of wine types, including uncommon regions, grapes, or blends. Here is some background on each:

Uncommon Grapes and Regions—This category includes the grapes Albarino (from Spain), Pinot Blanc, Gewurztraminer, Gruner-Veltliner (from Austria; beloved by sommeliers and called by its pet name, Gru-V, like groovy), Torrontes (from Argentina), Moscofilero (from Greece), and Viognier (indigenous to France's Rhone Valley), all definitely worth your attention. The other-than-Pinot-Grigio Italian whites are also here, along with Spanish regional whites. (See the "Wine List Decoder" for more on these.)

Unique Blends—France's Alsace wineries sometimes blend the local grapes of the region - Riesling, Gewurztraminer, Pinot Gris and Pinot Blanc. This category also includes a growing crop of specialty multi-grape blends from Oregon, California and Italy that are well worth trying. Maybe it's a sign that consumers are continuing to branch out. Yay!

Serve: Well chilled.

When: The uncommon grapes (like Gewurztraminer) and unique blends are wonderful when you want to surprise guests with a different flavor experience.

With: In my opinion, Gewurztraminer, Albarino, Gruner-Veltliner, Torrontes and the unusual grape blends are some of the most fun food partners out there. They are especially suited to spicy ethnic fare such as Chinese, Thai and Indian. Also them with barbecue and even the Thanksgiving feast!

In: The One™ glass for white, or an all-purpose wineglass.

Anselmi Soave, Veneto, Italy 2007	$	Pts
	17	88

👍 🎿 The quintessential citrus-peel, chalk- and mineral-scented Soave. Melony flavors on the palate make it a great match with prosciutto or smoked sausages.
Kitchen Survivor™ Grade: B
Your notes: _____

Bastianich Tocai Friulano, Friuli Italy 2008	$	Pts
	15	89

🍺 I'd buy anything from famed restaurateur Joe Bastianich. This great entry point wine (look for his Vespa Bianco blend as well) is all fresh almond, floral, ripe pear freshness. A choice chaser for prosciutto.
Kitchen Survivor™ Grade: B+
Your notes: _____

Bodegas Avanthia Godello, Valdeorras, Spain 2008

$	Pts
65	96

A benchmark in the making, Yes it is pricey but I'd put it up against the best French Burgundy, Bordeaux and Rhone whites for sheer intensity and breed. Floral, tropical, thick and honeyed, yet with a backbone of minerality. Butter-poached lobster, truffled pasta and fine cheeses are the best pairing bets.

Kitchen Survivor™ Grade: B+

Your notes: _____

Bodegas Muga Rioja Blanco Barrel Fermented, Spain 2008

$	Pts
14	86

Ah, the buttermint candies I used to sneak from my Grandma's "company's coming" candy bowl: creamy, buttery, lemony-minty. This is all of that without the sugar! Fantastic with garlicky sauteed shrimp.

Kitchen Survivor™ Grade: B

Your notes: _____

Boutari Moschofilero, Mantinia, Greece 2008

$	Pts
17	86

Wish you were there? This wine is a vacation in a glass. Mo-sko-FEEL-er-o is the grape, a local specialty of the Mantinia district in Greece. The floral, rosehips and quince scent, and the bright pink grapefruit flavors, are like the Greek sunshine itself.

Kitchen Survivor™ Grade: B

Your notes: _____

Brundlmayer Gruner Veltliner Kamptaler Terrassen, Austria 2008

$	Pts
19	88

The siren song of GruV, in the hands of a great vintner like this one, seems to lure all sommeliers. This GruV is utterly distinct, with white pepper, sweet blossoms, grapefruit, crushed herb and earthy-mossy notes in the scent, zippy grapefruit, vitamin C, and quince on the bone-dry palate. Ideal with tuna ceviche, or pork with Pommery mustard sauce.

Kitchen Survivor™ Grade: B+

Your notes: _____

Burgans Albarino (*boor-GAHNS*   **$**   **Pts**
***all-bah-REEN-yoh*), Bodegas**   **14**   **86**
Vilarino-Cambados, Spain 2008
🍴👍 A great "starter" Albarino because it's bargain-priced, top quality, and true to the grape: that means zippy citrus, sweet hay, mineral and tangerine notes, with vibrant acidity tailor-made to cut through the brininess of bivalves or the richness of fried chicken.
Kitchen Survivor™ Grade: B+
Your notes: _____

Ca' del Solo Estate Muscat, Monterey,   **$**   **Pts**
California 2008   **18**   **88**
🍴 Here's an exotic wine worth seeking out. It is oak free and flavor-dense with Meyer lemon and grapefruit flavors, savory ginger and chutney notes, and a long peach finish. An ideal match for Indian food.
Kitchen Survivor™ Grade: B
Your notes: _____

Ceretto Blange Arneis,   **$**   **Pts**
Langhe, Italy 2008   **27**   **86**
🍴 *The* benchmark Arneis, a varietal local to the Langhe hills in the Piedmont region where Ceretto is famous for its Barbaresco reds. It is redolent with white blossoms and apricot. Perfect with dim sum.
Kitchen Survivor™ Grade: C
Your notes: _____

Chateau St. Jean Gewurztraminer,   **$**   **Pts**
Sonoma, California 2007   **15**   **85**
🍴 This wine's rose petal/spice scent and apricot fruit flavor make it great with Asian food in general.
Kitchen Survivor™ Grade: B
Your notes: _____

Chateau Ste. Michelle   **$**   **Pts**
Gewurztraminer, Washington 2008   **10**   **83**
The subtle candied apricot on the nose leads to a tropical fruit salad on the palate. Delicious with curries, tandoori, and Chinese food.
Kitchen Survivor™ Grade: B
Your notes: _____

Conundrum White Blend, $ Pts
California 2008   22   87

🍎 This wine enjoys practically a cult following, thanks to its "mystery blend" of up to 5 varietals, and its distinctive style: flowers, apricot, grapefruit, fig, fennel, tangerine, and more - an aromatherapy treatment in a glass. Its pairing potential is also vast: sushi, Asian food, Tex Mex, Latin, chicken, pork...
Kitchen Survivor™ Grade: B
Your notes: _____

Crios Torrontes, Cafayate, $ Pts
Mendoza, Argentina 2008   14   89

Ö ⚡ Drink more Torrontes! Argentina's signature white grape has irresistible floral, tutti-frutti and tangerine character that is great with BBQ, Chinese food, sushi, party hors d'oeuvres, or just for sipping. This is the best one made.
Kitchen Survivor™ Grade: A+
Your notes: _____

Dry Creek Vineyard Dry Chenin Blanc, $ Pts
Clarksburg, California 2007   11   86

Ö Like biting a Golden Delicious apple—juicy, with snappy acidity and a creamy-waxy finish. De-lish.
Kitchen Survivor™ Grade: B
Your notes: _____

Fetzer Valley Oaks Gewurztraminer, $ Pts
California 2008   9   86

Competes with the best GWZs for its varietal character - amazing ginger, allspice, apricot, lychee and rose petals on the nose. Soft apricot sweetness sparked with nice acidity make it great with curries.
Kitchen Survivor™ Grade: B
Your notes: _____

Guado al Tasso Vermentino, Bolgheri, $ Pts
Tuscany, Italy 2008   25   91

Ö ⚡ From nose to finish, a real "wow" wine. Intense aromatics of ripest peach, lemon oil and tropical blossoms are followed by pure Asian pear flavors and a long, almond brioche finish. Pair with herbed pastas and smoked fish, poultry or pork.
Kitchen Survivor™ Grade: A+
Your notes: _____

Heidi Schrock Ried Vogelsang blend,   **$**   **Pts**
Neusiedlersee-Hugelland, Austria 2007   **16**   **92**

🍎 The grapes - Welschriesling, Pinot Blanc, gold Muscat and Hungary's Furmint - are a frisky mouthful, and so is the wine. The opulent tutti-frutti flavors leap out of the glass and demand to dine with Chinese sesame noodles, sushi, or the blackened fish. The pure marzipan finish is simply amazing. A cheerful bird song in a glass? Yes: vogelsang means "bird song." Here's to beloved Heidi, a wine world gem.

Kitchen Survivor™ Grade: B

Your notes: _____

Hermanos Lurton Rueda,   **$**   **Pts**
Spain 2008   **14**   **83**

🖌 Super-crisp, with chalky-lemon flavors and snappy acidity that make it tasty with garlicky pastas.

Kitchen Survivor™ Grade: B

Your notes: _____

Hidalgo La Gitana (*ee-DAHL-go*   **$**   **Pts**
***la hee-TAH-nuh*) Manzanilla**   **16**   **89**
Sherry, Spain NV

🍴 🖌 👍 This sherry's clean nutty flavor and bracing tanginess are super with salty or fried foods, Manchego cheese, and Spanish Marcona almonds.

Kitchen Survivor™ Grade: A

Your notes: _____

Hirsch Gruner Veltliner #1, Kamptal,   **$**   **Pts**
Austria 2007   **16**   **89**

🍴 A great food wine with pink grapefruit on the palate, white pepper and ginger on the nose and finish. Break out the horseradishy cocktail sauce and chilled shrimp. If you prefer fried shrimp and the white stuff (tartar sauce), that's an amazing match, too.

Kitchen Survivor™ Grade: B+

Your notes: _____

Hogue Gewurztraminer, Columbia Valley.   **$**   **Pts**
Washington 2008   **10**   **85**

Ginger and cinnamon-spiced apricots on the nose, fresh peaches on the palate and a hint of sweetness. Pair with Chinese, Thai or Indian food.

Kitchen Survivor™ Grade: B

Your notes: _____

Hugel (*hew-GELL*) Gewurztraminer, $ Pts
France 2006   18   85

🍎 Textbook Alsace Gewurz: rose petal and sweet spice scent and lychee-nut/apricot flavors.
Kitchen Survivor™ Grade: A
Your notes: _____

Hugel Pinot Blanc Cuvee Les Amours, $ Pts
France 2007   14   85

The apple-pear flavor, mineral complexity, and liveliness of this Pinot Blanc are great for the price.
Kitchen Survivor™ Grade: B
Your notes: _____

Inama "Vin Soave," Soave Classico, $ Pts
Veneto, Italy 2008   17   90

Not your grandmother's Soave. This one is fantastic, with scents of Seckel pear, fennel, citrus peel and talcum powder that echo on the palate and into the long finish. A great match for fried foods and even tough-to-pair artichoke and asparagus dishes.
Kitchen Survivor™ Grade: B
Your notes: _____

Kunde Estate Viognier, Sonoma, $ Pts
Valley, California 2007   20   88

The Kundes are synonymous with Sonoma - committed to environmentally-sustainable farming and yummy, affordable wines. This Viognier is, as they say, aromatherapy in a glass - honeysuckle, spice and orange peel, with no heaviness. Just sip and sigh.
Kitchen Survivor™ Grade: B
Your notes: _____

Marc Kreydenweiss Kritt Gewurztraminer, $ Pts
Alsace, France 2007   41   88

Amazing complexity and character: candied peach, ginger, clove, beeswax and honey layers that beg for curried shrimp or a nutty aged Gouda cheese.
Kitchen Survivor™ Grade: C
Your notes: _____

Marques de Riscal Rueda (*mar-KESS* $ Pts
***deh ree-SCAHL roo-AY-duh*), Spain 2007**   9   85

This wine put Rueda (the region name) on the map, and now this white wine made from the local Verdejo grape is on fire. Riscal's key lime and kiwi fruit, without oak flavor, makes it a great food partner: salads, ceviche, goat cheese, garlicky pastas.

Kitchen Survivor™ Grade: B

Your notes: _____

Martin Codax Albarino, Rias Baixas (*all-buh-REEN-yo*), Spain 2008	$ 15	Pts 85

♟ Fragrant with scents of fresh hay and spring blossoms, and intense candied lemon peel notes. A natural with fresh shellfish, and great with spicy food..

Kitchen Survivor™ Grade: B

Your notes: _____

Miner Family Viognier Simpson Vineyard, California 2007	$ 20	Pts 94

Fantastic varietal character and utter deliciousness - apricot, honeysuckle, mango and lavender - make this one of CA's top Viogniers. Pair with fennel pizza or seared scallops with Pernod cream sauce.

Kitchen Survivor™ Grade: A

Your notes: _____

Pierre Sparr Alsace-One, France 2008	$ 14	Pts 85

A bouqet of fragrant local grapes, one tasty wine, with peach and tangerine fruit, ginger and honeysuckle. A great match with Thai, Chinese or Japanese food.

Kitchen Survivor™ Grade: B

Your notes: _____

Pierre Sparr Pinot Blanc Reserve, Alsace, France 2008	$ 14	Pts 86

There is no oak or high alcohol to distract from the lip-smacking pear and quince fruit. Pair with spicy sushi, chilled shrimp. blackened fish or BBQ.

Kitchen Survivor™ Grade: B

Your notes: _____

Qupe Marsanne, Santa Ynez, Valley, California 2008	$ 18	Pts 94

✍ For decades a sommelier favorite because it is so original, so delicious and so affordable. Hyacinth, peach, apricot and quince, with a hint of ginger make it a blast to pair with fusion flavors, whether Latin, Asian or Mediterranean. One sip and you're hooked!.

Kitchen Survivor™ Grade: B

Your notes: _____

Rocca delle Macie Occhio a Vento,   **$**   **Pts**
Vermentino, Tuscany, Italy 2008   **17**   **89**

♟ The bewitching scents and flavors of wild fennel, marzipan and Asian pear are perfect to pair with fennel salad, caramelized onion pizza, or sausage pasta.

Kitchen Survivor™ Grade: A

Your notes: _____

Ruffino Orvieto Classico,   **$**   **Pts**
Umbria, Italy 2007   **7**   **85**

☺ This wine's crisp acidity, clean pear fruit, and nutty qualities are what everyday Italian white wine should be. A great match for antipasti and fried foods.

Kitchen Survivor™ Grade: B

Your notes: _____

Santa Cristina (Antinori) Orvieto,   **$**   **Pts**
Campogrande, Umbria, Italy 2008   **12**   **83**

☺ The piercing minerality and citrus zest character make this a match for cured meats or garlicky pastas.

Kitchen Survivor™ Grade: B

Your notes: _____

Sauvion Muscadet de Sevre et Maine,   **$**   **Pts**
Loire Valley, France 2007   **11**   **84**

🍸 The ultimate carafe wine: crisp, lemony-mineral notes, easy price. Knock it back with some oysters on a breezy afternoon, and voila! You're in a Paris bistro.

Kitchen Survivor™ Grade: B

Your notes: _____

Schloss Gobelsburg Gruner-Veltliner   **$**   **Pts**
Steinsetz, Austria 2008   **29**   **88**

🍸 A real stunner with fried chicken: citrus acidity to cut through the richness, and its snappy grapefruit flavors kicked up the spice and subtle herbs in the crunchy crust. The budget-friendly "Gobelsburger" GruV from this estate is also worth seeking out.

Kitchen Survivor™ Grade: A

Your notes: _____

Sella & Mosca La Cala Vermentino,   **$**   **Pts**
Sardinia, Italy 2008   **13**   **85**

🍸 Lots of yum for the price with lively pear fruit and a hint of mineral that begs for clam-sauced pasta.

Kitchen Survivor™ Grade: A

Your notes: _____

Sokol Blosser Evolution, $ Pts
Oregon NV   15   85

🍎 ☺ Like an aromatherapy treatment—honeysuckle, peach, apricot, pear—but a lot cheaper!

Kitchen Survivor™ Grade: B

Your notes: _____

Tablas Creek Cotes de Tablas Blanc, $ Pts
Paso Robles, California 2008   25   90

🏆 French-style aromatic complexity - fennel, flowers, quince and pears, with California ripeness. It's a
blend of Viognier, Roussanne, Marsanne and Grenache Blanc that pairs great with ceviche and Tex Mex.

Kitchen Survivor™ Grade: A

Your notes: _____

Tilia Torrontes, Salta, $ Pts
Argentina 2008   10   87

🍎 Rivals the Crios for top Torrontes in my book. An
explosive scent of pineapple and tropical blossoms,
with pure and lively tangerine and passion fruit flavors. Wonderful with spicy Latin empanadas.

Kitchen Survivor™ Grade: A

Your notes: _____

Walter Glatzer Gruner-Veltliner $ Pts
Kabinett, Austria 2008   14   87

👌 A perfect GruV for newbies to the grape: loaded
with the classic grapefruit, ginger and white pepper
notes, totally dry, imminently affordable. Try it with
ceviche or nachos (seriously!), or fried chicken.

Kitchen Survivor™ Grade: A

Your notes: _____

BLUSH/PINK/ROSE WINES

Category Profile: Although many buyers are snobby
about the blush category, the truth is that for most of
us white Zinfandel was probably the first wine we
drank that had a cork. It's a juicy, uncomplicated style
that makes a lot of buyers, and their wallets, very
happy. Now for the gear switch—rose. The only thing
true roses have in common with the blush category is
appearance. Rose wines are classic to many world-
class European wine regions. They are absolutely dry,

tangy, crisp, and amazingly interesting wines for the money. I often say that with their spice and complexity they have red wine flavor, but the lightness of body and chillability gives them white wine style. They are *great* food wines. Don't miss the chance to try my recommendations or those of your favorite shop or restaurant. You will love them.

Serve: The colder the better.

When: The refreshing touch of sweetness in blush styles makes them great as an aperitif. Roses are great for both sipping and meals.

With: A touch of sweetness in wine can tone down heat, so spicy foods are an especially good partner for blush wine. Dry roses go with everything.

In: The One™ glass for white, or an all-purpose wineglass.

	$	Pts
Beringer White Zinfandel, California 2008	7	85

The standard-bearer White Zin is yummy and light 'n' easy as ever, with strawberry-watermelon flavors that say "bring on the spice!" Tame your hottest tandoori, curry or serrano salsa with a cool glass of this.
Kitchen Survivor™ Grade: B
Your notes: _____

	$	Pts
Big House Pink, California 2008	10	84

With flavors like the strawberry-watermelon bubble gum of your youth, what's not to love? Sip on a summer afternoon, paired with sunshine and a picnic.
Kitchen Survivor™ Grade: B
Your notes: _____

	$	Pts
Bodegas Muga Rioja Rosado, Spain 2008	12	87

An unusual "clarete" style, meaning red (Garnacha & Tempranillo) and white (Viura) grapes are blended. A strawberry-rhubarb-pomegranate "gulper" wine, delish with spicy foods like the Spain classic, chorizo.
Kitchen Survivor™ Grade: B
Your notes: _____

Bodegas Ochoa (oh-*CHOH*-uh)   **$**   **Pts**
Garnacha Rosado, Spain 2008   9   86

A wonderful summer rosé, completely dry with scents of strawberry and potpourri. Great with BBQ shrimp.
Kitchen Survivor™ Grade: B+
Your notes: _____

Bonny Doon Vin Gris de Cigare   **$**   **Pts**
Pink Wine, California 2008   12   85

This wine boldly put an American stamp on the dry European style of rose at a time when Americans were embracing sweet blush-style wines like white Zin. It succeeded because the tangy, savory pomegranate flavor is lively and lipsmacking.
Kitchen Survivor™ Grade: B
Your notes: _____

Chateau d'Aqueria Tavel Rose,   **$**   **Pts**
Provence, France 2008   19   86

Close your eyes and imagine some of the freshest summer flavors - raspberries, sweet tomatoes, watermelon; they're in this bottle, all kissed with an herbal hint that makes this wine a food-lover's ace-in-the-hole with anything Mediterranean, or grilled.
Kitchen Survivor™ Grade: B+
Your notes: _____

Domaine Tempier Bandol Rose,   **$**   **Pts**
Provence, France 2007   25   85

Expensive for rose, but this is the famous Grenache-based Provencal classic. Onion-skin color, pomegranate, white pepper and dried herb notes, lots of refreshing acidity; tailor-made for Nicoise salad.
Kitchen Survivor™ Grade: B
Your notes: _____

El Coto Rioja Rosado,   **$**   **Pts**
Spain 2008   11   86

One of my favorite roses, for its savory white pepper-on-strawberries flavor and snappy, spicy finish. Yum!
Kitchen Survivor™ Grade: A
Your notes: _____

Sutter Home White Zinfandel,	$	Pts
California 2008	7	84

This trailblazing WZ is still one of the best. Soft watermelon flavor and a hint of sweetness make it perfect for Tex Mex and other spicy fare.

Kitchen Survivor™ Grade: B

Your notes: _____

RED WINES

Beaujolais/Gamay

Category Profile: Beaujolais (*bow-jhoe-LAY*) Nouveau, the new wine of the vintage that each year is shipped from France on the third Thursday in November (just in time for Thanksgiving), dominates sales in this category. You can have fun with nouveau, but don't skip the real stuff—particularly Beaujolais-Villages (*vill-AHJH*) and Beaujolais Cru (named for the town where it is grown, for example, Morgon, Brouilly, and Moulin-à-Vent). These Beaujolais categories are a wine world rarity, in that they offer real character at a low price. The signature style of Beaujolais is a juicy, grapey fruit flavor and succulent texture with, in the crus, an added layer of earthy spiciness. All red Beaujolais is made from the Gamay grape.

Serve: Lightly chilled, to enhance the vibrant fruit.

When: Great as an aperitif and for alfresco occasions such as picnics and barbecues.

With: Many tasters said they swear by it for Thanksgiving. It's so soft, smooth, and juicy I think it goes with everything, from the simplest of sandwich meals to brunch, lunch, and beyond. It's often a great buy on restaurant wine lists and versatile for those really tough matching situations where you've ordered everything from oysters to osso bucco but you want one wine.

In: The One™ glass for red or an all-purpose wineglass.

Chateau de la Chaize Brouilly,   **$**   **Pts**
France 2008   **16**   **85**

This is classic Beaujolais, with lots of soft berry fruit and a smoky, earthy scent like autumn leaves.

Kitchen Survivor™ Grade: B

Your notes: _____

Duboeuf (Georges) Beaujolais-   **$**   **Pts**
Villages, France 2008   **11**   **85**

A great "house red," with soft plump berry flavor and nice acidity for matching with everyday dinners.

Kitchen Survivor™ Grade: B

Your notes: _____

Duboeuf (Georges) Moulin-A-Vent,   **$**   **Pts**
France 2008   **14**   **85**

Among the most powerful and expressive of the Beaujolais Crus, with leafy-mushroomey notes to compliment the plum fruit and subtle black pepper spice. Perfect with meatloaf or stuffed peppers.

Kitchen Survivor™ Grade: B

Your notes: _____

Louis Jadot Beaujolais-Villages,   **$**   **Pts**
France 2008   **14**   **83**

☺ Back to its classic style after an austere turn in the 2007 vintage. There's still leafy earthiness and pepper, but also plenty of plummy, grapey fruit.

Kitchen Survivor™ Grade: B

Your notes: _____

Pinot Noir

Category Profile: Pinot Noir is my favorite of the major classic red grape varieties, because I love its smoky-ripe scent; pure fruit flavor; and, most of all, silken texture. When well made, it offers red wine intensity and complexity, without being heavy. Although Pinot Noir's home turf is the Burgundy region of France, few of those wines make the list of top sellers in the United States, because production is tiny. The coolest parts of coastal California (especially the Russian River Valley, Carneros, Monterey, Sonoma Coast, and Santa Barbara County) specialize in Pinot Noir, as does Oregon's Willamette (*will-AM-ett*) Valley. New Zealand is also growing in importance as a Pinot source. Pinot Noir from all the major regions is typically oak aged, but as with other grapes the amount of oakiness is matched to the intensity of the fruit. Generally the budget bottlings are the least oaky.

Serve: *Cool* room temperature; don't hesitate to chill the bottle briefly if needed.

When: Although the silky texture makes Pinot Noir quite bewitching on its own, it is also the ultimate "food wine." It is my choice to take to dinner parties and to order in restaurants, because I know it will probably delight both white and red wine drinkers and will go with most any food.

With: Pinot's versatility is legendary, but it is *the* wine for mushroom dishes, salmon, rare tuna, and any bird (especially duck). Smoked meats and fish, too.

In: The One™ glass for red wines, or a larger-bowled red wineglass.

A by Acacia Pinot Noir,	$	Pts
California 2007	17	85

A soft and silky bottling with vivid red cherry fruit and a hint of dried potpourri and tea leaf scent, with a long, smoky finish. Pair with seared pork tenderloin.
Kitchen Survivor™ Grade: B
Your notes: _____

Acacia Carneros Pinot Noir,	$	Pts
California 2007	26	89

Still seductive after all these years. As always, a sexy gaminess envelops the silky raspberry fruit. Long and earthy, and great with Gruyere or Manchego cheese.
Kitchen Survivor™ Grade: B
Your notes: _____

Adelsheim Pinot Noir,	$	Pts
Oregon 2006	30	87

🍷 This Oregon classic's signature is subtlety - dried-cranberry fruit and a dusty-herbal-smoky scent.
Kitchen Survivor™ Grade: B
Your notes: _____

A to Z Pinot Noir,	$	Pts
Oregon 2007	15	86

This kind of value in Pinot Noir is all too rare. Straw-

berry-rhubarb flavors, satiny texture and a hint of savory consomme in the finish. *The* match for grilled salmon. Great with caramelized roasted veggies, too.
Kitchen Survivor™ Grade: B
Your notes: _____

Au Bon Climat Santa Barbara County   **$**   **Pts**
Pinot Noir, California 2008   **18**   **87**
    Oh-bohn-clee-MAHT has a cult following and a nickname. "ABC" (for short) is among the truly great American Pinots, with layers of strawberry-rhubarb fruit, tea, and potpourri, a slightly "animal" earthiness, and perfect balance. At this price? Yeah! True Pinot-philes will also want to check out their many single vineyards, and will want to cellar them. These definitely get better with age.
Kitchen Survivor™ Grade: B+
Your notes: _____

Beaulieu Vineyard (BV) Reserve Carneros   **$**   **Pts**
Pinot Noir, Napa, California 2006   **40**   **86**
Needs time to open up, then serves up flavors of Bing cherry tart with vanilla, cinnamon, and great length. A lovely match with red wine-braised duck.
Kitchen Survivor™ Grade: B+
Your notes: _____

Beringer Pinot Noir, Napa,   **$**   **Pts**
California 2007   **20**   **85**
A soft, fleshy, berry-flavored Pinot with a whiff of cardamom and vanilla scent. Pair with roasted veggies.
Kitchen Survivor™ Grade: C
Your notes: _____

Brancott Vineyards Marlborough   **$**   **Pts**
Reserve Pinot Noir, New Zealand 2007   **21**   **84**
This wine's cinnamon–red cherry flavors and tea-like tannins harmonize nicely when paired with salmon.
Kitchen Survivor™ Grade: B
Your notes: _____

Brancott Vineyards South Island   **$**   **Pts**
Pinot Noir, New Zealand 2007   **16**   **85**

🍴 A solid value offering, which is hard to find in Pinot Noir. Soft red cherry with a savory sundried tomato & smoky quality that would be great with Chinese BBQ spareribs or chicken teriyaki.

Kitchen Survivor™ Grade: B

Your notes: _____

Buena Vista Carneros Pinot Noir,   **$**   **Pts**
California 2006   **26**   **86**

From America's oldest winery, classic Carneros, with cherry candy and menthol notes and cinnamon spice. Pair with a lusty wine-rich stew like Coq au Vin.

Kitchen Survivor™ Grade: B

Your notes: _____

Calera Central Coast Pinot Noir,   **$**   **Pts**
California 2007   **24**   **90**

This long-time classic leaves many a more expensive Pinot in the dust. It's got silky strawberry-rhubarb on the palate, with a round, 3-D unctuousness that you simply never find at this price. It screams "Pinot" without being heavy. Pair with pork or grilled quail.

Kitchen Survivor™ Grade: B+

Your notes: _____

Cambria (*CAME-bree-uh*) Julia's   **$**   **Pts**
Vineyard Pinot Noir, California 2007   **21**   **86**

Oh, the cherry Lifesavers of my misspent youth. They weren't as good as this which has silky smokiness, too, but it's a fun memory, and a yummy wine.

Kitchen Survivor™ Grade: B

Your notes: _____

Castle Rock Pinot Noir, Mendocino   **$**   **Pts**
California 2007   **14**   **88**

👃 I give the excellent varietal character for this price very high marks. The cherry fruit, spice, and purity are exemplary. A great match for rare grilled tuna.

Kitchen Survivor™ Grade: C

Your notes: _____

Chalone Vineyard Estate Pinot Noir,   **$**   **Pts**
Chalone, California 2007   **40**   **87**

⌛ 🥄 This one needs time and air to harmonize the

sweet strawberry and red cherry, earth, mushroom and smoky notes. Pair with seared salmon or tuna.

Kitchen Survivor™ Grade: B

Your notes: _____

Chateau St. Jean Sonoma Pinot Noir,   **$**   **Pts**
California 2007   **20**   **91**

A heck of a Pinot for the price. It starts subtle with tea and fresh raspberry scents, then enriches after a day or so, when Asian spices emerge and the texture softens to pure silk. Pair with duck or salmon.

Kitchen Survivor™ Grade: B+

Your notes: _____

Clos du Bois North Coast   **$**   **Pts**
Pinot Noir, California 2007   **19.99**   **85**

Strawberry-rhubarb, and a snappy spicy note perfect to pair with teriyaki chicken or spicy tuna sushi rolls.

Kitchen Survivor™ Grade: B

Your notes: _____

Coldstream Hills Pinot Noir, Yarra   **$**   **Pts**
Valley, Australia 2007   **33**   **87**

🏆 👍 I love this Aussie offering for its Burgundian smokiness, and sun-dried tomato flavor with lots of smoky, earthy exoticism; pair with wild mushrooms.

Kitchen Survivor™ Grade: C

Your notes: _____

Cristom Jefferson Cuvee Pinot Noir,   **$**   **Pts**
Willamette Valley, Oregon 2006   **30**   **92**

🏆 🏆 This wine's signature smoky/cocoa scent, deep cherry fruit, and satiny texture are amazing. It cellars quite beautifully for up to 15 years in the best vintages. One of Oregon's crown jewels.

Kitchen Survivor™ Grade: B

Your notes: _____

Deloach Russian River Pinot Noir,   **$**   **Pts**
California 2007   **24**   **88**

🏆 🍎 This wine offers rich and crystalline cinnamon-spiced cherry flavor and silky texture, at a great price for the quality and pedigree.

Kitchen Survivor™ Grade: B

Your notes: _____

Domaine Carneros Estate Pinot Noir,   **$**   **Pts**
California 2007   **40**   **88**

My Grandma's strawberry jam on the scent! Sweet vanilla and red licorice notes that float, sleek and elegant, across the palate. Pair with duck confit or tuna.

Kitchen Survivor™ Grade: B

Your notes: _____

Domaine Drouhin (*droo-AHN*)   **$**   **Pts**
Willamette Valley Pinot Noir,   **45**   **89**
Oregon 2007

Needs aeration to unlock the layers: stewed cherry, truffle and cured meat. Pair with mushroom risotto.

Kitchen Survivor™ Grade: B+

Your notes: _____

Domaine Drouhin Laurene   **$**   **Pts**
Pinot Noir, Dundee Hills, Oregon 2006   **65**   **88**

Tight and smoky, with red currant and savory sun-dried tomato notes. I suspect it will be better in a year's time. Pair it with duck confit or beef stew.

Kitchen Survivor™ Grade: B

Your notes: _____

Domaine Faiveley Mercurey Clos des   **$**   **Pts**
Myglands, Burgundy, France 2007   **46**   **88**

As ever, a layered, smoky and savory intro to the Cote Chalonnaise Mercurey appellation. The pure cherry, mushroom and sundried tomato notes beg for roast duck or smoked pork with a dried cherry sauce.

Kitchen Survivor™ Grade: B

Your notes: _____

Edna Valley Vineyard Paragon Vineyard   **$**   **Pts**
Pinot Noir, California 2007   **20**   **84**

This one actually needed aeration to open and show its signature strawberry-rhubarb and smoky notes.

Kitchen Survivor™ Grade: B+

Your notes: _____

Erath Pinot Noir,   **$**   **Pts**
Oregon 2007   **16**   **84**

"Say hey..." to this value star that's classically Oregon with sundried tomato, pomegranate and smoky notes.

Kitchen Survivor™ Grade: B

Your notes: _____

Estancia Pinnacles Ranches Pinot Noir,   **$**   **Pts**
Monterey, California 2007   **21**   **85**

Pooh on the price increase, but the quality is still nice - strawberry, vanilla, tarragon, super-silky, long finish.

Kitchen Survivor™ Grade: B+

Your notes: _____

Etude Carneros Pinot Noir,   **$**   **Pts**
California 2007   **40**   **90**

👍 A study in elegance, with rose hips and orange peel, smoke and sweet tomatoes on the nose. More smoke and savor on the palate, with cardamom, white pepper, cherry-cranberry fruit and a long mineral-tarragon finish. Pair with a subtle cheese or rare tuna.

Kitchen Survivor™ Grade: A

Your notes: _____

Firesteed Pinot Noir,   **$**   **Pts**
Oregon 2007   **16**   **84**

☺ Nice for the price; the dried cranberry, earth, smoke and tomato notes pair great with goat cheese.

Kitchen Survivor™ Grade: C

Your notes: _____

Gary Farrell Russian River Selection Pinot   **$**   **Pts**
Noir, Russian River, California 2006   **42**   **89**

Sumptuous Asian spice route scents and satiny cherry fruit make this a pure, perfumed and elegant example of RRV PN. Pair with duck or spice-rubbed pork.

Kitchen Survivor™ Grade: B

Your notes: _____

Goldeneye Pinot Noir, Anderson Valley,   **$**   **Pts**
California 2006   **50**   **89**

🏅 Anderson Valley is a rockstar of PN regions in my book, and this wine is one of the reasons. Cardamom, tea, rhubarb and cherry, all on a sleek and structured frame. Delicious with duck (it'll age, too).

Kitchen Survivor™ Grade: B

Your notes: _____

Iron Horse Estate Pinot Noir, Green Valley of $ Pts
Russian River Valley, California 2007 40 89
🍎 The snappy rhubarb and heady cherry cola scents and flavors, with fragrant notes of rose petals in the finish, lure you back to the glass. Silky, delish.
Kitchen Survivor™ Grade: B
Your notes: _____

J Vineyard & Winery Company Russian $ Pts
River Pinot Noir, Sonoma, California 2007 35 89
🍎 Satiny raspberry and spiced tea notes, with floral and cardamom layers; lovely with smoked duck.
Kitchen Survivor™ Grade: B
Your notes: _____

Kendall-Jackson Vintner's Reserve $ Pts
Pinot Noir, California 2007 18 87
☺ This is a superb intro to Pinot, with classic silky cherry and spice character at an affordable price.
Kitchen Survivor™ Grade: B
Your notes: _____

King Estate Signature Pinot Noir, $ Pts
Oregon 2007 25 85
Lively acidity, with a smoky minerality and red cherry-sundried tomato character. A great match for salmon.
Kitchen Survivor™ Grade: B
Your notes: _____

La Crema Sonoma Coast Pinot Noir, $ Pts
California 2007 22 88
Close your eyes and think Burgundy. The taut, ash-and-roses scent and spiced cherry fruit could fool a pro palate. It needs time and food: duck or pork.
Kitchen Survivor™ Grade: C
Your notes: _____

Lindemans Bin 99 Pinot Noir, South $ Pts
Eastern Australia 2007 9 86
Real Pinot for under $10? Honest! The cherry candy and rose petal scent and satiny-smooth, juicy cherry palate are the real-deal in both taste and cost. Chill lightly and sip solo, or pair with smoked chicken.
Kitchen Survivor™ Grade: C
Your notes: _____

MacMurray Ranch Central Coast
Pinot Noir, California 2007

	$	Pts
	20	87

Dark cherry-cola scents, cinnamon spice, a mush-roomey-truffly finish, and silky texture, all at a price that loves you back. Pair with rare-seared tuna.

Kitchen Survivor™ Grade: B

Your notes: _____

MacMurray Ranch Sonoma Coast
Pinot Noir, California 2007

	$	Pts
	24	85

The earthiest in the MacMurray lineup, with chalky-cherry, tea and mushroom notes. Needs aeration to show its best (and maybe a rare-seared duck breast!).

Kitchen Survivor™ Grade: B+

Your notes: _____

Mark West Pinot Noir,
California 2007

	$	Pts
	15	86

This wine earns its "great value" raves in spades. It is incredibly silky and languid on the palate, with gorgeous strawberry-vanilla scents and flavors. De-lish.

Kitchen Survivor™ Grade: A+

Your notes: _____

Merry Edwards Russian River
Valley Pinot Noir, California 2006

	$	Pts
	42	89

Elegance in a bottle, with perfumey layers of cola, red cherry, cinnamon and sassafras giving it depth. Merry Edwards is a Pinot rockstar. Pair with salmon.

Kitchen Survivor™ Grade: B

Your notes: _____

Miner Garys' Vineyard Pinot Noir, Santa
Lucia Highlands, California 2007

	$	Pts
	60	94

Many wineries produce an over-blown Garys' Vineyard-designate. Not here. While super-ripe, plummy and lushly oaked, this keeps the elegance that Pinot should have. Big enough to match lamb.

Kitchen Survivor™ Grade: B

Your notes: _____

Morgan 12 Clones Pinot Noir,   **$**   **Pts**
California 2007   31   87

Although the price has gone up, the mouthwatering strawberry-rhubarb fruit and sleek texture are irresistible. A great match for mushroom ravioli.

Kitchen Survivor™ Grade: B+

Your notes: _____

Patz & Hall Sonoma Coast Pinot Noir,   **$**   **Pts**
Sonoma Coast, California 2007   45   89

I'd buy any of the Patz & Hall Pinots but this SC shows they know how to bring out the style of the growing district: strawberry-pomegranate scents and flavors, and of course the signature silkiness of Pinot.

Kitchen Survivor™ Grade: B

Your notes: _____

Ponzi Pinot Noir, Willamette Valley,   **$**   **Pts**
Oregon 2006   35   89

In the classic charming Ponzi style: fragrant spice, floral and cherry aromas, sleek texture, bright berry fruit and a coffee earthiness in the finish.

Kitchen Survivor™ Grade: C

Your notes: _____

Rex Hill Willamette Valley   **$**   **Pts**
Pinot Noir, Oregon 2007   24   86

Textbook OR PN: wood ash, smoked tomato and dried cherry, plus cardamom spice and orange peel; lively and tangy on the palate; smoky finish.

Kitchen Survivor™ Grade: B

Your notes: _____

Robert Mondavi Pinot Noir,   **$**   **Pts**
Los Carneros, California 2007   27   92

Hello, gorgeous! Let's cozy up to a nice roast salmon and enjoy your succulent cherry-vanilla, sweet spice and anise perfume, and smooth body. Ya, mon! The best PN in years from Mondavi.

Kitchen Survivor™ Grade: B

Your notes: _____

Robert Mondavi Private Selection | **$** | **Pts**
Pinot Noir, California 2007 | **11** | **87**

♕ Simply the best value-priced Pinot there is. In fact it kicks many more expensive Pinots' you-know-whats. Delicious silky cherry-strawberry-rhubarb flavors with a hint of vanilla. Lovely on its own but bring on the salmon or tuna sushi for real flavor fireworks.

Kitchen Survivor™ Grade: A

Your notes: _____

Robert Sinskey Los Carneros | **$** | **Pts**
Pinot Noir, California 2007 | **38** | **86**

The Sinskey style features sweet oak and cinnamon-spiced, supple, dark berry fruit with grace notes of orange peel and incense. Pair with tea-smoked duck.

Kitchen Survivor™ Grade: B

Your notes: _____

Rochioli Russian River Pinot Noir, | **$** | **Pts**
California 2007 | **60** | **88**

☝ This vintage took a day after opening for the black tea, rose petal potpourri, cinnamon stick and orange scents to come through. The structure and depth of pure cherry fruit suggest this will age well.

Kitchen Survivor™ Grade: B+

Your notes: _____

Rosemount Diamond Label Pinot Noir, | **$** | **Pts**
South Eastern Australia 2007 | **11** | **84**

Intriguing gamy, minty cardamom scents, cherry and sweet balsamic flavors on the palate, silky texture. A yummy budget Pinot perfect for teriyaki.

Kitchen Survivor™ Grade: C

Your notes: _____

Saintsbury Carneros Pinot Noir, | **$** | **Pts**
California 2007 | **35** | **87**

☝ This Carneros classic maintains its signature elegance, with perfumed notes of violets, soft allspice, and strawberry-rhubarb fruit. Pair with salmon on a bed of wild mushrooms and melted leeks

Kitchen Survivor™ Grade: B+

Your notes: _____

Saintsbury Garnet Pinot Noir, | **$** | **Pts**
California 2008 | **20** | **85**

☝ The first PN that showed you could stay true to the cherry fruit purity and potpourri perfume of the grape, for a great price. Pair with smoked chicken.

Kitchen Survivor™ Grade: B+

Your notes: _____

Sanford Pinot Noir, Santa Rita | **$** | **Pts**
Hills, California 2007 | **40** | **84**

The snappy cranberry-earthy notes are a little more austere than in past vintages. Needs air to open up.

Kitchen Survivor™ Grade: B+

Your notes: _____

Sea Smoke Southing Pinot Noir, Santa | **$** | **Pts**
Rita Hills, Santa Barbara, California 2007 | **50** | **88**

☝ The movie *Sideways* gave this wine a cult following. The fruit purity—spiced cherry, strawberries— and complex earthy-smoky-black tea scents are exactly what Pinot Noir lovers are looking for. Pair with pork.

Kitchen Survivor™ Grade: B+

Your notes: _____

Sebastiani Sonoma County Pinot | **$** | **Pts**
Noir, California 2006 | **18** | **85**

☛ A price/value star, with sleek mineral-dark cherry-strawberry compote flavors and a spicy scent.

Kitchen Survivor™ Grade: B+

Your notes: _____

Sokol-Blosser Dundee Hills Pinot Noir, | **$** | **Pts**
Willamette Valley, Oregon 2007 | **38** | **91**

☛ ⚒ The best yet from S-B and that's sayin' somethin'. I love the laser-pure cherry fruit, campfire smoke and potpourri notes, and the pure satin texture. A fantastic pair with wood-grilled salmon.

Kitchen Survivor™ Grade: B+

Your notes: _____

Sonoma Coast Vineyards Pinot Noir | **$** | **Pts**
Peterson Vineyard, California 2006 | **65** | **91**

☛ A relative newcomer whose aim for "Grand Cru Burgundian" concentration, smokiness and intensity partners nicely with the super-ripe cherry and cola

notes typical of the Sonoma Coast. Give it some aeration, and a tender table-mate: duck leg or salmon.
Kitchen Survivor™ Grade: B+
Your notes: _____

Sterling Vintner's Collection Pinot Noir,	$	Pts
Central Coast, California 2007	16	84

Searching for "value Pinot" is often a fool's errand, but this one's an exception to the rule. The snappy cherry fruit, cinnamon and silkiness impress for less.
Kitchen Survivor™ Grade: C
Your notes: _____

Stoneleigh Pinot Noir, Marlborough,	$	Pts
New Zealand 2007	16	86

Silky and fragrant with rose petals and fresh cherry in the scent, a soft white pepper-cranberry flavor and long finish. Perfect with seared pork chops.
Kitchen Survivor™ Grade: A
Your notes: _____

Taz Pinot Noir, Santa Barbara,	$	Pts
California 2006	25	87

Classic Santa Barbara style: Bing cherry fruit and smokiness slaked with lively acidity that prolongs the red-licorice finish. Great with rare duck breast.
Kitchen Survivor™ Grade: ?
Your notes: _____

Whitehaven Pinot Noir, Marlborough,	$	Pts
New Zealand 2006	25	86

I continue to differ with pros who rave about NZ's Central Otago Pinots. This wine is another datapoint in favor of Marlborough. Red cherry and red currant flavors, sleek and taut acidity, with a touch of smoke.
Kitchen Survivor™ Grade: B+
Your notes: _____

WillaKenzie Willamette Valley	$	Pts
Pinot Noir, Oregon 2007	28	85

More sprightly, lean and restrained than past vintages, with frisky acidity and bright red cherry fruit.
Kitchen Survivor™ Grade: B
Your notes: _____

Willamette Valley Vineyards Reserve   **$**   **Pts**
Pinot Noir, Oregon 2006   **25**   **88**

An affordable reserve that delivers: plump black cherry fruit, cola and wet stone notes, sleek texture.
Kitchen Survivor™ Grade: B+

Your notes: _____

Willamette Valley Vineyards Whole   **$**   **Pts**
Cluster Pinot Noir, Oregon 2007   **19**   **84**

☺ The juicy cherry-grapey flavors and cherry-candy scent are great for just sipping. Great price, too.
Kitchen Survivor™ Grade: C

Your notes: _____

Williams-Selyem Pinot Noir,   **$**   **Pts**
Russian River Valley, California 2007   **45**   **93**

Bob Cabral is Pinot-Maestro in my book. His wines set the standard for American PNs, without hewing to the big alcohol, over-extracted style that pleases some critics. This one is sleek, elegant and charged-up, with orange peel, cardamom, vibrant cherry and dried mushroom notes. Cellar if you can!
Kitchen Survivor™ Grade: B+

Your notes: _____

Chianti, Sangiovese & Other Italian Reds

Category Profile: Remember the days when "Chianti" meant those kitschy straw-covered bottles? Tuscany's signature red has come a long way in quality since then, pulling much of the Italian wine world with it. But let me clear up some understandable confusion about the labels and styles. As quality has improved, Chianti has "morphed" into three tiers of wine—varietal Sangiovese (*san-joe-VAY-zay*), labeled with the grape name; traditional Chianti in a range of styles; and the luxury tier, which includes top regional wines like Brunello, and the so-called Super Tuscan reds (see below). Many of the major Tuscan wineries produce wines in all three categories. The basic Sangioveses largely populate the budget price tier, and some offer good value. (Most are, in my opinion, just "red wine" without a lot of character.) Chianti itself now spans the entire price and quality spectrum from budget quaff to boutique collectible, with the top-quality *classico* and *riserva* versions worthy of aging in the cellar. Finally, the Super Tuscans emerged because wineries wanted creative license to use international grapes outside the traditional Chianti "recipe" (and, I guess, with fantasy names like Summus, Sassicaia, and Luce, poetic license, too!). What they all have in common is that Italian "zest"—savory rustic spice in the scent, plus vibrant acidity—and international sophistication from the use of French oak barrels for aging and some French grapes (like Cab and Merlot) for blending. The wines are often cellar worthy and nearly always pricey—I've listed the deals in this section.

I have also included the rest of the world of Italian red wines, including the great wines of the Piedmont district, and many interesting emerging regional wines. These are often some of the best deals in red wine, period, and almost always very food-friendly, so check them out.

Serve: Cool room temperature (the budget-priced wines are generally nice with a light chill); the "bigger" wines—classicos, riservas, Super Tuscans, and Barolos—benefit from aeration (pour into the glass and swirl or decant into a pitcher or carafe with plenty of air space).

When: Any food occasion, from snack to supper to celebration.

With: Almost anything; truthfully, nearly every wine in this section warrants the "Food Friendly" symbol. Especially great wherever tomato sauce, cheese, olive oil, or savory herbs (rosemary, basil, oregano, sage) are present.

In: The One™ glass for red or a larger-bowled red wineglass.

Allegrini Valpolicella, Veneto,	$	Pts
Italy 2007	13	84

The classic Valpolicella, with cherry & amaretto scents and flavors and soft tannins. Perfect with tortellini and other cheesy pastas, or takeout pizza.
Kitchen Survivor™ Grade: B
Your notes: _____

Arnaldo Caprai Sagrantino di Montefalco   **$**   **Pts**
Basilicata, Italy 2004   **59**   **90**

Suede slipcovers for your tongue. This wine is all
about texture and the full-blooded intensity of the
Sagrantino grape: black olive, dark fig, raspberry fruit
leather and a loooong finish. Pair with braised beef.
Kitchen Survivor™ Grade: B
Your notes: _____

Avignonesi Rosso di Montepulciano,   **$**   **Pts**
Tuscany, Italy 2007   **18**   **88**

This is the Sangiovese grape? Surely one of the most
fruit-forward versions ever, with blueberry, licorice
and savory cured meat notes that are smokin' good!
Kitchen Survivor™ Grade: C
Your notes: _____

Avignonesi Vino Nobile di Montepulciano,   **$**   **Pts**
Tuscany, Italy 2006   **28**   **88**

One of *the* names in the Vino Nobile region, and a
great intro to the style: red cherry and red plum fruit,
with notes of licorice, savory herbs and black olive.
Kitchen Survivor™ Grade: B+
Your notes: _____

Badia a Coltibuono Chianti Classico,   **$**   **Pts**
Tuscany, Italy 2007   **25**   **85**

Textbook Chianti Classico with lots of dried
strawberry and red licorice flavor hiding under a taut,
spicy, chalky cloak. Pair with grilled chicken skew-
ered with bacon and sage, or a cheesy tomato-y pasta.
Kitchen Survivor™ Grade: B+
Your notes: _____

Badia a Coltibuono Chianti Classico   **$**   **Pts**
Riserva, Tuscany, Italy 2005   **35**   **87**

Classy, thick and taut, with sassafras, dark cherry
and balsamic notes that cry out for rosemary-scented
meats or a great pecorino cheese. Will age well.
Kitchen Survivor™ Grade: B+
Your notes: _____

Badia a Coltibuono Sangioveto, $ Pts
Tuscany, Italy 2003 60 90

A classical Sangiovese-based super Tuscan with lots of leather and herb complexity, deep dark cherry fruit and impressive ageability, for a good price.

Kitchen Survivor™ Grade: B

Your notes: _____

Badia a Passignano Chianti Classico Riserva, $ Pts
Tuscany, Italy 2005 50 87

Heady notes of olives cured meat, with a deep core of cherry kirsch and even hints of chocolate, give your senses a workout, Tuscan style. Pair with a slow-braised meat dish, or Pecorino & olive oil.

Kitchen Survivor™ Grade: B+

Your notes: _____

Castelgiocondo Brunello di Montalcino, $ Pts
(Frescobaldi) Tuscany, Italy 2004 65 89

While intended for aging, this wine shows complex layers of cocoa, charred wood, dried cherries and figs and coriander spice, even in youth. Decant it for aeration and pair with a well-marbled steak.

Kitchen Survivor™ Grade: B+

Your notes: _____

Castellare di Castellina Chianti Classico, $ Pts
Tuscany, Italy 2007 19 86

Lively and spicy, with the old-style Chianti character that I love.

Kitchen Survivor™ Grade: B+

Your notes: _____

Castellare di Castellina Chianti Classico $ Pts
Riserva, Tuscany, Italy 2005 22 91

A supremely expressive Chianti Classico, heady with balsamic, licorice, leather and deep plum notes, with a savory-spicy finish tailor-made for a meaty stew.

Kitchen Survivor™ Grade: A+

Your notes: _____

Castello Banfi Brunello di Montalcino,　　**$**　**Pts**
Tuscany, Italy 2004　　　　　　　　　　　　　　**70**　**86**

🍷 Taut and structured, with palate-coating tannin, dense fig and mocha flavors and herb/olive tapenade notes. Pair with rich cheeses or slow-braised meats.

Kitchen Survivor™ Grade: B+

Your notes: _____

Castello Banfi Chianti Classico Riserva,　**$**　**Pts**
Tuscany, Italy 2006　　　　　　　　　　　　　　**18**　**85**

🍷 Classic Chianti with savory spice and dried herb notes, and mouthwatering strawberry fruit. A perfect choice for homemade lasagne or a simple pasta with butter and sage.

Kitchen Survivor™ Grade: A

Your notes: _____

Castello Banfi Cum Laude Super Tuscan,　**$**　**Pts**
Tuscany, Italy 2007　　　　　　　　　　　　　　**35**　**89**

🍷 Spicy, plummy and tarry, with dried spices, heady herbs and a licorice note. It's a great value for the complexity, and very food friendly. Pair with rich meat stews or slow-braised short ribs or lamb shanks.

Kitchen Survivor™ Grade: B+

Your notes: _____

Castello di Gabbiano Alleanza,　　　　　　**$**　**Pts**
Tuscany, Italy 2006　　　　　　　　　　　　　　**35**　**92**

🍶🍎 Why pay more? This super Tuscan hits on all cylinders: old world chalkiness, new world fruit, and layers of anise, vanilla bean, plum and dried spices. I suspect it will age into something even more special, if you can resist drinking it now with sage rubbed pork or a veal chop. The name refers to the winemaking alliance (*alleanza* in Italian) between Beringer and Castello di Gabbiano. Che bella!

Kitchen Survivor™ Grade: A+

Your notes: _____

Castello di Gabbiano Chianti　　　　　　　**$**　**Pts**
Classico, Tuscany, Italy 2005　　　　　　　　**13**　**88**

☺ A soft, light Chianti, with red cherry flavors and spicy notes that "can't be beat for the price." Bravo!

Kitchen Survivor™ Grade: B+

Your notes: _____

Castello di Gabbiano Chianti $ Pts
Classico Riserva, Italy 2005   23 89
♟ Old world without being austere, and a true rendition of classic riserva. That means ripe red cherry fruit, red licorice, black pepper and cumin with silky tannins and a spicy-smoky finish. Pair with tomato sauced pastas (of course!) or cheesy risotto.
Kitchen Survivor™ Grade: B+
Your notes: _____

Castello di Volpaia Chianti Classico $ Pts
Riserva, Tuscany, Italy 2004   34 89
♟ Worth the trade-up (though the non-Riserva is exemplary), for its intense, brooding richness and layers: licorice, dark plum, dried spices. Pair with herbed lamb chops or spice-rubbed pork or chicken.
Kitchen Survivor™ Grade: B+
Your notes: _____

Ceretto Asij Barbaresco DOCG, $ Pts
Piedmont, Italy 2006   51 87
This vintage showcases the improvements in vineyard and winemaking practices at Ceretto. The nose shows the potential of this cellar-worthy wine: tar, bruised plum, leather and licorice. If you do drink it young, tame the tannin with risotto or short ribs.
Kitchen Survivor™ Grade: B
Your notes: _____

Ceretto Zonchera Barolo DOCG $ Pts
Piedmont, Italy 2004   51 88
👆 Tar, rose petal potpourri, roasted beets and balsamic-glazed plums - in short, quite a wine, and it will only get better with time. In youth it needs food - a rich and cheesy risotto, buttery pasta, or slow-cooked wine-braised meat - to soften and show its potential.
Kitchen Survivor™ Grade: B
Your notes: _____

Citra Montepulciano d'Abruzzo $ Pts
(*CHEE-truh mon-teh-pool-CHAH-no*   6 83
***dah-BROOT-so*), Italy 2007**
🏷 ☺ A yummy little wine for the money, whose fruity earthy spice make almost any dish taste better.
Kitchen Survivor™ Grade: B
Your notes: _____

Col d'Orcia Brunello di Montalcino,   **$**   **Pts**
Tuscany, Italy 2004   **55**   **87**

♟ Aerate to soften the grip of firm tannin and unlock the layered rosemary, earth, pepper and strawberry. Pair with a rich beef stew or grilled sausages.
Kitchen Survivor™ Grade: B+
Your notes: _____

Falesco Vitiano (*fuh-LESS-co*   **$**   **Pts**
***vee-tee-AH-no*), Umbria, Italy 2007**   **12**   **89**

♙☺ A full-blooded blend of Sangiovese, Merlot and Cab that bursts with dark jammy fruit: plums, cherries and blackberry. Pizza- priced, but good enough for gourmet food - the best risotto or pasta you can muster.
Kitchen Survivor™ Grade: B
Your notes: _____

Fonterutoli Chianti Classico,   **$**   **Pts**
Tuscany, Italy 2006   **25**   **87**

♟ Red fruits, lively acidity and a peppery note lead to a subtly chalky finish. Pair with some crusty bread dipped in great olive oil to let the flavors emerge.
Kitchen Survivor™ Grade: B
Your notes: _____

Frescobaldi Nipozzano Chianti   **$**   **Pts**
Rufina Riserva, Tuscany, Italy 2006   **25**   **89**

♙ Mmm...Chianti dressed in velvet, with plenty of ripe plum fruit, licorice, and black olive nuances, and a grip of tannin. Pair with fennel sausage on crostini.
Kitchen Survivor™ Grade: B+
Your notes: _____

Guado Al Tasso Red Blend, Bolgheri,   **$**   **Pts**
Tuscany, Italy 2006   **115**   **95**

♙ Fearlessly super Tuscan, with not a drop of a local varietal (Cab, Merlot & Syrah). Here's to originality! You still get the taut red fruits, fragrant floral-herbaceousness and chalky tannins of Tuscany, plus sweet vanilla from French oak, and cedar-smokiness of the Bordeaux varietals. A great match for rosemary lamb.
Kitchen Survivor™ Grade: B+
Your notes: _____

Il Poggione Brunello di Montalcino,   **$**   **Pts**
Tuscany, Italy 2004   **70** **88**

🏅 Brooding and savory, with layers of sassafras, earth, leather, tar and dried fig. The chewy tannins will soften with air and fare, such as a fennel foccacia with roasted figs and shaved Pecorino cheese.

Kitchen Survivor™ Grade: B+

Your notes: _____

La Vite Lucente, Tuscany,   **$**   **Pts**
Italy 2006   **25** **89**

🍷 I wish more Super Tuscans were as affordable as this Merlot/Sangiovese/Cab blend. Unmistakably Tuscan with its brown spice, clay and dried cherry scents, lively acidity and chalky texture. Deep cherry on the palate, delivering both lushness and finesse.

Kitchen Survivor™ Grade: A+

Your notes: _____

Le Volte (Ornellaia), Tuscany,   **$**   **Pts**
Italy 2007   **28** **87**

A nice "intro" Super Tuscan based on Sangiovese which gives it snappy cranberry and savory herb notes; plus Merlot and Cab that add a plummy, dusty quality. Like all good Italian wines, it's meant for food such as a tender pork roast with garlic and sage.

Kitchen Survivor™ Grade: B+

Your notes: _____

Luce della Vite Super Tuscan, Tuscany,   **$**   **Pts**
Italy 2006   **80** **94**

Simply one of the great Super Tuscans, and still one of the best-priced at this level of quality. It's a minty-spicy, blend of Merlot and Sangiovese, with rosemary and cedar notes and luscious red fruits on the palate. Pair with a top-quality grilled steak or pesto pasta.

Kitchen Survivor™ Grade: A+

Your notes: _____

Marchese Antinori Chianti Classico Riserva, **$**   **Pts**
Tuscany, Italy 2005   **35** **86**

Lots of old-world, classic Chianti character here: strawberry fruit leather, chalky tannins, sweet balsamic and peppery spice. Serve with a charred steak.

Kitchen Survivor™ Grade: B+

Your notes: _____

Marchesi di Barolo, Barolo DOCG,	$	Pts
Piedmont, Italy 2005	55	88

♆ Barolo is meant for aging and for food. This is one that shows its alluring black plum fruit, mushroom, smoke and tarry quality in youth, if you decant and pair with a cheesy or buttery risotto or pasta.

Kitchen Survivor™ Grade: B+

Your notes: _____

Marchesi di Gresy Barbaresco Martinenga,	$	Pts
Piedmont, Italy 2005	60	87

♆ From a classic maker, a nice intro to Barbaresco's tarry, taut cherry, smoky, tangy-balsamic style. Needs cellaring to really shine, but you can enjoy it young: aerate and pair with a rich meat braise or fine cheese.

Kitchen Survivor™ Grade: B+

Your notes: _____

Marchesi di Gresy Monte Aribaldo	$	Pts
Dolcetto d'Alba, Piedmont, Italy 2007	17	88

♆ If you want a dance partner for your tongue (and your plate) this wine is ready to cut in on your boring everyday dinner vino. It's solidly old world with an inky, tarry, violet fragrance and very savory, spicy plum and balsamic palate, all on a sprightly, soft frame.

Kitchen Survivor™ Grade: B+

Your notes: _____

Masi Amarone della Valpolicella Classico,	$	Pts
Veneto, Italy 2001	28	86

Classic Amarone character, with scents of almond liqueur, dark cherries, dried figs, chocolate and sweet spices. Pair with aged parmesan or braised beef.

Kitchen Survivor™ Grade: B+

Your notes: _____

Michele Chiarlo Barbera d'Asti	$	Pts
'Le Orme', Italy 2006	15	85

A lot of Italian character for the money! The lively acidity and flavor of dried cherries, sweet spice, and balsamic lingers into the finish and gets even better with aeration. Pair with a lusty sage-mushroom pasta.

Kitchen Survivor™ Grade: B+

Your notes: _____

Ornellaia Super Tuscan, Bolgheri, $ Pts
Tuscany, Italy 2006   125   91

Elegant, cedary and very Bordeaux-like (a Cab and Merlot-dominated blend with Cab Franc and Petit Verdot). The dense cassis fruit is layered with cinnamon spice, vanilla and dusty-leafy crushed mint notes, with the Tuscan touch: chalky texture and vibrant acidity. Pair with Tuscan steak, pecorino with olive oil and crusty bread, or basil pesto.

Kitchen Survivor™ Grade: B+

Your notes: _____

Pian delle Vigne Brunello di Montalcino, $ Pts
Tuscany, Italy 2004   65   88

♟ While nothing from Antinori is cheap any more, for good Brunello this is a deal. It opens up with aeration so you can see the majesty: cinnamon, sweet licorice, black pepper, dark figs. Just add cheese!

Kitchen Survivor™ Grade: B+

Your notes: _____

Poggio alla Badiola, Tuscany, $ Pts
Italy 2006   18   85

🍎 This Sangiovese/Merlot blend is the perfect combo of soft and dark fruit, with that Italian savor you expect from Tuscany: licorice, spice, a hint of tar. Great with fresh mozzarella, basil and tomato salad.

Kitchen Survivor™ Grade: B

Your notes: _____

Poliziano Vino Nobile di Montepulciano, $ Pts
Tuscany, Italy 2005   25   86

Of all the Tuscan reds, Vino Nobile shows the most dark ripe fruit when young - black plum and blackberry, with a dusty, forest floor note that's a great match for earthy dishes like wild mushroom ravioli.

Kitchen Survivor™ Grade: B+

Your notes: _____

Prunotto Barolo, Piedmont, $ Pts
Italy 2004   45   87

Fragrant anise, balsamic and black olive scents and dark plum fruit give this Barolo expression even in youth. Decant for aeration, and pair with a rich pasta such as Fettucine Alfredo or Linguine Carbonara.

Kitchen Survivor™ Grade: B+

Your notes: _____

Rocca delle Macie Chianti Classico, $ Pts
Tuscany, Italy 2006   18   86

☖ A savory and chalky Chianti, with scents of green herbs, leather and licorice gracing the peppery strawberry palate. Perfect with garlicky, cheesy pastas.

Kitchen Survivor™ Grade: C

Your notes: _____

Ruffino Aziano Chianti Classico, $ Pts
Tuscany, Italy 2007   13   83

Good basic Chianti for the price, with stewed tomato, spice and strawberry flavors and a chalky texture. The perfect pizza-pasta-panini wine.

Kitchen Survivor™ Grade: C

Your notes: _____

Ruffino Chianti Classico Riserva $ Pts
Ducale (*doo-CALL-eh*) Oro (Gold   40   89
Label), Tuscany, Italy 2006

Although it's pricey, this classic delivers leathery, roasted fig and spice complexity. Pair it with fresh figs with black pepper, balsamic and fresh mozzarella.

Kitchen Survivor™ Grade: A+

Your notes: _____

Santa Cristina Sangiovese, $ Pts
Antinori, Tuscany, Italy 2007   12   84

This easy to drink for everyday wine is better than ever, with earthy cherry fruit and lively acidity.

Kitchen Survivor™ Grade: C

Your notes: _____

Santa Cristina Chianti, Antinori, $ Pts
Tuscany, Italy 2007   16   86

Most Antinori Chiantis are now luxury wines, but this one is affordable and true to the Tuscan trattoria style: spicy, light cherry fruit, goes with anything.

Kitchen Survivor™ Grade: B

Your notes: _____

Solaia (Antinori), Tuscany, $ Pts
Italy 2006   285   97

☖ The nose is cult Cab-like: lavish with black cassis fruit, dark chocolate, allspice, sweet vanillin and a floral whiff of jasmine. On the palate it is subtle and smoky, with succulent black fruit in the mid-palate

and layered complexity in the finish: autumn leaves, lavender, cedar and rosemary (from the dollop of Sangiovese in the mostly-Cab blend). An amazing wine.
Kitchen Survivor™ Grade: A
Your notes: _____

Taurino Salice Salentino Rosso Riserva, Apulia, Italy 2006 $ 12 Pts 88
Ö A rustic, mouth-watering leather-and-berries vino that's tailor-made for garlicky pastas or roast chicken.
Kitchen Survivor™ Grade: B+
Your notes: _____

Tenuta del Terriccio Tassinaia, Tuscany, Italy 2004 $ 35 Pts 88
The cedary Cabernet shows in this Super Tuscan trio blend with Merlot and Sangiovese. The firm acidity and chalky tannin, and lively core of blackberry and cranberry fruit, are exemplary. Pair with pesto pasta.
Kitchen Survivor™ Grade: A
Your notes: _____

Tenuta Sette Ponti Crognolo, Tuscany, Italy 2007 $ 35 Pts 90
Ö One of the best value Super Tuscans on the market. A savory balsamic-strawberry-anise-scented blend of Sangiovese and Merlot that serves up cumin and cardamom spices with aeration. Pair with pasta with sausage and herbs or an array of fine cheeses.
Kitchen Survivor™ Grade: A
Your notes: _____

Tignanello, Tuscany, Italy 2006 $ 95 Pts 95
Ö The yin to sister wine Solaia's yang. This one is mostly Sangiovese with some Cab (Solaia is the opposite). The Sangiovese dominance shows as red fruits (cherry, currant, strawberry) and red licorice and gamy notes, with a bewitching vanilla-gardenia fragrance. The chalky tannins and charged-up acidity will sustain it for the long haul but it's wonderful now with herb-laced meats, or cheese and tomato pastas.
Kitchen Survivor™ Grade: A
Your notes: _____

Val di Suga Brunello di Montalcino,
Tuscany, Italy 2004

$	Pts
66	93

♉ A steal for great Brunello, and a find for its delicious drinkability. Serve some slow-braised short ribs to unlock the lusty layers: leather, chewy dark cherry, smoke, spice and anise. Buy some extra for the cellar.
Kitchen Survivor™ Grade: A
Your notes: _____

Val di Suga Rosso di Montalcino,
Tuscany, Italy 2006

$	Pts
26	90

"Baby Brunello," meaning it's made from younger vines, drinkable younger, and less expensive. Handsdown the most complex Rosso I have ever tasted: vanilla, coffee, ripe & dusky plum fruit, chalky finish.
Kitchen Survivor™ Grade: A
Your notes: _____

Merlot

Grape Profile: When early 1990s news reports linked heart health and moderate red wine drinking, Merlot joined the ranks of go-to wine grapes that inspire instant customer recognition. As producers scrambled to meet the new demand, a lot of so-so Merlot began to flood the market, making this a tricky category for finding quality and character. The selections in this section are the worthy ones. I also have to say that the grape is making a comeback with me, meaning I am finding the number of impressive, distinctive Merlots is really on the rise. That's great news!

As with other market-leading varietals like Chardonnay and Cabernet Sauvignon, Merlot can range both in price, from budget to boutique, and in complexity, from soft and simple to "serious." Across the spectrum, Merlot is modeled on the wines from its home region of Bordeaux, France. At the basic level, that means medium body and soft texture, with nice plum and berry fruit flavor.

The more ambitious versions have more body, tannin, and fruit concentration and usually a good bit of oakiness in the scent and taste. Washington State, California's Sonoma and Napa regions, and Chile are my favorite growing regions for varietal Merlot. Most Merlot producers follow the Bordeaux practice of blending in some Cabernet Sauvignon (or another of the classic Bordeaux red grapes) to complement and enhance the wines' taste and complexity.

Serve: *Cool* room temperature.

When: With meals, of course; and the basic bottlings are soft enough to enjoy on their own as a cocktail alternative.

With: Anything with which you enjoy red wine, especially cheeses, roasts, fuller-bodied fish, and grilled foods.

In: The One™ glass for red, or a larger-bowled red wine stem.

	$	Pts
Beringer Bancroft Ranch Merlot, Howell Mountain, Napa Valley, California 2006	75	92

♉ One of Napa's greatest Merlots, luxuriant with chocolate, blueberry, plum, wet stone and autumn leaf-pile notes. Truly meant for aging, and for pairing with prime steak, pesto pasta or lamb chops.
Kitchen Survivor™ Grade: C
Your notes: _____

	$	Pts
Blackstone Merlot, California 2007	12	82

A fruit bomb that's nice for the price. The spunky hint of black licorice makes it great with BBQ.
Kitchen Survivor™ Grade: C
Your notes: _____

	$	Pts
Bogle Merlot, California 2007	12	84

♉ This wine is hugely popular for its juicy berry fruit, smooth drinkability and solid value. Great for everyday meals like meatloaf, beef stew or spaghetti.
Kitchen Survivor™ Grade: C
Your notes: _____

Canoe Ridge Merlot, Columbia Valley, Washington 2006 $ 26   Pts 85

Although it's gotten pricey, this wine's a big seller for its classy mix of new world plummy fruit and old world earth, and dusty-smoky notes.

Kitchen Survivor™ Grade: C

Your notes: _____

Casa Lapostolle Cuvee Alexandre Merlot, California 2006 $ 20   Pts 87

New World ripe cherry fruit, Bordeaux-like mocha, earth, vanilla. Very classy. Pair with mushroom risotto.

Kitchen Survivor™ Grade: B

Your notes: _____

Chateau Ste. Michelle Canoe Ridge Estate Merlot, Horse Heaven Hills, WA 2006 $ 25   Pts 89

This is what Merlot wants to be: blueberry pie filling, licorice, coal dust and smoke, smooth and balanced.

Kitchen Survivor™ Grade: B

Your notes: _____

Chateau Ste. Michelle Columbia Valley Merlot, Washington 2006 $ 14   Pts 88

Once again, this was a winner in my blind tasting of benchmark Merlots at 2-3x the price. The earth, plum and sweet vanilla, rich texture and long finish - and the amazing value - earn this top marks

Kitchen Survivor™ Grade: B

Your notes: _____

Chateau Ste. Michelle Indian Wells Merlot, Columbia Valley, Washington 2006 $ 18   Pts 90

🍎 ☺ Serve this when you want to blow them away with sumptuous fruit, lush oak and chocolatey richness. Match it with cheeses or dark chocolate.

Kitchen Survivor™ Grade: B

Your notes: _____

Chateau St. Jean Merlot, Sonoma, California 2006 $ 25   Pts 89

This wine shows St. Jean's deft hand with the Bordeaux grapes. The dark berry, coffee and smoky notes are long and harmonious. Pair with fine cheeses.

Kitchen Survivor™ Grade: B+

Your notes: _____

MERLOT'S KISSING COUSINS: If you are looking for something different but similar to Merlot, check out two South American specialties. First, there's Argentina's Malbec (*MAHL-beck*), a red grape originally from Bordeaux. It's similar in body and smoothness to Merlot, with lots of smoky aromatic complexity. Some wineries to look for: Salentein, Navarro Correas, Catena, and Kaiken. Second, from Chile, try Carmenere (*car-muh-NAIR-eh*), also a Bordeaux import that was originally misidentified as Merlot in many Chilean vineyards. Its smooth texture and plum fruit are complemented by an exotically meaty-smoky scent. Look for Carmeneres from Concha y Toro, MontGras, Arboleda, and Veramonte Primus. Check out "Other Reds" for more on these.

	$	Pts
Clos du Bois North Coast Merlot, California 2006	16.99	82

Hugely popular for sure, and in the early days of my career it was a quality benchmark, too. Now I find the fruit a bit lighter than it used to be - I want more for the money.
Kitchen Survivor™ Grade: C
Your notes: _____

	$	Pts
Columbia Crest Grand Estates Merlot, Washington 2006	11	84

☺ Most in-the-know winegeeks avoid budget Merlot like the Plague, but this one is a credit to the category - smooth, plummy, a nice everyday meal partner.
Kitchen Survivor™ Grade: B
Your notes: _____

	$	Pts
Duckhorn Napa Merlot, Napa, California 2006	52	89

♉ Spicy! Cedar, cinnamon, sweet vanilla - all of these oak-sourced elements integrated with the fruit a day after opening, so decant! It is a Napa classic.
Kitchen Survivor™ Grade: B+
Your notes: _____

Ehlers Estate Merlot,
Napa, California 2005

$ **Pts**
55   89

🍎 It's pricey, but this sumptuously dark plum and fig-fruited Merlot is one of California's best. An impress-the-boss kind of wine that begs for prime rib.
Kitchen Survivor™ Grade: B+
Your notes: _____

Fetzer Valley Oaks Merlot,
California 2007

$ **Pts**
9   85

☺ One of the best basic California Merlots out there, with juicy berry flavors and a good survivor grade that makes it a great "house wine."
Kitchen Survivor™ Grade: A
Your notes: _____

Franciscan Merlot, Napa,
California 2006

$ **Pts**
24   83

While still marked by dusty plummy fruit, this wine is lighter and less lush than past vintages.
Kitchen Survivor™ Grade: B
Your notes: _____

Frei Brothers Reserve Merlot, Dry
Creek Valley, California 2006

$ **Pts**
20   88

Although the price has gone up, this wine delivers nice Merlot complexity: dark plum, dusty tobacco and red licorice. Pair it with fig-stuffed pork roast.
Kitchen Survivor™ Grade: B
Your notes: _____

Frog's Leap Merlot, Rutherford,
Napa Valley, California 2006

$ **Pts**
34   91

🍷 The complex fig and cassis fruit, layers of licorice and roasting coffee, and long finish, make this one of the best Merlots in America. Pair it with osso bucco, cheesy risottos, or grilled steak.
Kitchen Survivor™ Grade: B+
Your notes: _____

Grgich Hills Estate Merlot, Napa,
California 2005

$ **Pts**
42   94

🍷 🏆 A triumphant follow-up to the lovely 2004, showing the all-too-rarely reached potential of the Merlot grape. The dusty minerality framing plum

and violet notes is met on the palate with dusty cocoa, smoke and cassis flavors.   Really fantastic.
Kitchen Survivor™ Grade: B

Your notes: _____

Kendall-Jackson Vintner's Reserve   **$**   **Pts**
Merlot, California 2006   **18**   **86**

This is Merlot in the luscious style—redolent with black cherry flavor and smooth texture; the consistency and complexity for the money are exemplary.
Kitchen Survivor™ Grade: B+

Your notes: _____

Kenwood Merlot, Sonoma,   **$**   **Pts**
California 2006   **14**   **84**

☺ Smooth and plummy, with a hint of smokiness. A popular and worthy everyday Merlot
Kitchen Survivor™ Grade: C

Your notes: _____

L'Ecole No. 41 Seven Hills Vineyard Estate   **$**   **Pts**
Merlot, Walla Walla, Washington 2007   **36**   **88**

♀ This label was an early indicator of the potential for Merlot in the Walla Walla region. It remains a benchmark, offering so much chocolatey-dark cherry depth of fruit for the money. Rich and ripe enough to pair with chocolate. Great with spiced pork or duck.
Kitchen Survivor™ Grade: B

Your notes: _____

Marilyn Merlot, Napa,   **$**   **Pts**
California 2006   **27**   **86**

Although you pay for the name, this is a pleasant bottle, with voluptuous plum and dark cherry fruit and vanilla oakiness. Pair with pork roast or meaty pasta.
Kitchen Survivor™ Grade: B

Your notes: _____

Markham Merlot, Napa,   **$**   **Pts**
California 2005   **23**   **86**

Still a value compared to other high-end California Merlots, with smooth dark berry flavors, truffly earthiness and soft cinnamon spice. A great trade-up wine to keep on hand for drop-in guests, host gifts, or when you scored a deal on T-bone at the butcher.
Kitchen Survivor™ Grade: B

Your notes: _____

Matanzas Creek Merlot, Bennett Valley,   **$**   **Pts**
Sonoma, California 2005   35   90

☝ This wine has always had an impressive depth and benchmark quality. A hint of green herbs in the scent accents the very Sonoma boysenberry fruit and sweet oak. Delicious with grilled squab or duck.

Kitchen Survivor™ Grade: B+

Your notes: _____

Merryvale Starmont Merlot, Napa   **$**   **Pts**
California 2006   24   85

Although it's better-known for Chardonnay, Merry-vale makes a fine Merlot, with chocolatey-plummy fruit with a whiff of fresh herbs and vanilla. Nice!

Kitchen Survivor™ Grade: B

Your notes: _____

Northstar Merlot, Columbia Valley   **$**   **Pts**
Washington 2005   40   92

🍎 This wine bursts with plum and dark cherry fruit, while maintaining subtlety and layers of smoke, cocoa, and dusty-leafiness in the very long finish. Super now, and I suspect it will age very well.

Kitchen Survivor™ Grade: A

Your notes: _____

Pine Ridge Crimson Creek Merlot,   **$**   **Pts**
Napa, California 2006   32   86

The lively red fruits (cherry, cranberry) and savory herbal/peppery notes make this among the more food friendly CA Merlots. Even works with the Thanks-giving spread, from spicy stuffing to tart cranberries.

Kitchen Survivor™ Grade: B

Your notes: _____

Ravenswood Vintners Blend   **$**   **Pts**
Merlot, California 2007   10   85

☺ You can't do better for $10 than this plummy and juicy gulper; it's even better than the signature Zin.

Kitchen Survivor™ Grade: B

Your notes: _____

Raymond Reserve Merlot, Napa,   **$**   **Pts**
California 2005   24   90

Here is a reserve that earns the accolade and does the grape proud. The scent teems with cassis, clove and

cinnamon notes. The palate is fearlessly structured and smoky. The price, for this quality, is a gift!
Kitchen Survivor™ Grade: A

Your notes: _____

Robert Mondavi Winery Merlot, Napa, California 2006

$	Pts
23	85

☒ Velvety and soft, with red cherry, red licorice and savory herb notes, and soft vanilla oak in the finish.
Kitchen Survivor™ Grade: C

Your notes: _____

Rodney Strong Sonoma Merlot, California 2005

$	Pts
19	85

Lots of oak in the form of cedar, spice and coconut scents, but lots of dark blueberry fruit to match. Pair with jerk pork or beef braised in lots of red wine.
Kitchen Survivor™ Grade: C

Your notes: _____

Rutherford Hill Merlot, Napa Valley, California 2005

$	Pts
25	86

☺ Velvety-smooth, lush with plum and berry fruit and a nice vanilla-cocoa finish. Bring on the burgers!
Kitchen Survivor™ Grade: C

Your notes: _____

St. Clement Merlot, Napa, California 2006

$	Pts
36	91

♉ ☒ A stunner for the price, with complex gravelly, cedar-cinnamon scents and deeply textured, lush brandied-cherry fruit flavor. Gorgeous with pesto.
Kitchen Survivor™ Grade: B+

Your notes: _____

Sebastiani Sonoma County Merlot, California 2006

$	Pts
17	90

♉ 🍎 More CA Merlot for the money than any other in the book. Loads of blueberry fruit layered with bay leaf, tobacco, coconut and dark chocolate notes that linger in the long finish. Where so many Merlots have become mundane, this one rocks. At this price, it's a gift. Delicious on its own, but St. Andre cheese is the perfect, decadent pairing.
Kitchen Survivor™ Grade: B

Your notes: _____

Shafer Napa Merlot,   **$**   **Pts**
California 2006   46   87

This Napa classic rocks on, with lush crushed berry fruit, cinnamon spice, lavish vanilla oak and a dusty-cocoa, medium-length finish. Pair with filet mignon.

Kitchen Survivor™ Grade: B

Your notes: _____

Simi Merlot, Sonoma   **$**   **Pts**
California 2006   20   84

Lavishly oaked, with big blackberry fruit; vanilla, clove, and coconut scents. A nice match for big and juicy grilled blue cheese burgers, or rich cheeses.

Kitchen Survivor™ Grade: C

Your notes: _____

Souverain Alexander   **$**   **Pts**
Valley Merlot, California 2006   19   85

You get a lot for the money: sweet plum, dusty cocoa and tangy cured meat notes on the palate, plus a long smoky finish. A nice match for a wintry pot roast.

Kitchen Survivor™ Grade: B

Your notes: _____

Silverado Merlot Napa   **$**   **Pts**
Valley, California 2006   35   86

♉ Maybe it's the extra bottle age that gives this brambly-berry bottling a wine-braised beef richness. Its more subtle-earthy, old world style really sings with earthy foods like roasted eggplant or lentil stew.

Kitchen Survivor™ Grade: B

Your notes: _____

Stag's Leap Wine Cellars Napa   **$**   **Pts**
Merlot, California 2005   45   89

A real standout for its brambly-dusty tobacco, aged balsamic, coffee bean and plum complexity, and its old world subtlety and length. Pair with seared hanger steak with Bearnaise sauce.

Kitchen Survivor™ Grade: C

Your notes: _____

Sterling Vineyards Merlot, Napa   **$**   **Pts**
California 2006   22   86

Sterling's best Napa bottling in years, with velvety-cocoa tannins, black plum fruit and a smoky finish.

Kitchen Survivor™ Grade: B+

Your notes: _____

Twomey Merlot, Napa $ Pts
California 2005 50 87

🍷 🏅 The dash of Cabernet Franc gives a violets and mint lift to the subtle plum, earthy and charcoal note of this exemplary Napa Merlot. Pair with a creamy goat cheese or velvety prime rib.

Kitchen Survivor™ Grade: B

Your notes: _____

Cabernet Sauvignon and Blends

Grape Profile: Although Merlot ranks above it, Cabernet Sauvignon remains a top-selling red varietal wine. It grows well virtually all over the wine world and gives good to excellent quality and flavor at every price level, from steal to splurge. Its style can vary, based on the wine's quality level, from uncomplicated everyday styles to the super-intense boutique bottlings. The most famous and plentiful sources of Cabernet are Bordeaux in France, California (especially Sonoma and Napa), Washington State, and Italy on the high end with its Super Tuscan versions; and I think Chile shines in the low- to mid-priced category. Classically, it has a scent and taste of dark berries (black cherry, blackberry), plus notes of spice, earth, cocoa, cedar, and even mint that can be very layered and complex in the best wines. It has medium to very full body and often more tannin—that bit of a tongue-gripping sensation that one of my waiters once described, perfectly I think, as "a slipcover for the tongue, ranging from terry cloth to suede to velvet," depending on the wine in question. Oakiness, either a little or a lot depending on the growing region and price category, is also a common Cabernet feature. Combined, these can make for a primo mouthful of wine, which surely explains why Cabernet is king of collectible wines.

A note about blends: As described previously for Merlot, Cabernet Sauvignon wines often follow the Bordeaux blending model, with one or more of the traditional Bordeaux red grapes—Merlot, Cabernet Franc, Petit Verdot, and Malbec—blended in for balance and complexity. Australia pioneered blending Cabernet Sauvignon with Shiraz—a delicious combination that the wine buying market has embraced. Those blends are listed either here or in the Shiraz section, according to which of the two grapes is dominant in the blend (it will be listed first on the label, too).

Serve: Cool room temperature; the fuller-bodied styles benefit from aeration—pour into the glass a bit ahead of time or decant into a carafe (but if you forget, don't sweat it; if you care to, swirling the glass does help).

When: With your favorite red wine meals, but the everyday bottlings are soft enough for cocktail-hour sipping.

With: Anything you'd serve alongside a red; especially complements beef, lamb, goat cheese and hard cheeses, pesto sauce, and dishes scented with basil, rosemary, sage, or oregano.

In: The One™ glass for red or a larger-bowled red wineglass.

	$	Pts
Alexander Valley Vineyards Cabernet Sauvignon, California, Alex. Valley 2006	20	85

A Cab for fans of the elegant and earthy style, with blackberry fruit, velvety tannins, vanilla oak and a touch of cedar.
Kitchen Survivor™ Grade: C
Your notes: _____

	$	Pts
Alice White Cabernet Sauvignon, Australia 2007	7	82

Another solid offering from this value brand, with soft blackberry fruit and a hint of cedar and mint.
Kitchen Survivor™ Grade: C
Your notes: _____

	$	Pts
Alice White Cabernet Shiraz, Australia 2007	7	84

☺ This yummy budget choice has nice plum fruit and a touch of cedar in the scent.
Kitchen Survivor™ Grade: C
Your notes: _____

Araujo Cabernet Sauvignon Eisele Vineyard $ Pts
Napa Valley, California 2005 250 98
♀ A "cult" Cab since before the term was invented. It has to be the Eisele vineyard source that makes this, along with Dalla Valle and Staglin, a wine apart from the uber-Napa Cab pack. The incredible power and decadence comes from the expression of fruit and terroir rather than alcohol and oak: flavors and scents of deep figs, dark chocolate fudge, and spicy-savory notes of cinnamon and cedar; velvet texture.
Kitchen Survivor™ Grade: B
Your notes: _____

Baron Philippe de Rothschild, $ Pts
Escudo Rojo Cabernet Blend, Chile 2007 18 89
♀ 🏅 REALLY worth seeking out for its meaty-smoky yin-yang complexity: super-sweet plum fruit, countered by savory cumin and roasted meat notes. Pair with chicken mole poblano or pork chile verde.
Kitchen Survivor™ Grade: B+
Your notes: _____

Beaulieu Vineyard (BV) Coastal Estates $ Pts
Cabernet Sauvignon, California 2006 9 85
The nice blackberry and cedar varietal character makes this one of the best budget Cabs out there. Great as an everyday red with anything from grilled chicken to meatloaf to pesto pasta.
Kitchen Survivor™ Grade: C
Your notes: _____

Beaulieu Vineyard (BV) Georges $ Pts
de Latour Private Reserve Cabernet 115 95
Sauvignon, Napa, California 2006
♀ "Let them drink cake," and I mean Black Forest cherry cake (this wine, minus the sugar and fat). It is sumptuous, yet balanced, on the palate, needing only dark chocolate or a fine cheese. Instant special night!
Kitchen Survivor™ Grade: B
Your notes: _____

Beaulieu Vineyard (BV) Rutherford   **$**   **Pts**
Cabernet Sauvignon, California 2006   **27**   **89**

♉ The best in years, and that's something since this classic is always rock-solid. This bottling is dusty and smoky with lead pencil, dense blackberry, cedar and cinnamon notes, and a wonderful palate-coating texture and richness that lingers into the finish. Pair with a great cheese or simply a rare, well-charred steak.

Kitchen Survivor™ Grade: B+

Your notes: _____

Beaulieu Vineyard (BV) Tapestry Reserve   **$**   **Pts**
Red Blend, California 2006   **55**   **91**

A blend of the Bordeaux grapes (Cab, Merlot, Cabernet Franc, Malbec and Petit Verdot) that shows layers of dusty earth, ripe and dark berry fruit, smoke and lead pencil, with a velvety texture. Delicious young, but it ages really well, too. Fantastic with sage- and thyme-rubbed pork roast.

Kitchen Survivor™ Grade: B

Your notes: _____

Benziger Cabernet Sauvignon,   **$**   **Pts**
Sonoma, California 2006   **18**   **89**

An exemplary Sonoma Cab for the price, with succulent boysenberry and dark plum fruit, a whisper of licorice and a velvety-juicy, drink-me texture. Pair with hoisin and soy-glazed duck.

Kitchen Survivor™ Grade: B

Your notes: _____

Beringer Alluvium Red Blend,   **$**   **Pts**
Napa, California 2006   **30**   **89**

Figs, blackberries, velvet, smoke. This is a delicious wine with wonderful earthiness and lusciousness - the perfect balance between old world elegance and new world fruit intensity. Pesto, mild cheeses or olive tapenade would set off the flavors beautifully.

Kitchen Survivor™ Grade: B+

Your notes: _____

Beringer Knights Valley Cabernet　　$　Pts
Sauvignon, Sonoma, California 2007　27　93

Three cheers: for Laurie Hook (the winemaker), Knights Valley (the source), and a price you can swallow. There is major character and complexity here: scents of hardwood charcoal with cassis fruit, fragrant cedar, chocolate and licorice notes, plush velvety tannins and a really long finish. The wine's a deal, so splurge on the best prime steak you can buy.
Kitchen Survivor™ Grade: A

Your notes: _____

Beringer Private Reserve Cabernet　　$　Pts
Sauvignon, California 2005　116　94

⏳ One whiff brings a wave of layers: cedar, olives, tobacco, mint, smoke, cocoa and black currants. Sip after sip is an exercise in "name that essence." Once the fun of the game is over, the joy of the wine is not. Break out your best cheeses or prime rib, and settle in for some languorous sipping.
Kitchen Survivor™ Grade: B+

Your notes: _____

Blackstone Cabernet　　$　Pts
Sauvignon, California 2006　12　84

☺ Although they're better known for the Merlot, I prefer this Cab for its varietal character - blackberry fruit and dustiness that matches nicely with the char of grill fare: eggplant, chicken, beef, mushrooms.
Kitchen Survivor™ Grade: B

Your notes: _____

Cain Cuvee Bordeaux Style Red,　　$　Pts
California NV6　34　86

A fragrance-forward wine, with meaty-herbaceous accents to the plummy fruit. NV6 means it's mostly from the 2006 vintage. It's Merlot-dominated, and thus a smoothy! Pair with slow-cooker beef stew.
Kitchen Survivor™ Grade: B+

Your notes: _____

Cain Five Bordeaux Style Red,   **$**   **Pts**
Napa Valley, California 2005   **125**   **89**

One of the early Napa notables, and still special. Sleek & fragrant with rosemary, demi-glace and caramelized shallot notes to compliment the violets and black fruits. Pair with braised short ribs to bring out all the layers.

Kitchen Survivor™ Grade: B+

Your notes: _____

Cakebread Cellars Napa Cabernet   **$**   **Pts**
Sauvignon, California 2006   **75**   **86**

The licorice, syrupy blackberry fruit, and cedary complexity show its Napa pedigree. The structure and power suggest this one will cellar well if you can wait.

Kitchen Survivor™ Grade: B+

Your notes: _____

Caro Red Blend (Catena-Rothschild),   **$**   **Pts**
Mendoza, Argentina 2006   **45**   **89**

♟ A super-sophisticated, dusty coffee and black cherry-flavored blend of Cabernet and Malbec from the famed Catena winemaking family of Argentina and the (Lafite) Rothschilds of Bordeaux. Concentrated, powerful and refined; built for the cellar.

Kitchen Survivor™ Grade: B+

Your notes: _____

Caymus Napa Cabernet   **$**   **Pts**
Sauvignon, California 2006   **70**   **93**

🍎👍 Simply awesome Cab and every bit as complex and layered as neighbors at 2-3x the price. Cedary, with fudgy, black cherry Kirsch flavors and velour tannins. Stunning with pesto pasta and flatiron steak.

Kitchen Survivor™ Grade: B+

Your notes: _____

Chalk Hill Estate Cabernet Sauvignon,   **$**   **Pts**
Chalk Hill, Sonoma, California 2006   **70**   **97**

♟ Although it's not cheap, the quality equals that of cults at 4-5x the price. It is exotic, hedonistic and yet structured for cellaring. Coffee bean, mocha, chocolate and cassis scents, palate-coating, thick and luxuriant dark fruit and chocolate flavors - all without being cloying and gooey, or over-oaked. Bravo!

Kitchen Survivor™ Grade: A

Your notes: _____

Chappellet Signature Cabernet Sauvignon, Napa, California 2006

	$	Pts
	42	90

A steal at this price! The dusky blackcurrant fruit, smoky-cedar notes and incredible depth and structure make this delicious now, and a great cellar candidate. A velvet cloak for your tongue.

Kitchen Survivor™ Grade: B+

Your notes: _____

Chateau Clerc-Milon, Pauillac, Bordeaux, France 2004

	$	Pts
	50	87

A great way to affordably buy Bordeaux is from a solid chateau without rockstar status, like this one. The 2004 vintage is beginning to show nicely, with scents of warm brick and flavors of warm berries, with a coffee finish. Pair with rare prime rib or lamb.

Kitchen Survivor™ Grade: B

Your notes: _____

Chateau Cos d'Estournel, Ste. Estephe, Bordeaux, France 2004

	$	Pts
	130	89

Although the great 2005 vintage is impossibly expensive, this so-called "off" vintage makes a worthy splurge. Its dusty cedar, cassis, sweet tobacco, anise, and coffee bean character are classic Cos (rhymes with "boss"), as fans call it. Top vintages age 25+ years; lesser vintages still improve for a decade or so.

Kitchen Survivor™ Grade: B+

Your notes: _____

Chateau d'Issan Bordeaux, Margaux, France 2005

	$	Pts
	80	90

One of the more affordable 2005s that also happens to be awesome - power and elegance in perfect harmony. The seductive mocha, toast, blackcurrant and anise layers are luxuriant and long. If you can find the 2002, it is half the price, and also delicious.

Kitchen Survivor™ Grade: B+

Your notes: _____

Chateau Duhart-Milon Rothschild   **$**   **Pts**
Bordeaux, France 2004   **55**   **87**

⚜ 🏆 Another great bet for affordable Bordeaux.
This wine is tightly-wound and intense, with chewy-dusty tannins, dark cherry and currant fruit, and lots
of cedar and sandalwood in the scent and finish.
Kitchen Survivor™ Grade: B

Your notes: _____

Chateau Greysac Medoc, Bordeaux,   **$**   **Pts**
France 2005   **22**   **88**

🏆 A fantastic wine from a world-class vintage. Text-book Medoc Bordeaux with autumn leaf pile, roasted
espresso and cedar, and subtle blackcurrant fruit. Long,
smoky, and tailor-made for a simple roast or aged cheese.
Kitchen Survivor™ Grade: B

Your notes: _____

Chateau Gruaud-Larose, St. Julien,   **$**   **Pts**
Bordeaux, France 2005   **75**   **89**

🏆 Pricey, but more affordable than many Bordeaux
of comparable quality, with palate-coating tannins,
dark cassis fruit, cedar-coffee scents, and a long finish.
Kitchen Survivor™ Grade: A

Your notes: _____

Chateau Lagrange, St. Julien,   **$**   **Pts**
Bordeaux, France 2005   **65**   **88**

🏆 *Affordable* classic Bordeaux, with a textbook dusty,
blackcurrant, and roasted coffee character. One of
the few good ones that's fairly affordable in the
highly-regarded 2005 vintage. Pair with braised short
ribs.
Kitchen Survivor™ Grade: B+

Your notes: _____

Chateau Lascombes, Margaux,   **$**   **Pts**
Bordeaux, France 2003   **59**   **87**

🍎 Like so many 2003s (a ripe vintage), up-front and
sexy now. Classic Medoc character of roasted coffee
bean, mocha and cassis. Check my Web site for the
complete note, and ageability recommendations.
Kitchen Survivor™ Grade: B

Your notes: _____

Chateau Les Ormes de Pez, Ste.   **$**   **Pts**
Estephe, Bordeaux, France 2006   **40**   **87**

♟ Austere and classic, showing autumn leaves and wet clay earthiness on the nose, with stony dark plum and sweet vanilla notes. Aerate well and pair with a velvety prime rib or pan-roasted duck or quail.
Kitchen Survivor™ Grade: B

Your notes: _____

Chateau Lynch-Bages, Pauillac,   **$**   **Pts**
Bordeaux, France 2006   **60**   **89**

♟ The cassis, coffee bean, cedar and wine-braised beef-in-a-glass notes are classic Lynch-Bages. It has the depth of flavor and structure to age 15 years+. A Bordeaux classic at a fair price if you shop around.
Kitchen Survivor™ Grade: B+

Your notes: _____

Chateau Meyney, Haut-Medoc,   **$**   **Pts**
Bordeaux, France 2005   **24**   **88**

♟ I think this will drink well for ten years or so, and it's nice now. The charry, smoky layers and fine core of dark cherry fruit lifted with cedar and lively acidity would pair deliciously with herb-crusted veal chops.
Kitchen Survivor™ Grade: B

Your notes: _____

Chateau Ste. Michelle Canoe Ridge Estate   **$**   **Pts**
Cabernet Sauvignon, Washington 2006   **22**   **89**

The incredibly sweet fruit and spice make this one of the most drinkable Cabs on the market. The depth and dustiness suggest it will age nicely for a few years. Every bit as good as many Cabs at 2X the price, so why pay more? Pair with filet with red wine sauce.
Kitchen Survivor™ Grade: B

Your notes: _____

Chateau Ste. Michelle Columbia Valley   **$**   **Pts**
Cabernet Sauvignon, Washington 2006   **16**   **85**

Always a favorite of mine because it offers real dusty, leafy blackberry Cab character for a fantastic price.
Kitchen Survivor™ Grade: B

Your notes: _____

Chateau St. Jean Cabernet Sauvignon   **$**   **Pts**
Sonoma, California 2006   **27**   **90**

Fantastic varietal character - blackcurrant, cedar, roasted coffee and autumn leaves, with a very silky texture that makes it a true pleasure to drink on its own. That said, a pairing with pesto takes it to a whole new level. Needs aeration to show its classic suppleness and layers of pencil lead, tobacco, cedar and dark cherry. A steal for the quality.

Kitchen Survivor™ Grade: B

Your notes: _____

Chateau St. Jean Cinq Cepages   **$**   **Pts**
(*sank seh-PAHJH*) Cabernet   **75**   **89**
Blend, California 2006

🏆 Needs aeration to show its classic suppleness and layers of pencil lead, tobacco, cedar and dark cherry.

Kitchen Survivor™ Grade: B+

Your notes: _____

Clos du Bois Marlstone, Alexander Valley,   **$**   **Pts**
California 2005   **50**   **86**

Chewy and brooding, with a mineral, briary scent and layers of black olive, balsamic, cherry and tobacco.

Kitchen Survivor™ Grade: B+

Your notes: _____

Clos du Bois Reserve Cabernet Sauvignon,   **$**   **Pts**
Alexander Valley, California 2005   **20**   **88**

A "reserve" that earns the billing is rare, and laudable. At this price the luscious cassis fruit, fragrant violets and vanilla spice, and the velvety richness, are a gift. Pair with pesto, prime steak or rich cheeses.

Kitchen Survivor™ Grade: B

Your notes: _____

Clos du Bois Sonoma Cabernet   **$**   **Pts**
Sauvignon, California 2004   **18**   **83**

Although the Merlot is far more popular, I think the wild berry and anise character of this wine makes it the true Clos du Bois calling card. Pair with charred steaks or earthy dishes like black bean stew or mushroom-barley soup.

Kitchen Survivor™ Grade: C

Your notes: _____

Clos du Val Napa Cabernet
Sauvignon, California 2006

$ 35   Pts 86

As ever, marching to its own drumbeat - elegance and dusty subtlety with soft plum fruit - rather than hewing to the "monster Cab" style of many in Napa.
Kitchen Survivor™ Grade: B
Your notes: _____

Col Solare Red Blend, Columbia Valley,
Washington 2006

$ 55   Pts 89

A mix of Cab, Merlot, Cab Franc, Petit Verdot and a touch of Syrah, that's classically Washington: new world dark plum and cocoa notes; old world trufflydusty tannins. Pair with great cheese or braised meat dishes. Will cellar well for at least 10 years.
Kitchen Survivor™ Grade: B+
Your notes: _____

Columbia Crest Grand Estates Cabernet
Sauvignon, Columbia Valley, Washington 2006

$ 11   Pts 84

☺ Really nice for the price thanks to its smoothness and blackberry-and-earth Cab character. A good Cab for everyday meals from meatloaf to pot roast.
Kitchen Survivor™ Grade: B+
Your notes: _____

Concha y Toro Casillero del Diablo Reserva
Privada Cabernet Syrah Maipo, Chile 2007

$ 16   Pts 87

A real bargain at this price, and a window on the greatness of the 2007 vintage. Dark fig, tar and licorice notes with a hint of pepper and velvety texture.
Kitchen Survivor™ Grade: B
Your notes: _____

Concha y Toro Don Melchor Cabernet
Cabernet Sauvignon Reserva, Maipo, Chile 2006

$ 65   Pts 87

♟ The roasted coffee, lead pencil and cassis sophistication are typical of this wine, though it is less Bordeaux-like than in past vintages. Smooth & classy.
Kitchen Survivor™ Grade: A
Your notes: _____

Concha y Toro Marques de Casa **$** **Pts**
Concha Cabernet Sauvignon, Maipo, Chile 2006 **14** **85**

♟ Aptly known as a "baby Don Melchor," this wine's subtle lead pencil, coffee bean and cassis notes are almost Bordeaux-like. Great value for the price.

Kitchen Survivor™ Grade: C

Your notes: _____

Duckhorn Estate Grown Patzimaro **$** **Pts**
Cabernet Sauvignon, Napa, California 2005 **95** **94**

Although famous for Merlot, Duckhorn makes smokin' Cabs. This one's got densely concentrated, brambly blackberry fruit, tarry anise tobacco notes, and massive velvety richness, all in balance.

Kitchen Survivor™ Grade: A+

Your notes: _____

Esser Cabernet Sauvignon, **$** **Pts**
California 2007 **11** **84**

It's hard to find a better Cab at this price. It's got some smoky dustiness, soft plum fruit and a touch of tannin for structure. Pair it with pesto or steak.

Kitchen Survivor™ Grade: C

Your notes: _____

Estancia Reserve Meritage, Alexander **$** **Pts**
Valley, California 2006 **32** **86**

Velvet and violets, dusty earth, dark plum fruit. The leafy, perfumey layers of this wine shine with slow-cooked meats such as braised short ribs or brisket.

Kitchen Survivor™ Grade: B+

Your notes: _____

Etude Cabernet Sauvignon, Napa **$** **Pts**
California 2005 **125** **92**

👍 Benchmark Napa Cab, defined: cedar, blackcurrant, mint, pencil lead; velvety-cocoa, and dense blackberry fruit on the palate. Long dusty-cherry finish. Pair this with a pesto-crusted, charred steak.

Kitchen Survivor™ Grade: B+

Your notes: _____

Far Niente Cabernet Sauvignon, **$** **Pts**
Napa, California 2006 **125** **89**

👍 Elegance and depth, restrained oak and structure,

make this a wine for the long-haul. But the pedigree and luxuriant fruit mean you'll see the current vintage being enjoyed on many a steakhouse table.

Kitchen Survivor™ Grade: A+

Your notes: _____

Ferrari-Carano Cabernet Sauvignon,	$	Pts
Alexander Valley, California 2005	38	86

A big and showy wine, with toffee-vanilla oak, rich dark fruit, anise and molasses, and plush tannins.

Kitchen Survivor™ Grade: C

Your notes: _____

Flora Springs Cabernet Sauvignon,	$	Pts
Napa, California 2006	32	85

♛ Excellent Napa Cab character with a nice balance of power with elegance. The tannins are smooth and velvety, the fruit dark and spicy..

Kitchen Survivor™ Grade: A+

Your notes: _____

Fetzer Valley Oaks Cabernet	$	Pts
Sauvignon, California 2007	9	83

Less varietally-distinct than in past vintages. For a smooth and drinkable everyday red choice, that's ok, but I hope to see this one re-emerge as a value/price leader. Pair with everyday fare like meatloaf or BBQ.

Kitchen Survivor™ Grade: C

Your notes: _____

Flora Springs Trilogy Red Table Wine,	$	Pts
California 2006	65	86

♛ A Napa classic Bordeaux-style blend styled more subtly than most. It's earthy and cedary, with chewy dark cherry on the palate and a dusty-cocoa finish.

Kitchen Survivor™ Grade: B

Your notes: _____

Franciscan Magnificat Meritage, Napa,	$	Pts
California 2005	50	87

With '05 still the current release, the extra year in bottle serves up the layered blackberry-cedar-vanilla notes, but with softer and finer tannins. Nice!

Kitchen Survivor™ Grade: B

Your notes: _____

Franciscan Cabernet Sauvignon,	$	Pts
Napa, California 2006	28	86

Still has the whiff of cedar and pencil lead, dark blackberry fruit, and sweet vanilla from oak, but slightly drier tannins than in past vintages. Pair it with pesto pasta, burgers or cheese to soften them.
Kitchen Survivor™ Grade: B

Your notes: _____

Frank Family Vineyards Cabernet	$	Pts
Sauvignon, Napa, California 2005	45	91

♈ This one dusted some big-name Napa neighbors at 2X the price in my blind tasting. The full-blooded, dense cassis and licorice flavors meld perfectly with lavish vanilla-cinnamon oakiness, plush tannins and fragrant notes of mint, violet and rosemary that echo in the finish. Pair with Tuscan-style herbed steak.
Kitchen Survivor™ Grade: B

Your notes: _____

Frei Brothers Reserve Cabernet Sauvignon,	$	Pts
Alexander Valley, California 2006	24	85

The cassis and smoky autumn leafiness are classic Alexander Valley. Nice fruit concentration and a long, smoky finish. Pair with grilled eggplant.
Kitchen Survivor™ Grade: C

Your notes: _____

Frog's Leap Cabernet Sauvignon,	$	Pts
Napa, California 2006	42	90

♈ One of Napa's most distinctive and worthy Cabs, jam-packed with blackberry flavor, kissed with vanilla, licorice, and black olive scents; impeccably balanced. I think it will age beautifully. In youth, pair with grilled lamb chops or pan-roasted quail with shallots.
Kitchen Survivor™ Grade: B

Your notes: _____

Gallo Family Vineyards Barelli Creek	$	Pts
Cabernet Sauvignon, Alex Vly, CA 2006	35	86

Compare this with the Frei (see next) to get Alexander versus Dry Creek Valley style differences. This one's got the classic leafy, herbaceous, dusty and dark berry notes, and the silky texture of Alexander Valley. Pair with rosemary-scented lamb to bring out the layers.
Kitchen Survivor™ Grade: B+

Your notes: _____

Gallo Family Vineyards Frei Ranch Cabernet Sauvignon, Dry Creek Vly, California 2006

	$	Pts
	35	88

Intense coconut, chocolate and black raspberry notes with a long, fudgy-creamy finish. Pair this with roast duck with berry sauce, or dark chocolate, or a big rich cheese (and a roaring fire and your lover!).

Kitchen Survivor™ Grade: B+

Your notes: _____

Grgich Hills Estate Cabernet Sauvignon, Napa, California 2005

	$	Pts
	60	92

♀ 👍 Grgich deftly eschews the "fruit bomb" model with this chewy and dense Cab that's built for aging. The dark cherry and blackcurrant fruit and tobacco character, plus a mushroomy earthiness, are almost old world in style. Pair it with slow-braised lamb or duck.

Kitchen Survivor™ Grade: A

Your notes: _____

Groth Napa Cabernet Sauvignon, Oakville, California 2006

	$	Pts
	58	88

👍 It's not cheap, but for a luxury Cab that ages well, it's reasonable. The plush tannins, deep cassis fruit, anise and licorice notes and lavish vanilla oak are classic Oakville. Pesto pasta or gnocchi with herbs and olive oil would be great table-mates.

Kitchen Survivor™ Grade: B+

Your notes: _____

Heitz Cellars Cabernet Sauvignon, Napa, California 2005

	$	Pts
	42	93

👍 Although there is a hint of the signature mint fragrance of the famed Martha's Vineyard bottling, this is its own, very special, thing. The scents of tar, black olive, bramble and blackstrap molasses preface similarly layered and lusty notes on the palate and finish, which then reverberates with a subtle charcoal-earthiness. Cellar if you can. Pair with lamb with black olives and rosemary, or venison with juniper berry *jus*.

Kitchen Survivor™ Grade: B+

Your notes: _____

Heitz Cellars Martha's Vineyard Cabernet Sauvignon, Napa, California 2004 — $ 125 — Pts 95

👍 A true classic, by any measure. California Cab lovers can guess it blind because of the fragrance of mint, cedar and eucalyptus, and the powerful, brooding blackberry on the palate. Ages beautifully.

Kitchen Survivor™ Grade: B+

Your notes: _____

Hess Cabernet Sauvignon, California 2006 — $ 17 — Pts 85

☺ As its predecessor Hess Select this bottling was a value favorite. Although the price has crept up, it remains a tasty wine with medium-weight dusty-cassis Cab character. A wine list favorite.

Kitchen Survivor™ Grade: B

Your notes: _____

Jacob's Creek Reserve Cabernet Sauvignon, Australia 2007 — $ 12 — Pts 87

Fragrant minty-berry notes, soft and juicy texture. This one is consistently tops in value for the money.

Kitchen Survivor™ Grade: B

Your notes: _____

J. Lohr 7 Oaks Cabernet Sauvignon, Paso Robles, California 2006 — $ 17 — Pts 84

🍎 Always a solid price/value with wild berry fruit and a sweet coconut cream scent from American oak.

Kitchen Survivor™ Grade: B+

Your notes: _____

Jordan Cabernet Sauvignon, California 2005 — $ 50 — Pts 85

♨ The quality can vary by vintage, but the elegant leafy-earthy, red fruit style of this Cab distinguishes it from the huge "fruit and oak bomb" Cabs that critics love. Ages well in top years. Pair with duck.

Kitchen Survivor™ Grade: B+

Your notes: _____

Joseph Phelps Insignia Cabernet Blend, California 2006 — $ 200 — Pts 96

♨ 🍎 👍 A Napa blockbuster, with potent black fig and cherry fruit, licorice, toasted-coconutty oak, and plush tannins. The wine wears its opulence with grace; while it's a decadent drink when young, it ages beautifully. Given that it always comes in tops in our blind tastings (even against more expensive - ouch! - wines), this is one of the most "worth it" splurges out there. How about a blowout pairing? How about gnocchi with parmesan and truffles; or, if you're a traditionalist, prime steak, charred to perfection.

Kitchen Survivor™ Grade: B+

Your notes: _____

Joseph Phelps Napa Cabernet	$	Pts
Sauvignon, California 2006	54	89

Real Napa Cab that's consistent every year for its structured mint, cedar, coffee-spice, and blackberry notes. Pair with pork or duck in red wine sauce.

Kitchen Survivor™ Grade: B

Your notes: _____

Justin Isosceles Cabernet Blend,	$	Pts
Paso Robles, California 2006	62	95

☝ This wine put Paso Robles on the map, and still stands apart in the region. With this vintage it also stands with the big boys of Cab in Napa and Sonoma. Briary dark blackberry fruit, black olive, cedar, licorice and myriad spices and herbs keep you sipping, guessing and marveling as you drink this wine. You could pay 5-7x the price in Napa, and find less character. Pair with great cheese or prime steak.

Kitchen Survivor™ Grade: A

Your notes: _____

Kendall-Jackson Vintner's Reserve	$	Pts
Cabernet Sauvignon, California 2006	18	86

A textbook example of classic California Cab style: blackberry, cedar, a hint of licorice and cocoa.

Kitchen Survivor™ Grade: B

Your notes: _____

Kenwood Jack London Cabernet Sauvignon,	$	Pts
Sonoma, California 2006	38	86

This wine's signature is savory sassafras and balsamic notes, chewy tannins, red currant fruit and coriander spice. A great pick for barbecued ribs.

Kitchen Survivor™ Grade: B+

Your notes: _____

Ladera Howell Mountain Cabernet,   **$**   **Pts**
Sauvignon, Napa, California 2005   60   96

Monumental quality and complexity. Dark fudge, black raspberry, tar and bramble notes, with amazing concentration and velvety, mouth-coating tannins. The flavor density and structure suggest it will age beautifully. One of the best CA Cabs, period.

Kitchen Survivor™ Grade: B+

Your notes: _____

Liberty School Cabernet Sauvignon,   **$**   **Pts**
Paso Robles, California 2006   18   85

☺ As it has for years, this wine offers good Cab character—dark plum fruit and spice—for the price.

Kitchen Survivor™ Grade: C

Your notes: _____

Los Vascos Cabernet Sauvignon,   **$**   **Pts**
Chile 2007   10   85

One of Chile's best budget Cabernets, with dark cherry fruit, a cedary scent, and smooth tannins.

Kitchen Survivor™ Grade: B

Your notes: _____

Louis Martini Alexander Valley Cabernet   **$**   **Pts**
Sauvignon Reserve, California 2006   35   88

Tasted blind against Cabs at twice the price, this bottling stands up tall, with coconutty-spicy oak, huge but dark berry compote flavors and a rosemary herbaceousness that cries out for lamb chops.

Kitchen Survivor™ Grade: B+

Your notes: _____

Louis Martini Napa Valley Reserve   **$**   **Pts**
Cabernet Sauvignon, Napa, California 2006   25   87

As always, lots of dusty-cedary Napa-ness for the price. The sweet cinnamon-spiced blackberry and cassis and velvet texture scream for a great or burger.

Kitchen Survivor™ Grade: B+

Your notes: _____

Louis Martini Sonoma Cabernet
Sauvignon, California 2007 $ 17   Pts 88

A juicy mouthful of wild berries, bramble, tar and
dust - lots for the money. Pair it with a charred steak.
Kitchen Survivor™ Grade: C
Your notes: _____

Markham Vineyards Cabernet Sauvignon,
Napa, California 2006 $ 31   Pts 86

☺ A great tradeup bet because it offers nice black-
berry, cinnamon and cedar layers, at a decent price.
The tannins are soft, so you can pair with pork or even
salmon, or an earthy dish like red beans and rice.
Kitchen Survivor™ Grade: C
Your notes: _____

McWilliam's Hanwood Estate
Cabernet Sauvignon, Australia 2007 $ 12   Pts 84

A budget Aussie Cab with real varietal character:
dustiness, crushed mint and dark berries.
Kitchen Survivor™ Grade: B
Your notes: _____

Mt. Veeder Cabernet Sauvignon,
Napa, California 2006 $ 40   Pts 90

🍷 One of my favorite Cabs, period. The firm, chewy
tannins, dense fig fruit, tobacco and cedar, long finish
and good ageability. out-perform many a more expensive Cabernet. Pairing it with a charred steak or
smoked brisket brings out the wine's tarry smokiness.
Kitchen Survivor™ Grade: A
Your notes: _____

Opus One Cabernet Blend,
California 2005 $ 170   Pts 92

A Napa benchmark that gets overlooked by many critics, but I think the Bordeaux-like coffee/lead-pencil,
leafy earthiness and the cedar and cassis on the palate, are exemplary. The wine is structured and powerful, but doesn't knock you over the head with its
oak or overripeness. In other words, it stays true to its
time-tested pedigreed, balanced, age-worthy style.
Kitchen Survivor™ Grade: B
Your notes: _____

Penfolds Bin 389 Cabernet Shiraz, $ Pts
South Australia 2006 37 94

♉ I am not the tattoo type but if I were, I might consider these 3 digits. Where? On my tongue, of course. Luckily we can all just drink the wine, which makes a similarly indelible impression. It is complete and impeccably balanced, but full of sensory abundance. Nose: coconut, eucalyptus, chocolate, molasses, black olive, pepper. Palate: figs, balsamic, sweet plums, vanilla, cocoa and dust. A natural for world-class cheeses, roasted game, lamb, or dark chocolate.

Kitchen Survivor™ Grade: A+

Your notes: _____

Penfolds Bin 707 Cabernet Sauvignon, $ Pts
South Australia 2006 140 92

♉ Sweetness, then depth, then smoke. This wine is a continuum experience, beginning with the nose of coconut and sweet Black Forest cherry cake. On the palate comes blackberry, mint, aged balsamic, eucalyptus, vanilla and smoke. Complicated food would detract; go with prime steak.

Kitchen Survivor™ Grade: A+

Your notes: _____

Provenance Vineyards Cabernet $ Pts
Sauvignon, Rutherford, California 2006 42 90

The classic cedar and charcoal dust notes of Rutherford Cab, with opulent dark cherry and cassis fruit, cinnamon spice and plush tannins. A great match for roast chicken with black olives and herbs.

Kitchen Survivor™ Grade: B

Your notes: _____

Quintessa Cabernet Blend, Napa Valley, $ Pts
California 2006 130 91

The best yet from Quintessa, with a new dose of mid-palate fruit richness that's a gorgeous accent to its trademark earthy/elegant profile of dust, cocoa and autumn leaf-pile. Pair with rosemary-scented lamb.

Kitchen Survivor™ Grade: B+

Your notes: _____

Ravenswood Vintners Blend $ Pts
Cabernet Sauvignon, California 2007 10 85

Real dusty-smoky Cab character like this for $10 is

unheard of. The lovely blackcurrant fruit and rich mouthfeel are tailor-made for braised beef.

Kitchen Survivor™ Grade: B

Your notes: _____

	$	Pts
Raymond Reserve Cabernet Sauvignon, Napa, California 2005	35	88

Here's to an affordable wine that really drinks like a reserve, with lots of dark-fruited richness, lavish vanilla and cinnamon spice, and a plush texture.

Kitchen Survivor™ Grade: B

Your notes: _____

	$	Pts
Robert Mondavi Cabernet Sauvignon Reserve, Napa, California 2006	135	94

A Napa blue chip that's stylish and layered, with briary cedar, dark berry, and bitter chocolate and cassis; delicious young, but it ages incredibly well, too.

Kitchen Survivor™ Grade: B+

Your notes: _____

	$	Pts
Robert Mondavi Cabernet Sauvignon, Napa, California 2006	28	88

The best vintage in years for this benchmark Napa Cab. There's a nice lift of acidity and fragrant cedar to the ripe cherry fruit, and softly earthy finish.

Kitchen Survivor™ Grade: C

Your notes: _____

	$	Pts
Robert Mondavi Oakville Cabernet Sauvignon, Napa, California 2006	45	90

From the vineyards right near the winery, which anchors Napa's chi-chi Oakville district (home to many of the "cults" like Harlan and Dalla Valle), this is the best vintage yet since the district bottling was introduced. It screams licorice/chocolate/dark cherry "Oakville-ness." The neighbors better take note!

Kitchen Survivor™ Grade: B+

Your notes: _____

	$	Pts
Robert Mondavi Private Selection Cabernet Sauvignon, California 2007	11	82

A little more austere than in past vintages. It's got soft dark fruit and a hint of dusty-earthiness.

Kitchen Survivor™ Grade: B

Your notes: _____

Rodney Strong Sonoma Cabernet Sauvignon, California 2006 $ 16 Pts 84

The coconutty oak dominates the style here, with a nice compliment of black raspberry fruit.

Kitchen Survivor™ Grade: B

Your notes: _____

Rodney Strong Symmetry Meritage red blend, Alexander Valley, California 2006 $ 60 Pts 92

A sensory smack-down, but the balance is so spot-on that you have to surrender. Liquefied velvet, with packed-in fig, licorice, fudge flavors and a smoky-cocoa-coconut finish. Pair it with dark chocolate.

Kitchen Survivor™ Grade: B+

Your notes: _____

Rosemount Diamond Label Cabernet Sauvignon Australia 2006 $ 10 Pts 86

☺ The best jammy, juicy Cab buy on the market!

Kitchen Survivor™ Grade: C

Your notes: _____

Rubicon Estate, California 2005 $ 145 Pts 89

♟ I'm always struck by this wine's distinctive, gamy notes of balsamic-marinated cherries and lavender. On the palate, plush tannins underpin the dark fruit, licorice and earth notes. Definitely a wine for the cellar. An unusual Rubicon blend of nearly all Cab (98.5%) with a touch of Petit Verdot (and no Merlot or Cab Franc - a first since the wine's 1978 inception).

Kitchen Survivor™ Grade: B+

Your notes: _____

Rust-en-Vrede Estate Red, South Africa 2005 $ 40 Pts 88

♟ Like a good Bordeaux in its complexity, but there's Shiraz mixed with the Cab and Merlot. It's very true to its South African roots, with velvety tannins and savory meaty and molasses notes atop the ripe fig fruit. Pair with spice-rubbed pork ribs.

Kitchen Survivor™ Grade: B+

Your notes: _____

St. Clement Cabernet Sauvignon,   **$**   **Pts**
Napa, California 2006   **35**   **90**

This Napa classic flies under the radar, hence the great price for what you get: classy real-deal Napa Cab. The cedar, violets, red cherry and warm brick scent unfolds to a palate of luxuriant dark fruit, velvety tannin and cinnamon spice. Delicious.

Kitchen Survivor™ Grade: B+

Your notes: _____

Santa Rita 120 Cabernet Sauvignon,   **$**   **Pts**
Rapel Valley, Chile 2007   **8**   **84**

☺ Plenty of quality and flavor punch for the price: soft blackberry fruit complimented by a meaty-spicy, dusty scent. Pair with a grilled anything: hanger steak, veggies, burgers, chicken.

Kitchen Survivor™ Grade: C

Your notes: _____

Sebastiani Sonoma Cabernet   **$**   **Pts**
Sauvignon, California 2006   **18**   **88**

🍎 I really think you can't find more character for the price. The wild berry-brambly fruit, clove and all-spice notes, and savory herbs and sassafras will stand up to a punchy pairing: jerk pork, blackened chicken or Moroccan lamb tagine.

Kitchen Survivor™ Grade: B

Your notes: _____

Sequoia Grove Cabernet Sauvignon   **$**   **Pts**
Napa, California 2006   **34**   **90**

So much better than a slew of Napa Cabs at 2-3X the price. It's harmonious, velvety and concentrated, with blackberry, cedar, gravelly earthiness and a long, smoky finish. I believe it will also cellar well for 5-7 years. Enjoy it in youth with rare duck breast or seared quail.

Kitchen Survivor™ Grade: B

Your notes: _____

Sequoia Grove Rutherford Bench Reserve   **$**   **Pts**
Cabernet Sauvignon, California 2004   **65**   **93**

♂ An amazing wine for a keep-it-to-yourself price. Serve this blind to any wine snob. The packed-in blackberry and black cherry fruit are framed by tarry-dusty tannins and a host of fragrant layers: pencil lead, tar, licorice, anise...the list goes on. Pair this with a fine cheese or bittersweet chocolate to showcase the complexity. Will cellar for a decade or more.

Your notes: _____

Shafer Hillside Select Cabernet Sauvignon,   **$**   **Pts**
Stags Leap District, Napa, California 2005   **215**   **91**

♂ A mammoth wine that still nevertheless shows its Stag's Leap District terroir - sassafras, charcoal dust, wet metal, rosemary and anise. It coats the palate with black fruits, chocolate and sweet spices that echo into the smoky finish. One for the cellar, or a fine cheese and an evening of contemplation.

Kitchen Survivor™ Grade: B

Your notes: _____

Shafer One Point Five Cabernet Sauvignon,   **$**   **Pts**
Stags Leap District, Napa, California 2006   **65**   **86**

Big Cab lovers will fawn over the roasted coffee bean scent and intense, sweet oak on the nose and palate, respectively. Plan accordingly and invite a ribeye..

Kitchen Survivor™ Grade: B

Your notes: _____

Silverado Napa Cabernet   **$**   **Pts**
Sauvignon, California 2005   **43**   **88**

Silverado is a vintage behind many of its peers, and it makes a big difference. There is more subtlety, layers and harmony in the already subtle style with dense cassis, cedar, sweet-vanilla oak, and a leafy earthiness, all in seamless balance. Pair with sage pasta.

Kitchen Survivor™ Grade: B

Your notes: _____

Silver Oak Alexander Valley   **$**   **Pts**
Cabernet Sauvignon, California 2005   **70**   **91**

♂ 🍎 I love the wild berry fruit, cardamom-coconut-dill scent coming from American oak barrels, and rich, smooth tannins on this wine. It delivers much pleasure now, but also has an excellent track record for aging if you've got the discipline. Irresistible with pasta with olive oil, prosciutto, sage and garlic.

Kitchen Survivor™ Grade: B

Your notes: _____

Silver Oak Napa Valley   **$**   **Pts**
Cabernet Sauvignon, California 2004   **100**   **94**

🍎 The extra year in bottle compared to other big Cabs gives this extra nuances of brambly gaminess to compliment the succulent dark cherry fruit, and signature coconut and allspice notes. Pair with dark chocolate, or prime rib with caramelized shallots.

Kitchen Survivor™ Grade: B

Your notes: _____

Simi Cabernet Sauvignon, Alexander   **$**   **Pts**
Valley, Sonoma, California 2006   **25**   **86**

☺Lavish vanilla oak frames the very Sonoma Cab flavors of warm wild berries and sweet spice.

Kitchen Survivor™ Grade: B

Your notes: _____

Souverain Alexander Valley   **$**   **Pts**
Cabernet Sauvignon, California 2006   **20**   **90**

⏱ Cab balance and elegance, defined. You get all the leafy-dusty, dark cassis fruit and sweet vanilla of classic CA Cab, without heaviness. Velvety, smooth and loooong. Pair with rosemary pork tenderloin.

Kitchen Survivor™ Grade: B

Your notes: _____

Staglin Family Estate Cabernet Sauvignon,   **$**   **Pts**
Napa Valley, California 2005   **175**   **98**

⏱ 👍 They drink this in Heaven. One can dream, right? Wines rarely achieve such an impeccable balance of opulence, power and grace. Nose: fig syrup and chocolate, vanilla, spice, tar, cedar, violets. Palate: a dark velvet sarong for your tongue, echoing all that came before in the nose, with nuances of vanilla and smoke that carry into the finish. The wine deserves all of your attention, so keep the pairing simple - a fine cheese or prime steak.

Kitchen Survivor™ Grade: B

Your notes: _____

Stag's Leap Artemis Cabernet Sauvignon, | $ | Pts
Napa, California 2006 | 55 | 90

A mini-splurge compared to the winery's famous SLV, Cask 23 and Fay Vineyard bottlings. That said, it's a wow for the price, and a great rendition of the Stag's Leap style which emphasizes an old world-like balance of power between subtlety and intensity. It also emphasizes gorgeous, layered aromatics - bay leaf, olive, cedar, and violets. On the palate the flavor of brooding dark berries combines with notes of roasted meat and aged balsamic. Pair with lamb shanks.

Kitchen Survivor™ Grade: C

Your notes: _____

Sterling Vineyards Cabernet Sauvignon | $ | Pts
Reserve, Napa, California 2006 | 75 | 90

Hello, hedonism...in the form of lavish coconut oakiness, black cherry-kirsch notes, and plenty of Napa dusty-cedar on the finish. Pair with rosemary lamb.

Kitchen Survivor™ Grade: B+

Your notes: _____

Sterling Vineyards Napa Cabernet | $ | Pts
Sauvignon, California 2006 | 26 | 85

Jammy and velvety, with chewy tannins, plummy cedar flavors and a spicy-oaky-vanilla finish.

Kitchen Survivor™ Grade: B

Your notes: _____

Sterling Vintner's Collection Cabernet | $ | Pts
Sauvignon, Central Coast, California 2006 | 15 | 84

☺ Soft and plump, with nice dusty blackberry fruit.

Kitchen Survivor™ Grade: C

Your notes: _____

Stonestreet Alexander Valley | $ | Pts
Cabernet Sauvignon, California 2005 | 42 | 86

The elegance and scents of vanilla, damp earth, crushed mint, and blackberry are classic Alexander Valley, and pair nicely with herb-crusted lamb chops.

Kitchen Survivor™ Grade: C

Your notes: _____

Trefethen Estate Cabernet Sauvignon, | $ | Pts
Oak Knoll District, Napa California 2005 | 50 | 94

Such a finessed wine, and true to its signa-

tures of violets, lavender, dark plum, blackberry and sprightly cedar. All that complexity makes it a stunner with Tuscan steak or soy-marinated duck, but this wine ages surprisingly well, too. Amazing value.
Kitchen Survivor™ Grade: B
Your notes: _____

| Veramonte Cabernet Sauvignon, | $ | Pts |
| Reserva, Colchagua Valley, Chile 2006 | 13 | 86 |

The licorice-berry flavors, chewy tannin, and savory spice and black olive notes taste like twice the price.
Kitchen Survivor™ Grade: C
Your notes: _____

| Viader Napa Valley Red Blend, | $ | Pts |
| Napa, California 2005 | 90 | 89 |

🍎 A luxuriant 69% Cab/31% Cab Franc blend that needed at least an hour to open up. Violets, intensely sweet licorice-oak and black fruit show the touch of consultant Michel Rolland, as does the price!
Kitchen Survivor™ Grade: A+
Your notes: _____

Rioja, Ribera del Duero, and Other Spanish Reds

Category Profile: Like other classic European wines, it's the place—called a Denominación de Origen (DO)—rather than the grape on a Spanish wine label, in most cases. Spain's signature red grape, used in both the Rioja (*ree-OH-huh*) and the Ribera del Duero (*ree-BEAR-uh dell DWAIR-oh*) DOs, is called Tempranillo (*temp-rah-NEE-oh*). Depending on quality level, the style of Rioja ranges from easy drinking and spicy to seriously rich, leathery/toffee. Ribera del Duero is generally big and tannic. The other Spanish reds here are from Priorat (*pre-oh-RAHT*), known for strong, inky-dark cellar candidates (usually made from Tempranillo, Cabernet, and/or Grenache). Though not represented in the top red wine sellers, Penedes (*pen-eh-DESS*), which is better known for Cava sparkling wines, is also an outstanding source of values in every style and color.

Serve: Cool room temperature; as a rule Spanish reds are exemplary food wines, but basic reds from Penedes and Rioja (with the word *Cosecha* or *Crianza* on the label), and emerging regions like Navarra, Toro, and Somontano, are good "anytime" wines and tasty on their own.

When: If you dine out often in wine-focused restaurants, Spanish reds are *the* red wine category for world-class drinking that's also affordable.

With: The classic matches are pork and lamb, either roasted or grilled; also amazing with slow-roasted chicken or turkey and hams, sausages, and other cured meats. Finally, try a Spanish Ribera del Duero, Priorat, or Rioja Reserva or Gran Reserva with good-quality cheese. (Spanish Manchego is wonderful and available in supermarkets.)

In: The One™ glass for red wines, or a larger-bowled red wine stem.

	$	Pts
Abadia Retuerta Rivola, **Sardon de Duero, Spain 2006**	14	89

This 60/40 Tempranillo/Cab blend is exotic and juicy, with lively red berry, mint, floral and spice notes - in other words, a lot of complexity for the price!
Kitchen Survivor™ Grade: A+
Your notes: _____

	$	Pts
Abadia Retuerta Seleccion Especial, **Sardon de Duero, Spain 2006**	20	90

👍 This Tempranillo with a touch of Merlot and Cab is dark and lusty, with brandied cherry, chocolate and cinnamon kissed with a savory black olive note. Aeration shows off all those layers, hinting that it will age.
Kitchen Survivor™ Grade: A+
Your notes: _____

	$	Pts
Baron de Ley Rioja Gran Reserva, **Spain 1998**	24	92

🍷 Great bottle-aged character for this price? Yes! Leather, mushrooms, meat stock, tobacco and dark cherries; satin texture. Magic with wild mushrooms.
Kitchen Survivor™ Grade: B+
Your notes: _____

Borsao Tinto Garnacha/Tempranillo,
Campo de Borja, Spain 2007

$	Pts
8	86

🍎 ☺ The fruit-bomb ripeness and nice spice of this wine let you "yum out" on the cheap. Pair with chili, burritos, blackened chicken or barbecue.

Kitchen Survivor™ Grade: B+

Your notes: _____

Campo Viejo Tempranillo Rioja,
Crianza, Spain 2006

$	Pts
9	84

🍴⚡ 🍷 This big offers great value for the price. The dusty coriander and white pepper spice are a nice grace note to the red cherry fruit. Pair with pizza!

Kitchen Survivor™ Grade: B

Your notes: _____

Campo Viejo Tempranillo Rioja
Reserva, Spain 2004

$	Pts
13	86

🍴⚡ 🍷 Savory and spicy, with notes of rosemary, coriander and beef stock along with the balsamic-marinated strawberry flavor. A real find for the price.

Kitchen Survivor™ Grade: B

Your notes: _____

Comenge Ribera del Duero,
Spain 2006

$	Pts
30	88

🍷 A dense wine, with gamy molasses, toffee, charcoal and leather on those, and dark plum, balsamic and black pepper notes on the palate. Mustard-crusted lamb chops would be a perfect partner.

Kitchen Survivor™ Grade: B+

Your notes: _____

El Coto de Imaz Rioja Reserva,
Spain 2004

$	Pts
14.99	88

El Coto is a perfect mix of modern and traditional style Rioja (bright strawberry fruit, hints of leather and spice, silky texture), at a great price.

Kitchen Survivor™ Grade: B+

Your notes: _____

Faustino V Rioja Reserva, Rioja,
Spain 2004

$	Pts
21	88

🍷 A great price for all the leather and toffee, pepper and silkiness of traditional Rioja. Pair with lamb.

Kitchen Survivor™ Grade: B+

Your notes: _____

La Rioja Alta Vina Ardanza Reserva, $ 35 | Pts 92
Spain 2000

♟ Textbook traditional Rioja Reserva: tangy cranberry, sweet caramel, leather and caramelized onion notes that make it a stunning match with roast lamb.
Kitchen Survivor™ Grade: B
Your notes: _____

Marques de Caceres (*mahr-KESS* $ 14 | Pts 84
***deh CAH-sair-ess*) Rioja Crianza,**
Spain 2005

🍃 As always, a zippy strawberries-and-pepper quaffer that's perfect for everyday fare like pizza or pasta.
Kitchen Survivor™ Grade: B
Your notes: _____

Marques de Murrieta Castillo Ygay Rioja, $ 54 | Pts 91
Gran Reserva Especial, Spain 2001

♟ Traditional-style Rioja at its best, with leather, spice, tobacco, toffee, and lots of time left to go. Delicious now with slow-braised lamb or beef.
Kitchen Survivor™ Grade: B
Your notes: _____

Marques de Riscal (*mahr-KESS* $ 8 | Pts 85
***deh ree-SKALL*) Rioja Crianza, Spain 2004**

This wine earns praise for its lovely spicy nose, silken texture, lively acidity and savory-strawberry flavor.
Kitchen Survivor™ Grade: B+
Your notes: _____

Marques de Riscal Rioja Gran $ 35 | Pts 89
Reserva, Spain 2000

Traditional Rioja at its best: date and dried figs; leather, chewy tannins; and great spice, with a long buttery-coconut finish. A great match for sauteed mushrooms with garlic, or grilled lamb chops.
Kitchen Survivor™ Grade: B
Your notes: _____

Marques de Riscal Rioja Reserva, $ 18 | Pts 87
Spain 2004

A nice mix of old-style and new: toffee/coconut scents, raisiny and chocolatey flavor, spicy finish.
Kitchen Survivor™ Grade: B
Your notes: _____

Montecillo (*mohn-teh-SEE-yoh*) $ Pts
Rioja Crianza, Spain 2005 11   84

🌱 A favorite of wine geeks, for its Old-World pepper-on-strawberries flavors and snappy texture that loves food like grilled eggplant or stuffed peppers.

Kitchen Survivor™ Grade: C

Your notes: _____

Muga (*MOO-guh*) Rioja Reserva, $ Pts
Spain 2005 30   90

🏆 👍 "Muga" is Spanish for world-class quality, even in this entry-point red with stunning fig, prune, and dried cherry fruit and dense but suede-smooth tannins. Pair with manchego cheese, bread and olive oil.

Kitchen Survivor™ Grade: A+

Your notes: _____

Palacios Remondo La Montesa Rioja $ Pts
Crianza, Spain 2006 20   89

👍 Unusually for Rioja, this is a Garnacha-dominated blend (45%), with 40% Tempranillo plus Mazuelo and Graciano. The result is lots of savor and character with scents and flavors of red berries, and looots of spice! The gentle tug of earthy tannin makes it a great match for pork chops with mustard sauce.

Kitchen Survivor™ Grade: C

Your notes: _____

Palacios Remondo La Vendimia Rioja, $ Pts
Spain 2008 14   86

🌱 This 50/50 blend of Garnacha and Tempranillo in the *joven* (young) style of Rioja is just fun, with frisky red fruits and piquant black pepper and cumin notes just made for pairing with barbecued chicken or ribs.

Kitchen Survivor™ Grade: C

Your notes: _____

Pesquera (*pess-CARE-uh*) Crianza, Ribera $ Pts
del Duero, Spain 2006 35   91

🏆 A big and brooding wine. The scents of violets, tar and dark berries, and palate of dense tannins and plum liqueur, will harmonize with cellaring. When young, pair with roast game or rich cheeses.

Kitchen Survivor™ Grade: B

Your notes: _____

R. Lopez de Heredia Vina Bosconia Rioja   **$**   **Pts**
Reserva, Spain 2001   **37**   **91**

♉ A young wine for Lopez de Heredia, the classic traditionalist: aged forever yet seemingly ageless. Start with this silky, mushroomey, leathery classic and a great cheese - but try 'em all, white and rose, too.

Kitchen Survivor™ *Grade: B*

Your notes: _____

Torre Muga Rioja,   **$**   **Pts**
Spain 2004   **93**   **94**

♉ ♉ 👍 Perfumed and majestic, with jasmine, fig, leather and pepper scents and deep, chewy fig, sassafras and aged balsamic flavors. A wine for the cellar that's a favorite in our family for its nothing-quite-like-it singularly Spanish style. Pair with roast lamb.

Kitchen Survivor™ *Grade: A+*

Your notes: _____

Val Llach Embruix (*em-BROOSH*) Priorat,   **$**   **Pts**
Spain 2006   **34**   **89**

👍 Classic Priorat without the sticker shock. This one's heady with dark fig, molasses, fudge and allspice notes, with meaty-mushroomy undertones. Pair it with rich meats like braised duck or lamb shanks.

Kitchen Survivor™ *Grade: B+*

Your notes: _____

Uncommon Red Grapes and Blends

Category Profile: As with the whites, this isn't a cohesive category but rather a spot to put worthy, reds that don't neatly fit a grape or region category—namely, proprietary blends, and uncommon varietals.

Proprietary Blends—These may be tasty, inexpensive blends or ambitious signature blends at luxury prices.

Uncommon Varietals—These are quite exciting. I introduced Malbec and Carmenere in the Merlot section, because I think they are distinctive and delicious alternatives for Merlot lovers. Although the names and even the style (bold and a little peppery) are similar, Petite Sirah and Syrah (Shiraz) are not the same grape.

Serve: Cool room temperature, or even slightly chilled.

When: Anytime you need an interesting, value-priced red.

With: Anything from snacks to fine meals. These are very food-friendly!

In: The One™ glass for red wines, an all-purpose wineglass or a larger-bowled wineglass.

Alamos (Catena) Malbec, Mendoza	**$**	**Pts**
Argentina 2008	13	85

The ideal style for basic Argentine Malbec: fruit-bomb blueberry notes and a soft texture so you can go either way, fleshy fish like salmon, or big beef. Yum!
Kitchen Survivor™ Grade: C
Your notes: _____

Arboleda Carmenere, Colchagua,	**$**	**Pts**
Chile 2007	19	90

Arboleda achieves awesome character for the price. This Carmenere is a meaty meal-in-a-glass, with notes of cumin, prosciutto, rosemary, blackberry and leather. Pair with meaty, mushroomy pastas.
Kitchen Survivor™ Grade: A+
Your notes: _____

Bogle Petite Sirah,	**$**	**Pts**
California 2007	12	87

A black pepper and berries mouthful that's always an awesome value, and great match for barbecue.
Kitchen Survivor™ Grade: B
Your notes: _____

Catena Alta Malbec, Mendoza,	**$**	**Pts**
Argentina 2007	24	90

From an Argentina pioneer. The dense black-berry fruit, velvet texture, vanilla-sweet oak and peppery-mineral finish are at once sleek and powerful.
Kitchen Survivor™ Grade: B
Your notes: _____

Cline Ancient Vines Mourvedre,   **$**   **Pts**
California 2007   **18**   **86**

Dark, decadent blueberry and spice cake scents and flavors - rich and lush without being too heavy. Perfect with fig-stuffed pork roast or Moroccan lamb.

Kitchen Survivor™ Grade: B+

Your notes: _____

Cline Cashmere Grenache-Syrah-   **$**   **Pts**
Mourvedre, Contra Costa, California 2007   **18**   **88**

🍎 It's hard to go wrong with the sweet-savory spice, mincemeat and Christmas pudding decadence of this wine. A great match for barbecue or teriyaki.

Kitchen Survivor™ Grade: B

Your notes: _____

Concha y Toro Terrunyo   **$**   **Pts**
Carmenere, Chile 2006   **40**   **91**

🍷 One of the most expensive Chilean Carmeneres, but something special. It's like the concentrated essence of wild berries (huckleberries, raspberries), with yin-yang notes of sweet cola and beef stock.

Kitchen Survivor™ Grade: B

Your notes: _____

Kaiken Ultra Malbec, Mendoza,   **$**   **Pts**
Argentina 2007   **12**   **88**

🍎 Inky, smoky, dusty and velvety - that characterizes the best of Argentinian Malbecs. On the palate the licorice and blueberry preserves flavor is balanced by a touch of balsamic and black olive savoriness.

Kitchen Survivor™ Grade: A+

Your notes: _____

Lang & Reed Cabernet Franc Premier   **$**   **Pts**
Etage, Napa 2004   **40**   **91**

🍎 I fell in love with this wine - sumptuous dark raspberry fruit, coffee bean scents and a texture that is obscenely luxuriant. A true Napa benchmark.

Kitchen Survivor™ Grade: A+

Your notes: _____

Miner Family Sangiovese Gibson Ranch,   **$**   **Pts**
Mendocino, California 2007   **20**   **90**

🍷 Outrageously delicious, with strawberry-rhubarb compote, black pepper, orange peel and ginger tickling all your senses. Pair with BBQ quail or salmon.

Kitchen Survivor™ Grade: B+
Your notes: _____

MontGras Carmenere Reserva, $ Pts
Colchagua, Chile 2007   14   88
Attention-getting flavors and scents of cumin,
smoke, meat stock and dark cherry. Have it with hard
cheeses or a beefy roast to showcase the flavor layers.
Kitchen Survivor™ Grade: C
Your notes: _____

Navarro Correas Malbec, Mendoza, $ Pts
Argentina 2007   13   87
Rustic but really inviting, with an earthy, leathery,
savory spice scent, and silky, subtle plum fruit.
Kitchen Survivor™ Grade: B
Your notes: _____

Salentein Malbec Reserve, $ Pts
Argentina 2007   20   90
Richer, more sophisticated and more complex
than most Argentinian Malbecs. Dark boysenberry
fruit with varietally-typical notes of pen ink, roast
beef and leather underneath the soft vanilla and
spice. A real attention-getter. Pair with a great steak.
Kitchen Survivor™ Grade: B+
Your notes: _____

Stags' Leap Winery Petite Sirah, $ Pts
Napa, California 2006   38   87
A specialty of this (the other) Stags' Leap (notice the
s-apostrophe). The licorice and blackberry scents
and flavors, chewy tannins, and smoky-tar finish are .
Pair it with black olive and fennel sausage pizza, or
rare burgers with blue cheese.
Kitchen Survivor™ Grade: B
Your notes: _____

Tablas Creek Cotes de Tablas red blend, $ Pts
Paso Robles, California 2007   25   91
Syrupy and luscious fruit kissed with layers of spice,
wild herbs and a briary note make this irresistible and
unique. Pair with grilled fennel or olive tapenade.
Kitchen Survivor™ Grade: B
Your notes: _____

Veramonte Primus,	$	Pts
Chile 2006	**22**	**89**

🍴 This pioneer Carmenere blend is still one of the best, with a lot of exotic berry fruit, both savory and sweet spices, and a smoky-meaty note.

Kitchen Survivor™ Grade: B

Your notes: _____

Syrah/Shiraz and Other Rhone-Style Reds

Category Profile: The varietal Shiraz, Australia's signature red, is so hot that many pros say it has unseated Merlot as consumers' go-to grape. Popularity has its price for Shiraz lovers, though, because many of the biggest brands have begun to taste like generic red wine rather than the spunky-spicy Shiraz with which we fell in love. I've focused on brands that have stayed true to the Shiraz taste. The same grape, under the French spelling *Syrah,* also forms the backbone for France's revered Rhone Valley reds with centuries-old reputations. These include Cotes-du-Rhone (*coat-duh-ROAN*), Cote-Rotie (*ro-TEE*), Hermitage (*uhr-muh-TAHJ*), and Chateauneuf-du-Pape (*shah-toe-NUFF-duh-POP*). Like basic Shiraz, Cotes-du-Rhone, with its lovely spicy fruit character, is a value star. The latter three are true French classics and, in my view, currently lead that elite group in quality for the money. They are full-bodied, powerful, peppery, earthy, concentrated, and oak aged. Finally, most major American wineries, and many smaller players, are bottling California or Washington State versions, often labeled with the Aussie spelling *Shiraz* rather than the French *Syrah.*

Serve: Cool room temperature; aeration enhances the aroma and flavor.

When: Basic Syrah/Shiraz and Cotes-du-Rhone are great everyday drinking wines; in restaurants, these are great go-to categories for relative value.

With: Grilled, barbecued, or roasted anything (including fish and vegetables); outstanding with steaks, fine cheeses, and other dishes that call for a full red wine; I also love these styles with traditional Thanksgiving fare.

In: The One™ glass for red wines, an all-purpose wineglass or a larger-bowled wineglass.

	$	Pts
Alice White Shiraz,		
Australia 2008	8	85

☺ The most bang for the buck in an under-$10 red, thanks to its spicy scent and wild raspberry fruit." Bring on the barbecue (or teriyaki, or meatloaf!).
Kitchen Survivor™ Grade: B
Your notes: _____

	$	Pts
Andrew Murray Syrah Tous Les Jours,		
Central Coast, California 2006	16	86

🍶🍴 One of the tastiest bets in CA Syrah for the money, with luscious raspberry-pomegranate fruit and a hint of white pepper spiciness. Great with pizza.
Kitchen Survivor™ Grade: B
Your notes: _____

	$	Pts
Beaulieu Vineyard (BV) Coastal		
Estates Shiraz, California 2006	9	86

🍎 ☺ Meaty, juicy dark plum and berries; a yummy steal that's the perfect house red if you like 'em lush.
Kitchen Survivor™ Grade: B
Your notes: _____

	$	Pts
Bonny Doon Le Cigare Volant,		
California 2005	30	86

Grenache, Syrah and Mourvedre dominate this blend, always notable for its spice, rhubarb and pomegranate notes. A great match for ratatouille.
Kitchen Survivor™ Grade: C
Your notes: _____

	$	Pts
Brokenwood Shiraz, McLaren Vale,		
Australia 2007	27	88

🍎 This is benchmark McLaren Vale Shiraz, with black licorice, anise and raspberry-vanilla on the palate, eucalyptus and pepper in the finish. A great match for barbecued tuna or tandoori chicken.
Kitchen Survivor™ Grade: B+
Your notes: _____

Chalone Vineyard Estate Syrah,   **$**   **Pts**
Chalone, California 2006   30   87

Power and subtlety: tarry, dark fig and black raspberry fruit. Very smoky, firm and velvety. Loooong finish.

Kitchen Survivor™ Grade: B

Your notes: _____

Chapoutier Chateauneuf-du-Pape   **$**   **Pts**
La Bernardine, Rhone, France 2006   60   90

♟ A fragrance riot of pomegranate, white pepper, caraway, sweet strawberry and rhubarb. On the palate, grippy and earthy, with snappy strawberry-rhubarb and black pepper flavors. Needs air (or time in the cellar) to soften. Pair with steak au poivre.

Kitchen Survivor™ Grade: B

Your notes: _____

Chapoutier Cotes-du-Rhone Rouge   **$**   **Pts**
Belleruche, Rhone, France 2007   13   89

🔥 Absolutely the best CdR I have had in years. Vibrantly ripe strawberry fruit on the nose and palate, along with scents of citrus peel, cumin, sweet spices, and a luscious texture. Pair with Provencal fish stew.

Kitchen Survivor™ Grade: B+

Your notes: _____

Chapoutier Hermitage Rouge Monier de,   **$**   **Pts**
la Sizeranne, Rhone, France 2005   115   92

♟ Majestic and powerful, with layered notes of leather, pipe tobacco, sun-warmed berries, caramelized shallots and veal stock. Pair with slow-braised lamb shanks or smoked duck.

Kitchen Survivor™ Grade: B

Your notes: _____

Chateau de Beaucastel   **$**   **Pts**
Chateauneuf-du-Pape, France 2006   100   92

👍 Although it's expensive, the exotic notes of jasmine, Asian spices, tobacco and pepper along with powerful fig and dark berry fruit are luxuriant, yet all underpinned by structure that's built for the longhaul, if you've got the discipline to cellar it. Pair with rosemary- and garlic-scented leg of lamb.

Kitchen Survivor™ Grade: A+

Your notes: _____

Chateau La Nerthe (*shah-TOE lah NAIRT*) **Chateauneuf-du-Pape, Rhone, France 2006**

	$	Pts
	42	88

🌿 ♟ The pepper/spicy/leathery scents, gripping tannins, and dried cranberry-anise flavors are textbook Chateauneuf, built for rich meats and stews.
Kitchen Survivor™ Grade: A

Your notes: _____

Cline Syrah, California 2007

	$	Pts
	12	86

☺ Cline puts lots of vibrant berry fruit flavor and spicy-zingy scent in the bottle for a great price. A delicious match for burgers or ribs on the grill.
Kitchen Survivor™ Grade: B+

Your notes: _____

D'Arenberg The Footbolt Shiraz, Australia 2007

	$	Pts
	20	89

I love the intensity and meaty-smoky-berry richness of this wine, kicked up more by the sweet and savory spices that make it an ideal match for BBQ or pizza.
Kitchen Survivor™ Grade: B

Your notes: _____

Duboeuf (Georges) Cotes-du-Rhone (*du-BUFF coat-duh-ROAN*), **France 2007**

	$	Pts
	10	86

Always juicy and fresh, with red cherry and spicy pomegranate flavors that make your mouth water. Delicious with most any food, but especially tomato-sauced dishes, goat cheese and grilled fish, chicken or pork.
Kitchen Survivor™ Grade: B

Your notes: _____

E & M Guigal (*ghee-GALL*) **Cotes-du-Rhone, Rhone, France 2007**

	$	Pts
	15	86

A value from the famous Guigal name, with strawberry fruit, rhubarb and pepper-spice. Delicious with herbed goat cheese or spicy grilled sausages.
Kitchen Survivor™ Grade: A

Your notes: _____

E & M Guigal Cote-Rotie Brune et $~~~~~$ **$** $~~~$ **Pts**
Blonde, Rhone, France 2005 $~~~~~~~~~~~~~~$ **60** $~~~$ **94**

👍 The benchmark Cote-Rotie, for good reason. It is always top-quality, and true to the appellation. That means loads of charry-tarry, black olive, pepper and jasmine perfume, plush blackberry fruit, grippy-spicy tannins and a long, lavender-pepper finish. It will age 20 years but if you can't wait, pair with braised lamb.

Kitchen Survivor™ Grade: B+

Your notes: _____

Goats Do Roam Red, Paarl $~~~~~~~~~~~~~~$ **$** $~~~$ **Pts**
South Africa 2007 $~~~~~~~~~~~~~~~~~~~~~~~$ **8** $~~~$ **86**

🍷 A tongue-in-cheek take on French Cotes-du-Rhone, with a South African flair from Pinotage in the blend. The result is snappy and alluring meaty-pepper and soft red fruit flavors, for a great price.

Kitchen Survivor™ Grade: C

Your notes: _____

Greg Norman Shiraz, $~~~~~~~~~~~~~~~~~~$ **$** $~~~$ **Pts**
Australia 2007 $~~~~~~~~~~~~~~~~~~~~~~~~~~$ **14** $~~~$ **85**

Not much Shiraz varietal character, but lots of soft raspberry fruit. A nice match with seared tuna.

Kitchen Survivor™ Grade: C

Your notes: _____

Hill of Content Grenache/Shiraz, $~~~~~~$ **$** $~~~$ **Pts**
Australia 2007 $~~~~~~~~~~~~~~~~~~~~~~~~~~$ **14** $~~~$ **87**

🍷 🍎 This wine's raspberry-floral scent, ripe, jammy berry fruit, and juicy texture are de-lish!

Kitchen Survivor™ Grade: A

Your notes: _____

Jaboulet (*jhah-boo-LAY*) Parallele 45 $~~$ **$** $~~~$ **Pts**
Cotes-du-Rhone, France 2007 $~~~~~~~~~~$ **17** $~~~$ **88**

🕯️ 🍷 The best of this classic in years. They've dialed up the red-plum fruit and licorice while preserving the leather, smoke and black pepper. Great with tapenade crostini, stuffed peppers, or pasta Bolognese.

Kitchen Survivor™ Grade: B

Your notes: _____

Jacob's Creek Shiraz/Cabernet   **$**   **Pts**
Sauvignon, Australia 2007   8   87
☺ This wine offers great taste and great value, with lush raspberry and eucalyptus and a plush texture.
Kitchen Survivor™ Grade: B+
Your notes: _____

Jade Mountain Napa Syrah,   **$**   **Pts**
California 2005   26   89
One of the best California Syrahs made. It's got rich raspberry fruit, a pepper-cumin-rosemary scent and an irresistible meaty-gaminess and mint on the palate. Bring on the leg of lamb or BBQ'd ribs!
Kitchen Survivor™ Grade: B+
Your notes: _____

La Vieille Ferme (*lah vee-yay*   **$**   **Pts**
***FAIRM;* means "the old farm")**   11   86
Cotes-du-Ventoux, France 2007
☺ This raspberry-pomegranate and spice-bomb is a value classic and one of the most food-friendly every-day wines around. Pair with pizza, panini, pasta...
Kitchen Survivor™ Grade: B+
Your notes: _____

Lindemans Bin 50 Shiraz,   **$**   **Pts**
Australia 2007   7   86
☺ Soft, ripe raspberry fruit and a black pepper scent; an all-around great drink and great buy.
Kitchen Survivor™ Grade: B+
Your notes: _____

Morgan Double "L" Syrah, Santa Lucia   **$**   **Pts**
Highlands, Monterey, California 2007   40   93
One of the most varietally distinct and delicious American Syrahs yet. Cardamom, black pepper and black tea scents contribute detail and intrigue to the ripe raspberry and fig fruit. Pair it with Jerk pork.
Kitchen Survivor™ Grade: B+
Your notes: _____

Morgan Syrah, Monterey,   **$**   **Pts**
California 2007   18   90

Either Syrah has found its second home (after the Rhone in France) in Monterey, or vintner Dan Lee just knows what he is doing (it's probably a little of both). This floral and alluring raspberry, red licorice and black pepper-scented version is silky and luscious on the palate. Pair it with duck confit or grilled quail.

Kitchen Survivor™ Grade: B

Your notes: _____

Penfolds Kalimna Shiraz Bin 28,   **$**   **Pts**
Australia 2006   26   89

I serve this to my wine students to teach them about real-deal Aussie Shiraz—it's full of black pepper, sweet black fig flavors, clove and allspice, and thick velvety tannins. Fantastic with jerk-spiced chicken, steak au poivre or stewed rabbit.

Kitchen Survivor™ Grade: B+

Your notes: _____

Penfolds Koonunga Hill Shiraz   **$**   **Pts**
Cabernet, Australia 2007   12   85

☺ You can't beat this plummy, slightly spicy red for easy drinkability, yet with some nice tannic grip.

Kitchen Survivor™ Grade: C

Your notes: _____

Penfolds St. Henri Shiraz, South   **$**   **Pts**
Australia 2005   26   90

Roots, herbs, leather, olives, spices, meat, aged balsamic: this wine is kaleidoscopically complex, without being the slightest bit heavy. And that is in youth. I have tasted decades-old bottles that are wonders to behold. A true original in the wine world.

Kitchen Survivor™ Grade: B+

Your notes: _____

Qupe Central Coast Syrah, Central   **$**   **Pts**
Coast, California 2007   18   87

A time-tested value that's tasting better than ever. Its signature is a floral and fruit-driven lavender-pomegranate-raspberry-white pepper style that says "fire up the grill." It's also great with Greek salad.

Kitchen Survivor™ Grade: B

Your notes: _____

Ravenswood Sonoma County Syrah, California 2007

	$	Pts
	15	86

A real stand-out among California Syrahs in this price point, with lots of wild boysenberry fruit and sweet spice, with a hint of pepper in the finish.

Kitchen Survivor™ Grade: B

Your notes: _____

Rosemount Diamond Label Shiraz, South Eastern Australia 2007

	$	Pts
	10	85

☺ This wine really put Shiraz on the US mass market wine map, and remains a great intro to Shiraz varietal character: raspberry-coconut scents and flavors, with pepper and eucalyptus. Here's to value, mate!

Kitchen Survivor™ Grade: B

Your notes: _____

Rosemount Diamond Label Shiraz/ Cabernet Sauvignon, Australia 2007

	$	Pts
	8	87

� My favorite of the Diamond Label reds. It's got juicy, mouthwatering berry fruit, a touch of mint in the scent, and a gentle tug of tannin.

Kitchen Survivor™ Grade: B

Your notes: _____

Rosemount Show Reserve McLaren Vale GSM (Grenache-Shiraz-Mourvedre), Australia 2007

	$	Pts
	24	86

🍎 Less spicy in this vintage, but still lively, with duck stock and raspberry scents and flavors built for pairing with cassoulet, or duck breast with berry sauce.

Kitchen Survivor™ Grade: B

Your notes: _____

Shingleback McLaren Vale Shiraz, Australia, California 2007

	$	Pts
	20	85

🍎 Real McLaren Vale character: clove spice, raspberry fruit, vanilla-coconut-licorice finish.

Kitchen Survivor™ Grade: C

Your notes: _____

Sterling Vintner's Collection Shiraz, Central Coast, California 2007

	$	Pts
	10	87

Balsamic-y fig fruit, vanilla, and licorice. A tasty buy.

Kitchen Survivor™ Grade: C

Your notes: _____

Wente Livermore Syrah,   **$**   **Pts**
California 2007   **10**   **87**
Ⓤ Impressive complexity for the $: lavender, plum
and pepper, with a raspberry juiciness on the palate
that's great for sipping, and paired with jerk chicken.
Kitchen Survivor™ Grade: C
Your notes: _____

Wolf Blass Yellow Label   **$**   **Pts**
Shiraz, Australia 2007   **13**   **89**
Ⓤ The black cherry and black pepper complexity,
with a velvety texture make this a top best buy among
Aussie Shirazes. So much better than 95% of the
wines at this price point. Pair with ribs and roasts.
Kitchen Survivor™ Grade: C
Your notes: _____

Yellowtail Shiraz,   **$**   **Pts**
Australia 2007   **7**   **85**
Although the Chardonnay is rightly this wine's calling
card, the soft plum flavor makes this Shiraz a solid
quaff for everyday drinking and casual meals.
Kitchen Survivor™ Grade: C
Your notes: _____

Red Zinfandel

Category Profile: *Groupie* is the apt moniker for devotees of this California specialty, which ranges in style
from medium-bodied, with bright and juicy raspberry
flavors, to lush, full-bodied, and high in alcohol with
intense blueberry, licorice, and even chocolate scents
and flavors. Many of the best vineyards have old vines
that produce some amazingly intense, complex wines.
Zins usually are oaky—a little or a lot, depending on
the intensity of the grapes used. The grape intensity is
a function of the vineyard—its age and its location.
California's most famous red Zinfandel areas are
Sonoma (especially the Dry Creek Valley subdistrict),
Napa, Amador, and the Sierra foothills. Lodi, in California's Central Valley, is also a good source.

Serve: Room temperature; aeration enhances the
aroma and flavor.

When: Value Zinfandels are excellent for everyday drinking; good restaurant lists usually have a selection worth exploring across the price spectrum.

With: Burgers, pizza, lamb (especially with Indian or Moroccan spices), and quality cheeses are favorites—even dark chocolate!

In: The One™ glass for red wines, or a larger-bowled red wine stem.

7 Deadly Zins Zinfandel, Lodi,	$	Pts
California 2007	15	85

Hugely popular and why not? It's fun, and juicy-slurpable in a big-Zin kinda way: that means licorice, blueberry compote and spice. BBQ, anyone?

Kitchen Survivor™ Grade: C

Your notes: _____

Alexander Valley Vineyards Sin Zin,	$	Pts
Alexander Valley, California 2007	20	85

What Zin should be - wild boysenberry fruit, black pepper, licorice and violets, without excessive alcohol. Nice with dark chocolate, burgers, big cheeses.

Kitchen Survivor™ Grade: C

Your notes: _____

Bogle Old Vines Zinfandel,	$	Pts
California 2007	9	86

One of the best-value Zins, with chewy sassafras, plum and pepper character. A natural for barbecue.

Kitchen Survivor™ Grade: C

Your notes: _____

Cline Zinfandel,	$	Pts
California 2007	18	86

This is a wine that remembers its Zinfandel identity. The oak and alcohol are subtle, letting the raspberry fruit and sweet spice come through. A great food partner for casual fare like pizza, pasta, Greek salad.

Kitchen Survivor™ Grade: A

Your notes: _____

Dancing Bull Zinfandel,   **$**   **Pts**
California 2007   12   84

A tasty little budget Zin with nice varietal character: pepper, dark wild berries and tar. Great with bold foods like barbecue and blackened chicken.

Kitchen Survivor™ Grade: B

Your notes: _____

Dashe Cellars Dry Creek Zinfandel,   **$**   **Pts**
California 2007   22   86

Uber-intense with black fig, licorice and pepper notes. Pair with barbecued ribs, or even dark chocolate.

Kitchen Survivor™ Grade: C

Your notes: _____

DeArie Zinfandel, Shenandoah   **$**   **Pts**
Valley, California 2007   22   89

♉ Great Zin character - boysenberry, molasses and black pepper, with some classy restraint thanks to the modest alcohol and fine-grained tannins.

Kitchen Survivor™ Grade: B

Your notes: _____

Deloach Vineyards Heritage Zinfandel,   **$**   **Pts**
California 2007   12   90

You can't get more Zin for the money. In fact this is one of the best reds for the money, period. Syrupy raspberry and strawberry compote flavors with a hint of sweet spice and a completely silken texture make it lipsmacking to sip on its own, or with the satiny texture and spice of kicked-up tuna sushi.

Kitchen Survivor™ Grade: B

Your notes: _____

Deloach Vineyards Zinfandel, Russian   **$**   **Pts**
River Valley, California 2007   18   92

♉ A yum-fest, with lush raspberry and boysenberry flavors and silky-soft body. Delish on its own and with my signature "Zin panini": strawberries with balsamic and black pepper, and fresh mozzarella. Try it!

Kitchen Survivor™ Grade: B

Your notes: _____

Dry Creek Vineyard Old Vine   **$**   **Pts**
Zinfandel, Sonoma, California 2007   **28**   **86**

🍎 A great example of Dry Creek Zin: "blueberries and chocolate," as one of my wine buddies describes it, with thick and velvety tannins. Serve with braised short ribs or a rich cheese such as Maytag blue.

Kitchen Survivor™ Grade: A

Your notes: _____

Ferrari-Carano Zinfandel, Alexander Valley   **$**   **Pts**
California 2006   **28**   **88**

Taut and tarry, with dark blackberry, cocoa and hoisin sauce notes, plus sweet vanilla and pepper in the finish. A perfect partner for falling-off-the-bone ribs, braised lamb shanks or Maytag blue cheese.

Kitchen Survivor™ Grade: B+

Your notes: _____

Fetzer Valley Oaks Zinfandel,   **$**   **Pts**
California 2007   **9**   **85**

☺ It's all there: juicy, spicy, nice wild berry flavors and the consistency you can count on from Fetzer's Valley Oaks line. A great "house red."

Kitchen Survivor™ Grade: B+

Your notes: _____

Frank Family Zinfandel, Napa Valley,   **$**   **Pts**
California 2007   **35**   **93**

Where great Zins like this one really shine is in their fleshy mid-palate fruit that's not at all gooey or syrupy, but gorgeously round and ripe like perfect sun-warmed dark berries. This is a "big" red that tastes delish on its own, yet has the structure and balance to share the table with game birds, red meats or risotto.

Kitchen Survivor™ Grade: B

Your notes: _____

Frog's Leap Zinfandel, Napa,   **$**   **Pts**
California 2007   **27**   **89**

Sweet restraint! And sweet fruit: blueberry and cassis kissed with soft vanilla oak and baking spices. A yummy match for blue cheese burgers, lamb curry, or moo shoo pork.

Kitchen Survivor™ Grade: B

Your notes: _____

Girard Old Vine Zinfandel,   **$**   **Pts**
California 2007   **24**   **89**

Chewy, dense and rich on the palate with pepper, dried fig, sassafras and tar notes. Perfect with white bean and duck confit stew, or olive tapenade crostini.

Kitchen Survivor™ Grade: B+

Your notes: _____

Grgich Hills Estate Zinfandel,   **$**   **Pts**
California 2006   **28**   **92**

♀ ♀ Zin the way it used to be, with both sweet ripe berry fruit, and savory sundried tomato, black pepper and leather notes. A great partner for lusty, rustic dishes like lamb stew, braised short ribs or farmstead cheeses.

Kitchen Survivor™ Grade: B+

Your notes: _____

Inspiration Vineyards Zinfandel,   **$**   **Pts**
Alexander Valley, California 2007   **23**   **90**

♀ ♀ Owner and vintner Jon Phillips seems to have the Midas touch - he gets old world smoky-tarry-truffly character into the wine, alongside dense Zin richness: fruitcake, spice, fig, raspberry and black pepper Zin flavors. Pair with moo shoo pork, spice-rubbed duck or Provencal lamb stew.

Kitchen Survivor™ Grade: B+

Your notes: _____

Joel Gott Zinfandel,   **$**   **Pts**
California 2007   **14**   **87**

🍎 The gulpable blueberry cobbler flavors and easy price make this great for barbecues and casual meals.

Kitchen Survivor™ Grade: B+

Your notes: _____

Kendall-Jackson Vintner's Reserve Zinfandel **$**   **Pts**
Mendocino County, California 2007   **16**   **87**

Proof that Zin doesn't have to be high in alcohol to be "Zinny." This is full-blooded, brambly boysenberry Zin fruit with a touch of pepper and juicy-satiny texture. A great match for ribs or burgers.

Kitchen Survivor™ Grade: C

Your notes: _____

Louis Martini Monte Rosso Gnarly   **$**   **Pts**
Vines Zinfandel, California 2006   **50**   **88**
A big-bodied Zin for a big price, with clove and pepper spice and intense fig and black licorice flavors.
Pair with a creamy cheese such as St. Andre or Maytag blue, or char-cooked beef and caramelized onions.
Kitchen Survivor™ Grade: B
Your notes: _____

Martinelli Jackass Vineyard Zinfandel,   **$**   **Pts**
Russian River Valley, California 2007   **100**   **96**
Yes, it is expensive, but the drinking experience is
transformational. In youth, the wine has decadent
notes of spice, rum-soaked raisins, Kirsch, and a
chocolate-covered cherry cordial flavor that never
seems to subside even as the wine ages to smoky,
truffly yumminess (7-10 years). Pair with dark chocolate or pork with a chocolatey mole poblano sauce.
Kitchen Survivor™ Grade: B+
Your notes: _____

Quivira Zinfandel Anderson Ranch, Dry   **$**   **Pts**
Creek Valley, Sonoma, California 2006   **34**   **90**
A super-drinkable and pair-able Zin thanks to the perfumy complexity. Red licorice, strawberry fruit
leather and cinnamon-vanilla on the nose, with a
juicy-lively palate and gentle tug of tannin that cries
out for hot-smoked salmon or rare duck breast.
Kitchen Survivor™ Grade: B
Your notes: _____

Rancho Zabaco Dry Creek Valley   **$**   **Pts**
Zinfandel, Sonoma, California 2007   **24**   **87**
Supple and succulent, with juicy berry compote, cinnamon spice and brambly balsamic notes. Complete,
balanced and not over-the-top Pair with blackened
chicken, spicy barbecued ribs, or chocolate.
Kitchen Survivor™ Grade: B
Your notes: _____

Ravenswood Sonoma County Old Vines   **$**   **Pts**
Zinfandel, California 2007   **15**   **89**

🍎 So worth the trade-up from the Vintners Blend (see below), even though that is quite good. The payoff is really layers and great structure - things you rarely get for $15. Red berry fruit (raspberry, cherry) with sweet spices, plus sweet vanilla and red licorice in the finish. A fun tasting is to compare this to the Napa and Lodi Old Vines bottlings - all great quality for the $.

Kitchen Survivor™ Grade: B

Your notes: _____

Ravenswood Vintners Blend   **$**   **Pts**
Zinfandel, California 2007   **10**   **84**

True to the Zin varietal character (dark blueberry-licorice), and you have to credit the quality consistency and price-value. A good "house red" candidate.

Kitchen Survivor™ Grade: C

Your notes: _____

Renwood Zinfandel, Shenandoah   **$**   **Pts**
California 2006   **20**   **86**

👆 Renwood's Zins are justly revered among Zin lovers; this one's lusciously jammy, with a savory backnote of black pepper. Pair it with herb-crusted lamb chops or steak with peppercorn sauce.

Kitchen Survivor™ Grade: C

Your notes: _____

Ridge Geyserville (Zinfandel),   **$**   **Pts**
Sonoma, California 2007   **32**   **86**

👆 CA's benchmark "Zin," though as a field blend with inter-planted grapes (Carignane, Mourvedre and Petite Sirah), it marches to its own drumbeat. The dark fig, sweet blackstrap molasses and spice notes need aeration or cellaring to open.

Kitchen Survivor™ Grade: C

Your notes: _____

Rodney Strong Zinfandel, Sonoma,   **$**   **Pts**
California 2007   **14**   **85**

🍎 It's hard to go wrong with the jammy berry fruit, sweet coconut-eucalyptus scent, and bargain price.

Kitchen Survivor™ Grade: C

Your notes: _____

Rodney Strong Knotty Vines Zinfandel,   **$**   **Pts**
Sonoma County, California 2007   **14**   **86**

Knotty and gnarled old vines give the best Zin character - black pepper, boysenberry fruit, chewy tannins and sweet balsamic. Perfect with big burgers.

Kitchen Survivor™ Grade: A

Your notes: _____

Rosenblum Zinfandel Vintner's   **$**   **Pts**
Cuvee, California NV   **12**   **85**

🍎 A big, blueberry-licorice mouthful, at a bargain price. A good house red choice if you like bold reds and bold foods like barbecue, curry, blackened chicken or jerk pork.

Kitchen Survivor™ Grade: C

Your notes: _____

St. Francis Old Vines Zinfandel,   **$**   **Pts**
Sonoma, California 2006   **25**   **86**

More structured and balanced than in past vintages, but still with big, jammy chocolate-dipped fig flavors. Chewy tannins and a smoky spiciness make it a good match for barbecued ribs or slow-smoked brisket.

Kitchen Survivor™ Grade: B

Your notes: _____

Simi Zinfandel, Sonoma,   **$**   **Pts**
California 2007   **20**   **87**

One of Simi's best reds, with lots of ripe boysenberry and raspberry fruit, lavish cinnamon spice and coconutty oak, and a juicy texture. A great partner for pesto pasta, pizza, curried chicken or rich cheeses.

Kitchen Survivor™ Grade: C

Your notes: _____

Sterling Vintner's Collection Zinfandel,   **$**   **Pts**
Central Coast, California 2007   **10**   **85**

Further proof that Sterling's Vintner's Collection line is one of the best budget brands out there. This is a best buy Zin in the "slurpable berries" style. Yum!

Kitchen Survivor™ Grade: C

Your notes: _____

Woodbridge by Robert Mondavi   **$**   **Pts**
Zinfandel, California 2008   **8**   **85**

I prefer the Woodbridge whites - in fact this is the only red that made the Guide this year. But it's deserved. Although none of the Mondavi family members remain involved with the Robert Mondavi brands, I have to credit Robert's son Michael with the "ultimate pizza wine" quote - he's right! Juicy, yummy and Zinny - meaning lots of wild berry fruit. Bravo!

Kitchen Survivor™ Grade: B

Your notes: _____

DESSERT WINES

Category Profile: There are plenty of great and available dessert wines to choose from, many of them affordable enough to enjoy often, with or instead of dessert (they're fat free!). In this lineup there are worthy and available choices in all price points, and in all of the classic dessert wine styles: a) fortified - alcohol added to stop the sugar fermentation; b) late harvest/botrytis - picked late, and possibly infected with a sugar-concentrating mold; c) frozen-grape wines - ice wines made from grapes frozen on the vine or in a freezer before pressing; or d) dried-grape wines - made from grapes that have been dried into raisins before pressing. I hope you'll try them, because they will really jazz up your wine and food life. They are fantastic for entertaining, because they are unique and memorable, putting a distinctive mark on your dinner parties and cocktail gatherings.

Serve: Serving temperature depends on the wine, so see the individual entries.

When: With dessert, or *as* dessert; the lighter ones also make nice aperitifs. If you like to entertain, they're great. Add fruit, cheese, or some cookies, and you have a very classy end to a meal with very low hassle.

With: Blue cheese, chocolate, or simple cookies (like biscotti or shortbread) are classic.

In: The One™ glass for white wines, or an all-purpose wineglass, or smaller dessert wineglass. (The standard serving is 3 ounces rather than the traditional 5-6 ounces for most wines, because of the sugar and/or alcohol intensity typical of most dessert wines.)

	$	Pts
Blandy's 10-Year-Old Malmsey Madeira, Portugal NV	**35**	**89**

Caramel, burnt sugar, toffee, candied orange peel, toasted nuts, spice, and a cut of tangy acidity - that's classic Madeira (a fortified wine). Pair it with caramel or nut desserts or, best of all, dark chocolate!

Kitchen Survivor™ Grade: A+

Your notes: ______________________

	$	Pts
Bonny Doon Muscat Vin de Glaciere (*van duh glahss-YAIR*), California 2007 (half bottle)	**20**	**87**

A wine list and wine-by-the-glass favorite made from frozen grapes, with lush passion fruit and peach flavor and fabulous acidity. Chill, and serve with fruit tart, biscotti or cheesecake.

Kitchen Survivor™ Grade: A

Your notes: ______________________

	$	Pts
Broadbent 3 Year Fine Rich Madeira, Portugal NV	**18**	**88**

A great starter Madeira (fortified wine), with classic candied orange peel–toffee-caramel character at an easy price. Serve room temp, and the wine stays fresh for months. Great with a cheese, fruit and nut platter.

Kitchen Survivor™ Grade: A+

Your notes: ______________________

	$	Pts
Campbell's Rutherglen Muscat, Australia NV (half bottle)	**20**	**90**

"Liquid Fig Newtons!" That's what one of my students aptly proclaimed after the first taste of this fortified wine made from partly-raisined grapes. There's also mincemeat, Christmas pudding and toffee notes, making it stunning with chocolate, pecan pie or aged cheddar cheese. Serve at cool room temperature.

Kitchen Survivor™ Grade: A+

Your notes: ______________________

Castello Banfi Brachetto d'Acqui Rosa   **$**   **Pts**
Regale, Piedmont, Italy 2007   **20**   **89**

☺ ⚱ The rosa regale (regal rose) on the label teases this wine's alluring rose petal scent, accented with Asian spices and juicy raspberry flavors on the palate. One of the most beloved pairings I ever gave on my TV show was this wine, with warm flourless chocolate cake. Serve chilled; also great as an aperitif.

Kitchen Survivor™ Grade: B

Your notes: _____

Chalk Hill Estate Botrytised Semillon, Chalk   **$**   **Pts**
Hill, Russian River Valley 2006 (half bottle)   **40**   **92**

⚱ The botrytis mold concentrates the grapes, giving quince paste, candied ginger and peach compote flavors, and an unctuous texture. Enjoy with vanilla ice cream, creme brulee, blue cheese, or just on its own.

Kitchen Survivor™ Grade: A

Your notes: _____

Chambers Rosewood Vineyards Rutherglen   **$**   **Pts**
Muscadelle, Australia NV (half bottle)   **15**   **89**

A fortified wine with a deep, viscous flavor of dried figs and toasted nuts. Serve at cool room temp, with chocolate or caramel desserts, or cheeses.

Kitchen Survivor™ Grade: A+

Your notes: _____

Chateau Ste. Michelle Reserve Late Harvest   **$**   **Pts**
Riesling, Washington 2006 (half bottle)   **18**   **93**

Pineapple and peach pie flavors, with floral honeysuckle nectar notes. Incredible concentration makes it delicious on its own, but also luscious with creme brulee, ice cream, or fruit tarts. Serve chilled.

Kitchen Survivor™ Grade: B

Your notes: _____

Cockburn's Fine Ruby Port,   **$**   **Pts**
Portugal NV   **16**   **85**

Enjoy this plum, fig-and-spice-flavored fortified wine at room temp over many weeks, as the leftovers hold up well. Delicious with dark chocolate or rich blue cheeses such as Stilton.

Kitchen Survivor™ Grade: A+

Your notes: _____

Domaine de Coyeaux Muscat de   **$**   **Pts**
Beaumes de Venise, France 2006   **28**   **89**

What an alluring mandarin orange and honeysuckle scent and peach flavor! It's a fortified wine, but still delicate, so serve lightly chilled with fruit or cream desserts, pound cake, or shortbread cookies.

Kitchen Survivor™ Grade: B

Your notes: _____

Dow's Colheita Tawny Port,   **$**   **Pts**
Portugal 1992   **40**   **89**

Vintage tawny (a fortified wine) is rare, yet a steal for the quality and complexity: toasted walnuts, caramel, toffee—wow! Serve cool room temperature with holiday desserts: pumpkin pie, apple pie or gingerbread.

Kitchen Survivor™ Grade: A

Your notes: _____

Emilio Lustau Pedro Ximenez   **$**   **Pts**
"San Emilio" (*eh-MEE-lee-oh*   **22**   **89**
LOO-stau Pedro Hee-MEN-ez san
***eh-MEE-lee-oh*) Sherry, Spain NV**

Redolent with fig flavors coming from the raisin-dried grapes. It's lovely with chocolate and nut desserts. In Spain they pour it over vanilla ice cream. Serve at cool room temp. It's also nice with biscotti cookies, banana bread, or apple tart.

Kitchen Survivor™ Grade: A+

Your notes: _____

Ferreira Doña Antonia Port,   **$**   **Pts**
Portugal NV   **19**   **86**

Tawny-style Port (a fortified wine)—all amber gold color, toasted nut, cinnamon sugar, cappuccino, and maple scents and flavors. Beautiful with milk chocolate or nut desserts, and with aged cheddar cheese.

Kitchen Survivor™ Grade: A+

Your notes: _____

Ficklin Tinta "Port,"   **$**   **Pts**
California NV   **18**   **86**

A very worthy version of the fortified Port style, with flavors of chocolate, nuts, dried figs, and sweet spices.

Kitchen Survivor™ Grade: A+

Your notes: _____

Fonseca Bin 27 Port,   **$**   **Pts**
Portugal NV   **18**   **88**

This is Port (fortified wine) in the ruby style, with flavors of ripest figs, licorice, and allspice. Delicious at cool room temp with blue cheeses, nut bread and fruit.

Kitchen Survivor™ Grade: A+

Your notes: _____

Graham's Late Bottled Vintage Port,   **$**   **Pts**
Portugal 1996   **24**   **88**

The dense chocolate-dipped fig and spicy plum pudding notes of this fortified wine are perfect with blue cheese or chocolate.

Kitchen Survivor™ Grade: A+

Your notes: _____

Grgich Hills Violetta Late Harvest,   **$**   **Pts**
Napa Valley 2006 (half bottle)   **85**   **94**

Botrytis fungus on the grape skins concentrates the fruit and intensity of this decadent almond-apricot-candied ginger-scented wine. It is expensive, but a true original of great pedigree among Napa wines.

Kitchen Survivor™ Grade: A+

Your notes: _____

Heitz Cellars Ink Grade Port, Napa   **$**   **Pts**
Valley NV (half bottle)   **14**   **88**

Almost as much a Heitz signature as the Martha's Vineyard Cab, this fortified dessert wine made from classic Portuguese grapes is like liquefied blackberry jam. Explosively juicy and sumptuous on the palate, it needs merely dark chocolate, or just a cool evening sunset, to turn the occasion into a special one.

Kitchen Survivor™ Grade: A

Your notes: _____

Hogue Late Harvest Riesling,   **$**   **Pts**
Washington 2007   **12**   **87**

Lightly sweet with a hint of malt flavor that makes it delicious with buttery desserts like pineapple upside down cake or pound cake. Great price and convenient screw-top package.

Kitchen Survivor™ Grade: C

Your notes: _____

Inniskillin Riesling Ice Wine,   **$**   **Pts**
Canada 2006 (half bottle)   **70**   **96**

Freezing the grapes concentrates the sugar but also preserves the zingy acidity of cool climate-grown Riesling. The result is breathtakingly pure passion fruit and peach flavors and a creamy texture. Enjoy this lightly chilled with ice cream, fruit tarts or cheesecake; or, a fine blue cheese.

Kitchen Survivor™ Grade: A

Your notes: _____

Leacock's Rainwater Madeira,   **$**   **Pts**
Portugal NV   **18**   **87**

"Rainwater" is the style of Madeira (a fortified wine) - with a touch of sweetness, toffee and citrus zest flavors and a tangy lemon drop finish. Serve cool room temperature pineapple upside down cake or almonds.

Kitchen Survivor™ Grade: A

Your notes: _____

Michele Chiarlo Nivole ("Clouds")   **$**   **Pts**
Moscato d'Asti, Piedmont, Italy 2007   **15**   **88**

Honeysuckle-scented, low in alcohol, high in apricot-orange fruit and refreshment. Served chilled, it makes a great brunch wine or light, festive aperitif.

Kitchen Survivor™ Grade: B

Your notes: _____

Paolo Saracco Moscato d'Asti,   **$**   **Pts**
Piedmont, Italy 2007   **16**   **90**

ꙮ Nutmeg spice, orange blossom, honeysuckle and peach, plus a light and delicate bubble, make this an irresistible quaff. The light sweetness cuts through spicy heat, compliments brunch fare perfectly, and makes a wonderful, unique aperitif.

Kitchen Survivor™ Grade: B

Your notes: _____

Rivetti Moscato d'Asti La Spinetta,   **$**   **Pts**
Italy 2007   **20**   **89**

Rivetti and Saracco are the maestros of moscato. This wine's honeysuckle, orange blossom, and apricot scent and flavor are gorgeous, and the light alcohol makes it a great brunch wine instead of mimosas.

Kitchen Survivor™ Grade: B

Your notes: _____

Royal Tokaji Wine Company Red Label,   **$**   **Pts**
Tokaji Aszu, Hungary 2005 (half bottle)   **41**   **92**

⛎ *Aszu* refers to the noble rot-affected grapes that give this wine its legendary character: honey, dried and caramelized apples, and major mushroom. Pair with pate, blue cheese or creme brulee, or sip solo.

Kitchen Survivor™ Grade: B

Your notes: _____

St. Supery Moscato,   **$**   **Pts**
California 2007   **18**   **88**

Fragrant with honeysuckle and spiced apricot flavors, with just a touch of sweetness. Serve chilled with fruit tarts or cheesecake for dessert, or with beignets and omelets at brunch.

Kitchen Survivor™ Grade: B

Your notes: _____

Smith Woodhouse Lodge Reserve   **$**   **Pts**
Port, Portugal NV   **22**   **87**

The flavors of dried figs, dates, and berry syrup and long finish make this fortified wine great for sipping with Stilton cheese. Serve cool room temp; it stays fresh for weeks.

Kitchen Survivor™ Grade: A

Your notes: _____

Taylor Fladgate 20 Year Tawny   **$**   **Pts**
Port, Portugal NV   **60**   **92**

While it's pricey due to the decades of aging, it's also amazingly complex—toasted walnuts, streusel, toffee, cappuccino and caramel. Lovely for sipping at cool room temp on its own, or with milk chocolate desserts, nut cookies or flan.

Kitchen Survivor™ Grade: A

Your notes: _____

Warre 10-Year-Old Otima Tawny   **$**   **Pts**
Port, Portugal NV   **28**   **88**

I love the toasted nut flavors and satiny texture of this wine. I also love the price. Serve cool room temp with banana nut cake or carrot cake.

Kitchen Survivor™ Grade: A+

Your notes: _____

THE
COMPLETE WINE COURSE
MINI-COURSE:
A WINE CLASS IN A GLASS

How do you go about choosing wine? The best way to ensure you'll be happy with your wine choices is to learn your taste.

Here are two quick wine lessons, adapted from my *Complete Wine Course DVD*, that will let you do exactly that. You're probably thinking, Will there be a test? In a way, every pulled cork is a test, but for the *wine:* Are you happy with what you got for the price you paid, and would you buy it again? This mini-course will teach you to pick wines that pass muster by helping you learn what styles and tastes you like in a wine and how to use the label to help you find them.

If you want, you can complete each lesson in a matter of minutes. As with food, tasting impressions form quickly with wine. Then you can get dinner on the table, accompanied by your wine picks. Start by doing the first lesson, "White Wine Made Simple," one evening, and then Lesson 2, "Red Wine Made Simple," another time. Or you can invite friends over and make it a party. Everyone will learn a little bit about wine, while having fun.

Setup
Glassware: You will need three glasses per taster. A simple all-purpose wineglass is ideal, but clear disposables are fine, too.

Pouring: Start with a tasting portion (about an ounce of each wine). Tasters can re-pour more of their favorite to enjoy with hors d'oeuvres or dinner.

Flights: Taste the Lesson 1 whites first and then the Lesson 2 reds (pros call each sequence of wine a *flight*). There is no need to wash or rinse the glasses.

To Taste It Is to Know It

Tasting is the fastest way to learn about wine. My wine students tell me this all the time: They know what wines they like when they try them. The trick is in understanding the style and knowing how to ask for it and get it again: "I'd like a Chardonnay with lots of buttery, toasty oak and gobs of creamy, tropical fruit flavors." If you don't know what it means, you might feel silly offering a description like that when wine shopping. But those words really are in the glass, and these easy-to-follow tasting lessons will help you recognize the styles and learn which ones are your favorites.

The Lessons

What You'll Do:

For Lesson 1, "White Wine Made Simple," you will comparison-taste three major white wine grapes: Riesling, Sauvignon Blanc, and Chardonnay. For Lesson 2, "Red Wine Made Simple," you will compare three major reds: Pinot Noir, Merlot, and Cabernet Sauvignon. Follow these easy steps:

1. Buy your wines. Make your choice from the varietal sections of this book. It's best to choose wines in the same price category—for example, all under-$15 wines.
2. Chill (even the reds can take a light chill; they warm up quickly and can taste out of balance if too warm), pour, and taste the wines in the order of body, light to full, as shown in the tasting notes.
3. Use the tasting notes as a guide, and record your own if you want.

What You'll Learn:

Body styles of the major grapes—light, medium, or full. You'll see that Riesling is lighter (less heavy) than Chardonnay, in the same way that, for example, skim milk is lighter than heavy cream.

What the major grapes taste like—When tasted side by side, the grapes are quite distinctive, just as a pear tastes different from an apple, a strawberry tastes different from a blueberry, and so on.

What other wine flavor words taste like—Specifically, you'll experience these tastes: oaky, tannic, crisp, and fruity. Knowing them is helpful because they're used a lot in this book, on wine bottle labels, and by sellers of wine—merchants, waiters, and so on.

Getting comfortable with these basics will equip you to describe the wine styles you like to a waiter or wine merchant and to use the information on a bottle label to find those styles on your own. In the "Buying Lingo" section that follows, I've defined lots of other style words and listed some wine types you can try to experience them.

Tasting Lesson 1
WHITE WINE MADE SIMPLE

Instructions: Taste the wines in numbered order. Note your impressions of:

Color: Which is lightest and which is darkest? Whites can range from pale straw to deep yellow-gold. The darker the color, the fuller the body.

Scent: While they all smell like white wine, the aromas differ, from delicate and tangy to rich and fruity.

Taste and Body: In the same way that fruits range from crisp and tart (like apples) to ripe and lush (like mangoes), the wine tastes will vary along with the body styles of the grapes, from light to full.

Which grape and style do you like best? If you like more than one style, that's great, too!

The White Wines

Grape 1: Riesling (any region)—light bodied

Description: Crisp and refreshing, with vibrant fruit flavor ranging from apple to peach.

Brand name:_____

Your notes: _____

_____

Grape 2: Sauvignon Blanc (France or New Zealand)— medium bodied

Description: Very distinctive! The smell is exotically pungent, the taste tangy and mouthwatering, like citrus fruit (lime and grapefruit).

Brand name:_____

Your notes: _____

_____

Grape 3: Chardonnay (California)—full bodied

Description: The richest scent and taste, with fruit flavor ranging from ripe apples to peaches to tropical fruits. You can feel the full-bodied texture, too. "Oaky" scents come through as a sweet, buttery, or toasty impression.

Brand name:_____

Your notes: _____

_____

Tasting Lesson 2
RED WINE MADE SIMPLE

Instructions: Again, taste the wines in numbered order and note your impressions.

Color: Red wines range in color from transparent ruby, like the Pinot Noir, to inky dark purple—the darker the color, the fuller the body.

Scent: In addition to the smell of "red wine," you'll get the cherrylike smell of Pinot Noir, perhaps plum character in the Merlot, and a rich dark-berry smell in the Cabernet. There are other scents, too, so enjoy them. You can also compare your impressions with those included in the reviews section of the book.

Taste and Body: Like white wines, red wines range from light and delicate to rich and intense. You'll note the differences in body from light to full and the distinctive taste character of each grape. As you can see, tasting them side by side makes it easy to detect and compare the differences.

The Red Wines

Grape 1: Pinot Noir (any region)—light bodied

Description: Delicate cherrylike fruit flavor, silky-smooth texture, mouthwatering acidity, all of which make Pinot Noir a versatile wine for most types of food.

Brand name:_____

Your notes: _____

_____

Grape 2: Merlot (California, Chile, or Washington)—medium bodied

Description: More intense than Pinot Noir: rich "red wine" flavor, yet not too heavy. That's probably why it's so popular!

Brand name:_____

Your notes: _____

_____

Grape 3: Cabernet Sauvignon (Chile or California)—full bodied

Description: The fullest-bodied, most intense taste. Notice the drying sensation it leaves on your tongue? That's tannin, a natural grape component that, like color, comes from the skin. As you can see, more color and more tannin come together. Tasting high-tannin wines with fat or protein counters that drying sensation (that's why Cabernet and red meat are considered classic partners). In reds, an "oaky" character comes through as one or more of these scents: spice, cedar, smoke, toastiness, vanilla, and coconut. No wonder buyers love it!

Brand name:_____

Your notes: _____

_____

Wine Glossary

Here are the meanings of some of the major wine style words that you see in this book, on wine bottles and in wine shops.

Acidity—The tangy, tart, crisp, mouthwatering component in wine. It's a prominent characteristic of Riesling, Sauvignon Blanc, and Pinot Grigio whites and Pinot Noir and Chianti/Sangiovese reds.

Bag-in-a-Box—A box with a wine-filled bag inside that deflates as the wine is consumed, preventing oxidation.

Balance—The harmony of all the wine's main components: fruit, alcohol, and acidity, plus sweetness (if any), oak (if used in the wine making), and tannin (in reds). As with food, balance in the wine is important to your enjoyment, and a sign of quality. But it's also a matter of taste—the dish may taste "too salty" and the wine "too oaky" for one person but be fine to another.

Barrel aged / barrel fermented—The wine was aged or fermented (or both) in oak barrels. The barrels give fuller body as well as an "oaky" character to the wine's scent and flavor, making it seem richer. "Oaky" scents are often in the sweet family—but *not* sugary. Rather, *toasty, spicy, vanilla, buttery,* and *coconut* are the common wine words to describe "oaky" character. Other label signals that mean "oaky": Barrel Fermented, Barrel Select, Barrel Cuvee, Cask Fermented.

Bouquet—All of the wine's scents, which come from the grape(s) used, the techniques (like oak aging), the age of the wine, and the vineyard characteristics (like soil and climate).

Bright—Vivid and vibrant. Usually used as a modifier, like "bright fruit" or "bright acidity."

Buttery—Literally, the creamy-sweet smell of butter. One by-product of fermentation is an ester that mimics the butter smell, so you may well notice this in some wines, especially barrel-fermented Chardonnays.

Corked, corky—Refers to a wine whose scent or taste has been tainted by corks or wine-making equipment infected with a bacteria called TCA. While not harmful to health, TCA gives wines a musty smell and taste.

Creamy—Can mean a smell similar to fresh cream or a smooth and lush texture. In sparkling wines, it's a textural delicacy and smoothness of the bubbles.

Crisp—See ACIDITY.

Dry—A wine without sweetness (though not without fruit; see FRUITY for more on this).

Earthy—As with cheeses, potatoes, mushrooms, and other good consumables, wines can have scents and flavors reminiscent of, or owing to, the soil. The "earth" terms commonly attributed to wine include *mushrooms, truffles, flint, dusty, gravelly, chalky, slaty, wet leaves,* and even *barnyard*.

Exotic—Just as it applies to other things, this description suggests unusual and alluring characteristics in wine. Quite often refers to wines with a floral or spicy style or flavors beyond your typical fruit bowl, such as tropical fruits or rare berries.

Floral—Having scents that mimic flower scents, whether fresh (as in the honeysuckle scent of some Rieslings) or dried (as in the wilted rose petal scent of some Gewurztraminers).

Food friendly—Food-friendly wines have taste characteristics that pair well with a wide variety of foods without clashing or overpowering—namely, good acidity and moderate (not too heavy) body. The food-friendly whites include Riesling and Sauvignon Blanc; the reds include Chianti, Spanish Rioja, red Rhone, and Pinot Noir wines.

Fruity—Marked by a prominent smell and taste of fruit. In whites the fruit tastes can range from lean and tangy (like lemons and crisp apples) to medium (like melons and peaches) to lush (like mangoes and pineapples). In reds, think cranberries and cherries, plums and blueberries, figs and prunes. Note that *fruity* doesn't mean "sweet." The taste and smell of ripe fruit are perceived as sweet, but they're not sugary. Most wines on the market are at once dry (meaning not sweet) and fruity, with lots of fruit flavor.

Grassy—Describes a wine marked with scents of fresh-cut grass or herbs or even green vegetables (like green pepper and asparagus). It's a signature of Sauvignon Blanc wines, especially those grown in New Zealand and France. *Herbal* and *herbaceous* are close synonyms.

Herbal, herbaceous—See GRASSY.

Legs—The drips running down the inside of the wineglass after you swirl it. Not a sign of quality (as in "good legs") but of viscosity. Fast-running legs indicate a low-viscosity wine and slow legs a high-viscosity wine. The higher the viscosity, the richer and fuller the wine feels in your mouth.

Nose—The smell of the wine. Isn't it interesting how wines have a nose, legs, and body? As you've no doubt discovered, they have personalities, too!

Oaky—See BARREL AGED.

Off-dry—A lightly sweet wine.

Old vines—Refers to wine from vines significantly older than average, usually at least 30 years old and sometimes far older. Older vines yield a smaller, but often more intensely flavored, crop of grapes.

Regional wine—A wine named for the region where the grapes are grown, such as Champagne, Chianti, and Pouilly-Fuisse.

Spicy—A wine with scents and flavors reminiscent of spices, both sweet (cinnamon, ginger, cardamom, clove) and savory (pepper, cumin, curry).

Sweet—A wine that has perceptible sugar, called *residual sugar* because it is left over from fermentation and not converted to alcohol. A wine can be lightly sweet like a Moscato or very sweet like a Port or Sauternes.

Tannic—A red wine whose tannin is noticeable—a little or a lot—as a drying sensation on your tongue ranging from gentle (lightly tannic) to velvety (richly tannic) to harsh (too tannic).

Terroir—The distinctive flavors, scents, and character of a wine owing to its vineyard source. For example, the terroir of French red Burgundies is sometimes described as *earthy*.

Toasty—Wines with a toasty, roasted, caramelized, or smoky scent reminiscent of coffee beans, toasted nuts or spices, or burnt sugar.

Unfiltered—A wine that has not been filtered before bottling (which is common practice). Some say filtering the wine strips out flavor, but not everyone agrees. I think most tasters cannot tell the difference.

Varietal wine—A wine named for the grape used to make it, such as Chardonnay or Merlot.

Handling Wine Leftovers

I developed the Kitchen Survivor™ grades to give you an idea of how long each wine stays in good drinking condition if you don't finish the bottle. In the same way that resealing the cereal box or wrapping and refrigerating leftovers will extend their freshness window, you can do the same for wine by handling the leftovers as follows:

Still Wines

Re-cork—At a minimum, close the bottle with its original cork. Most wines will stay fresh a day or two at normal room temperature. To extend that freshness-window, purchase a vacuum-sealer (available in kitchenware shops and wine shops). You simply cork the bottle with the purchased rubber stopper, which has a one-way valve. The accompanying plastic vacuum pump is then placed on top of the stopper; you pump the handle repeatedly until the resistance tightens, indicating the air has been pumped out of the bottle. (Note: A few wine experts don't think rubber stoppers work, but I have used them for years. In my restaurants, I have found they extended the life of bottles opened for by-the-glass service at least two days longer than just sealing with the original cork.)

Refrigerate stoppered (and vacuum-sealed) bottles, whether white, pink, or red. Refrigeration of anything slows the spoilage, and your red wine, once removed from the fridge and poured in the glass, will quickly come to serving temperature.

For even longer shelf-life, you can preserve partial bottles with inert gas. I recommend this especially for more expensive wines. Wine Life and Private Preserve are two brands that I have used (sold in wine shops and accessories catalogs). They come in a can that feels light, as if it were empty. Inside is an inert gas mixture that is heavier than air. The can's spray nozzle is inserted into the bottle. A one-second spray fills the empty bottle space with the inert gas, displacing the air inside, which is the key because no air in contact with the wine means no oxidation. Then you quickly replace the cork (make sure the fit is tight). My experience in restaurants using gas systems for very upscale wines by the glass is that they keep well for a week or more.

Sparkling Wines

Your best bet is to purchase "clam shell" Champagne stoppers, with one or two hinged metal clamps attached to a stopper top that has a rubber or plastic gasket for a tight seal. You place the stopper on top, press down, and then anchor the clamps to the bottle lip. If you open your sparkler carefully and don't "pop" the cork, losing precious carbonation, a stoppered partial bottle will keep its effervescence for at least a few days, and sometimes much longer.

SAVVY SHOPPER: RETAIL WINE BUYING

Supermarkets, pharmacies, price clubs, catalogs, state stores, mega-stores, dot.coms, and boutiques . . . where you shop for wine depends a lot on the state where you live, because selling wine requires a state license. What many people don't realize is how much the wine laws vary from one state to the next.

In most states, the regulations affect the prices you pay for wine, what wines are available, and how you get your hands on them (ideally, they are delivered to your door or poured at your table, but this isn't always legal). Here is a quick summary of the retail scene to help you make the most of your buying power wherever you live.

Wine Availability The single biggest frustration for every wine buyer and winery is bureaucracy. To ensure the collection of excise taxes, in nearly all states every single wine must be registered and approved in some way before it can be sold. If a wine you're seeking isn't available in your area, this is probably the reason. For many small boutique wineries, it just isn't worth the bother and expense to get legal approval for the few cases of wine they would sell in a particular state. One extreme example is Pennsylvania, a "control state" where wine is sold exclusively by a state-run monopoly that, without competition, has little incentive to source a lot of boutique wines. By contrast, California, New York, and Chicago, with high demand and competition, are good markets for wine availability.

Wine Prices and Discounts Wine prices can vary from one state to the next due to different tax rates. And in general, prices are lower in competitive markets, where stores can use discounts, sale prices, and so on to vie for your business.

Where they are legal, case discounts of 10% to 15% are a great way to get the best possible prices for your favorite wines. On the more expensive wines, many people I know coordinate their buying with friends and family so they can buy full cases and get these discounts.

Delivery and Wine-by-Mail In many states, it is not legal for stores or other retailers to deliver wine to the purchaser.

Many catalogs and Web sites sell wine by mail. Some are affiliated with retail stores or wineries, whereas others are strictly virtual stores. The conveniences include shopping on your own time and terms, from home or office, helpful buying recommendations and information, and usually home delivery. Keep in mind that the laws governing such shipping are complex, and vary from state to state (in some states it is completely prohibited).

Mail-order wine clubs are an interesting option when you are looking for new wines to try. For information on my own wine club, Andrea's A-List,™ visit my Web site, www.andreawine.com.

Where Should I Shop? That depends on what you're buying. If you know what you want, then price is your main consideration, and you'll get your best deals at venues that concentrate on volume sales—discount stores, price clubs, and so on. If you want buying advice, or are buying rare wines, you're better off in a wine shop or merchant specializing in collectible wines. These stores have trained buyers who taste and know their inventory well; they can help you with your decision. The better stores also have temperature-controlled storage for their rare wines, which is critical to ensure you get a product in good condition. There are also Web-based fine and rare wine specialists, but that is a fairly new market. I suggest you purchase fine and rare wines only through sources with a good track record of customer service. In that way, if you have problems with a shipment, you will have some recourse.

Can I Take That Bottle on the Wine List Home with Me? In most states, restaurants' wine licenses allow for sale and consumption "on-premise" only, meaning they cannot sell you a bottle to take home.

Burgundy Buyers, Beware With the exception of volume categories such as Beaujolais, Macon, and

Pouilly-Fuissé, buyers of French white and red Burgundy should shop only at fine wine merchants, preferably those that specialize in Burgundy, for two reasons. First, Burgundy is simply too fragile to handle the storage conditions in most stores. Burgundy specialists ensure temperature-controlled storage. Second, selection is a major factor, because quality varies a lot from one winery to the next, and from one vintage to the next. Specialist stores have the needed buying expertise to ensure the quality of their offerings.

Is That a Deal or a Disaster? Floor stacks, "end caps," private labels, and bin ends can be a boon for the buyer, or a bust, depending on where you are shopping. Here's what you need to know about them:

"Floor Stacks" of large-volume categories and brands (e.g., branded varietal wines)—These are a best bet in supermarkets and other volume-based venues, where they're used to draw your attention to a price markdown. Take advantage of it to stock up for everyday or party wines.

"End Cap" wine displays featured at the ends of aisles—A good bet, especially in fine wine shops. You may not have heard of the wine, but they're usually "hidden gems" that the buyer discovered and bought in volume, to offer you quality and uniqueness at a savings.

"Bin Ends"—Retailers often clear out the last few bottles of something by discounting the price. In reputable retail stores, they are usually still good quality, and thus a good bet. Otherwise, steer clear.

Private labels—These are wines blended and bottled exclusively for the retailer—again, good bets in reputable stores, who stake their reputation on your satisfaction with their private labels.

"Shelf-talkers"—Written signs, reviews, and ratings. Good shops offer their own recommendations in lieu of, or along with, critics' scores. If the only information is a critic's score, check to be sure that the vintage being sold matches that of the wine that was reviewed.

BUYING WINE IN RESTAURANTS

Wine List Strategy Session

A lot of us have a love–hate relationship with the wine list. On the one hand, we know it holds the potential to enhance the evening, impress the date or client, broaden our horizons, or all three. But it also makes us feel intimidated, inadequate, overwhelmed, and . . .

Panicked by prices—That goes for both the cheapest wines *and* the most expensive ones; we're leery of extremes.

Pressured by pairing—Will this wine "go with" our food?

Overwhelmed by options—Can this wine I've never heard of possibly be any good? Does my selection measure up? (Remember, the restaurant is supposed to impress *you,* not the other way around.) This "phone book" wine list makes me want to dial 911.

Stumped by Styles—Food menus are easy because we understand the key terms: appetizer, entree, dessert, salad, soup, fish, meat, and so on. But after *white* and *red,* most of us get lost pretty quickly with wine categories. (Burgundy . . . is that a style, a color, a place, or all three?)

Let's deal with the first three above. For the lowdown on wine list terms, use the decoder that follows to pinpoint the grapes and styles behind all the major wine names.

Wine List Prices
The prices on wine lists reflect three things:

- *The dining-out experience*—The restaurant wine markup is higher than in retail stores because the decor is (usually) nicer, and you get to stay a while, during which time they open the wine, serve it in a nice glass, and clean up afterward. They also may have invested in the cost and expertise to select and store the wine properly. Consequently those who enjoy drinking wine in restaurants are accustomed to being charged more for the wine than you would pay to drink the same bottle at home. That said, exorbitant mark-ups are, in my opinion, the biggest deterrent to more guests enjoying wine in restaurants (which is both good for the guests and good for business). You can always vote with your wallet and dine in restaurants with guest-friendly wine pricing.

- *Location*—Restaurants in exclusive resorts, in urban centers with a business clientele, or with a star chef behind them, tend toward higher wine markups, because they can get away with it. The logic, so to speak, is that if you're on vacation, it's on the company, or it's just the "in" place, high markups (on everything) are part of the price of admission. However, I don't really think that's right, and I do think these places would sell more wine with lower markups.

- *The rarity of the wine*—Often, the rarer the wine (either because it's in high demand due to crit-ics' hype or because it's old and just a few bottles remain), the higher the markup. It's a form of rationing in the face of high demand/low supply. Food can be the same way (lobsters, truffles, caviar, etc.).

Getting the Most Restaurant Wine for Your Money

Seeking value doesn't make you a cheapskate. Here are the best strategies to keep in mind:

1. Take the road less traveled—Chardonnay and Cabernet Sauvignon are what I call "comfort wines" because they're so well known. But their prices often reflect a "comfort premium" (in the same way that a name-brand toothpaste costs more than the store brand). These spec-tacular wine styles often give better value for the money, because they're less widely known:

   Whites
   Riesling
   Sauvignon Blanc and Fume Blanc
   Sancerre (a French Loire Valley wine made from the Sauvignon Blanc grape)
   Anything from Washington State or New Zealand

Reds
Cotes-du-Rhone and other French Rhone
   Valley reds
Red Zinfandel from California
Spanish Rioja and other reds from Spain
Cabernet Sauvignon from Chile

2. Savvy Splurging—There's no doubt about it:
   nothing commemorates, celebrates, or
   impresses better than a special wine. Since
   splurging on wine in a restaurant can mean
   especially big bucks, here are the "trophy" wine
   styles that give you the most for your money on
   wine lists:

   > French Champagne—I think that Cham-
   > pagne (the real stuff from France's Cham-
   > pagne region) is among the most affordable
   > luxuries on the planet, and its wine list
   > prices are often among the best of all the
   > "badge" wine categories (such as French
   > Bordeaux and Burgundy, cult California
   > Cabernets, and boutique Italian wines).

   > California's Blue Chip Cabernets—I don't
   > mean the tiny-production cult-movement
   > Cabernets but rather the classics that have
   > been around for decades, and still make
   > world-class wine at a fair price. Names
   > like Beringer, BV, Franciscan, Mt. Veeder,
   > Robert Mondavi, Silver Oak, Simi, and
   > Stag's Leap all made the survey, and for
   > good reason: they're excellent and available.

   > Italian Chianti Classico Riserva—This
   > recommendation may surprise you, but I
   > include it because the quality for the price
   > is better than ever, and recent vintages
   > have been great. I also think that across the
   > country a lot of people celebrate and do
   > business in steak houses and Italian restau-
   > rants, which tend to carry this wine cate-
   > gory because it complements their food.

3. The Mid-price/Mid-style "Safety Zone"—This
   is a strategy I first developed not for dining
   guests but for our *waiters* trying to help diners

choose a bottle, usually with very little to go on (many people aren't comfortable describing their taste preference, and they rarely broadcast their budget for fear of looking cheap). The mid-price/mid-style strategy is this: in any wine list category (e.g., Chardonnays and Italian reds), if you go for the mid-price range in that section, odds are good the wine will be mid-style. Mid-style is my shorthand for the most typical, crowd-pleasing version, likely to satisfy a high proportion of guests and to be sticker shock free. The fact is that the more expensive the wine is, the more distinctive and even unusual its style is likely to be. If it's not to your taste *and* you've spent a lot, you're doubly disappointed.

4. Ask—With wine more popular than ever, restaurants are the most proactive they've ever been in seeking to put quality and value on their wine lists. So ask for it: "What's the best red wine deal on your list right now?" Or, if you have a style preference, say something like "We want to spend $XX. Which of these Chardonnays do you think is the best for the money?"

Pairing Wine and Food

Worrying a lot about this is a big waste of time, because most wines complement most foods, regardless of wine color, center-of-the-plate protein, and all that other stuff. How well? Their affinity can range from "fine" to "Omigod." You can pretty much expect at least a nice combination every time you have wine with food and great matches from time to time (of course, frequent experimentation ups your odds). The point is, your style preference is a lot more important than the pairing, per se, because if you hate the dish or the wine, you're hardly likely to enjoy the pairing. That said, here is a list of wine styles that are especially favored by sommeliers and chefs for their exceptional food affinity and versatility, along with a few best-bet food recommendations:

Favorite "Food Wines"	Best-Bet Food Matches
White	
Champagne and Sparkling Wine—So many people save bubbly just for toasts, but it's an amazing "food wine"	Sushi All shellfish Cheeses (even stinky ones) Omelets and other egg dishes Mushroom sauces (on risotto, pasta or whatever)
Riesling from Germany, Alsace (France), America, Australia	Mexican, southwestern, and other spicy foods Shellfish Cured meats and sausages
Alsace (France) White Wines—Riesling, Pinot Gris, and Gewurztraminer	Pacific Rim foods—Japanese, Thai, Korean, Chinese Indian food Smoked meats and charcuterie Meat stews (really!)
Sauvignon Blanc and wines made from it (French Sancerre, Pouilly-Fume, and white Bordeaux)	Goat cheese Salads Herbed sauces (like pesto) Tomato dishes (salads, soups, sauces)
Red	
Beaujolais (from France)	Mushroom dishes
Pinot Noir	Fish (especially rich ones like tuna, salmon, and cod) Smoked meats Grilled vegetables Duck
Chianti, Rosso di Montalcino, and other Italian reds made from the Sangiovese grape	Pizza, eggplant parmigiana (and other Italian-American–inspired tastes) Cheesy dishes Spicy sausages
Rioja from Spain	Roasted and grilled meats

Choosing from the Wine List

You've got the wine list. Unless you know a lot about wine, you now face at least one of these dilemmas:

- You've never heard of any of the wines listed or at least none of those in your price range. (Okay, maybe you've heard of Dom Pérignon, but let's be real.) Or the names you do recognize don't interest you.

- You have no idea how much a decent selection should cost. But you *do* know you want to keep to your budget, without broadcasting it to your guests and the entire dining room.
- The wine list is so huge you don't even want to open it.

Wine List Playbook

Remember, you're the buyer. Good restaurants want you to enjoy wine and to feel comfortable with the list, your budget, and so on. As far as the wine-snobby ones go, what are you doing there anyway? (Okay, if you took a gamble on a new place or somebody else picked it, the strategies here can help.)

The basics:

1. *Don't worry if you haven't heard of the names.* There are literally thousands of worthy wines beyond the big brand names, and many restaurants feature them to spice up their selection.

2. *Determine what you want to spend.* I think most people want the best deal they can get. With that in mind, here are some price/value rules of thumb. In most restaurants the wine prices tend to relate to the food prices, as follows:
   - Wines by-the-glass: The price window for good-quality wines that please a high percentage of diners usually parallels the restaurant's mid- to top-priced appetizers. So if the Caesar salad (or wings or whatever) is $5.95, expect to spend that, plus or minus a dollar or two, for a good glass of wine. This goes for dessert wine, too. Champagne and sparkling wines can be more, due to the cost of the product and greater waste because it goes flat.
   - Bottles: This is far more variable, but in general most restaurants try to offer an ample selection of good-quality bottles priced in what I call a "selling zone" that's benchmarked to their highest entree price, plus a margin. That's the variable part. It can range from $5–10 on average in national chain restaurants and their peers to at least $10–20 in luxury and destination restaurants. So if the

casual chain's steak-and-shrimp-scampi combo costs $17.95, the $20–30 zone on their wine list will likely hold plenty of good bottle choices. In an urban restaurant where the star chef's signature herb-crusted lamb costs $28, you could expect a cluster of worthy bottles in the $35–55 range.

We in the trade find it funny, and nearly universal, that guests shy away from the least expensive wines on our lists, suspicious that there's something "wrong" with the wine. But any restaurant that's committed to wine, whether casual chain or destination eatery, puts extra effort into finding top-quality wines at the lowest price points. They may come from grapes or regions you don't know, but my advice is to muster your sense of adventure and try them. In the worst-case scenario, you'll be underwhelmed, but since tastes vary, this can happen with wine at any price. I think the odds are better that you'll enjoy one of the best deals on the wine list.

The wine list transaction: You've set your budget. Now it's time to zero in on a selection. You've got two choices—go it alone or ask for help. In either case, here's what to do:

1. Ask for the wine list right away. It's a pet peeve of mine that guests even *need* to ask (rather than getting the list automatically with the food menus), because that can cause both service delays and anxiety. Many people are scared to request the list for fear it "commits" them to a purchase, before they can determine whether they'll be comfortable with the prices and choices available. As you're being handed the menus, say "We'll take a look at the wine list, too" to indicate you want a copy to review, not a pushy sales job. *Tip:* I always ask that the wine-by-the-glass list be brought, too. Since many places change them often, they may be on a separate card or a specials board. (I think verbal listings are the worst, because often key information, like the price or winery, can get lost in translation.)

2. Determine any style particulars you're in the mood for:
   - White or red?
   - A particular grape, region, or body style?

   If the table can't reach a consensus, look at wine-by-the-glass and half-bottle options. This can happen when preferences differ or food choices are all over the map ("I'm having the oysters, he's having the wild boar, we want one wine . . ." is a stumper I've actually faced!).

3. Find your style zone in the list. Turn to the section that represents your chosen category—e.g., whites, the wine-by-the-glass section, Chardonnays, Italian reds, or whatever—or let the server know what style particulars you have in mind.

4. Match your budget. Pick a wine priced accordingly, keeping in mind these "safety zones":
   - The wines recommended in this book
   - Winery or region names that you remember liking or hearing good things about (e.g., Chianti in Italy or a different offering from your favorite white Zinfandel producer)
   - The mid-price/mid-style zone (as I explained earlier, many lists have this "sweet spot" of well-made, moderately priced offerings)
   - Featured wine specials, if they meet your price parameters

   You can communicate your budget while keeping your dignity with this easy trick I teach waiters:
   - Find your style zone—e.g., Pinot Grigios—in the wine list.
   - With both you and the server looking at the list, *point to the price* of a wine that's close to what you want to spend and then say, "We were looking at this one. What do you think?"
   - Keep pointing long enough for the server to see the price, and you'll be understood without having to say (in front of your date or client), "No more than thirty bucks, okay?"

I ask my waiters to point to the price, starting at a moderate level, with their first wine suggestion. From there the guest's reaction shows his or her intentions, without the embarrassment of having to talk price.

There's no formula, but the bottom line is this: whether glass or bottle, it's hard to go wrong with popular grapes and styles, moderate prices, the "signature" or featured wine(s) of the restaurant, and/or the waiter's enthusiastic recommendation. If you don't like it, chalk it up to experience—the same could happen with a first-time food choice, right? Most of the time, experimentation pays off. So enjoy!

Wine List Decoder

Wine is like food—it's easy to choose from among the styles with which you're familiar. That's why wines like Pinot Grigio, Chardonnay, Chianti, and Merlot are such big sellers. But when navigating other parts of the list, namely less-common grape varieties and the classic European regional wines, I think many of us get lost pretty quickly. And yet these are major players in the wine world, without which buyers miss out on a whole array of delicious options, from classic to cutting edge.

This decoder gives you the tools you need to explore them. It reveals:

> *The grapes used* to make the classic wines—If it's a grape you've tried, then you'll have an idea of what the wine tastes like.
> *The body styles from light to full* of every major wine category—The waiters and wine students with whom I work always find this extremely helpful, because it breaks up the wine world into broad, logical categories that are easy to understand and similar to the way we classify other things. With food, for example, we have vegetables, meat, fish, and so on.
> *The taste profile,* in simple terms—The exact taste of any wine is subjective (I say apple, you say pear), but knowing how the tastes *compare* is a great tool to help you identify your preferred style.

The names are set up just as you might see them on a wine list, under the key country and region headings, and in each section they are arranged by body style from light to full. (For whites, Italy comes before France in body style, overall. Their order is reversed for reds.) Finally, where applicable I've highlighted the major grapes in italics in the column on the left to help you quickly see just how widely used these grapes are and thus how much you already know about these heretofore mystifying wine names.

Sparkling Wines

- **Italy**

Asti Spumante	Muscat (Moscato)	Light; floral, hint of sweetness
Prosecco	Prosecco	Delicate; crisp, tangy, the wine used in Bellini cocktails

- **Spain**

Cava	Locals: Xarel-lo, Parellada, Macabeo plus Chardonnay	Light; crisp, refreshing

- **France**

Champagne	The red (yes!) grapes Pinot Noir and Pinot Meunier, plus Chardonnay	To me, all are heavenly, but check the style on the label: Blanc de Blancs—delicate and tangy Brut NV, vintage and luxury—range from soft and creamy to rich and toasty

White Wines

- **Germany**

Riesling	Riesling rules Germany's quality wine scene	Feather-light but flavor-packed: fruit salad in a glass

- **Italy**

Frascati	Trebbiano, Malvasia	As you've noticed, mostly local grapes are used in Italy's whites. But the style of all these is easy to remember: light, tangy, and refreshing. Pinot Grigio, the best known, is also more distinctive—pleasant pear and lemon flavors, tasty but not heavy. The less common Pinot Bianco is similar.
Soave	Garganega, Trebbiano	
Orvieto	Grechetto, Procanico, and many others	
Gavi	Cortese	
Vernaccia	Vernaccia	
Pinot Grigio		

- **France**
  - ***Alsace—Grape names are on the label:***

	Pinot Blanc	Light; tangy, pleasant
Riesling	Riesling	Fuller than German Riesling but not heavy; citrus, apples, subtle but layered
	Pinot Gris	Smooth, richer texture; fruit compote flavors
	Gewurztraminer	Sweet spices, apricots, lychee fruit

  - ***Loire Valley***

Vouvray	Chenin Blanc	Look for the style name: Sec—dry and tangy; Demi-sec—baked apple, hint of sweetness; Moelleux—honeyed dessert style

Sauvignon Blanc

Sancerre and Pouilly-Fume	Sauvignon Blanc	Light to medium; subtle fruit, racy acidity

  - ***White Bordeaux***

Sauvignon Blanc & Semillon

Entre-Deux-Mers	Sauvignon Blanc and Semillon	Tangy, crisp, light
Graves Pessac-Leognan		Medium to full; ranging from creamy lemon-lime to lush fig flavors; pricey ones are usually oaky

  - ***Burgundy White***

Chardonnay

Macon St.-Veran Pouilly-Fuisse	Every Chardonnay in the world is modeled on white French Burgundy	Light; refreshing, citrus-apple flavors
Chablis		Subtle, mineral, green apple
St. Aubin Meursault Puligny-Mon-trachet Chassagne-Montrachet Corton-Charlemagne		Medium; pear, dried apple, nutty; complexity ranging from simple to sublime

- **France**

  - ***Red Burgundy***

Beaujolais Beaujolais-Villages	Gamay	Uncomplicated, light; fruity, pleasant

Beaujolais Cru:
  Morgon,
  Moulin-a-Vent, etc.
		More complex, plum-berry taste, smooth (the wines are named for their village)

  Pinot Noir

Cote de Beaune	Pinot Noir	Ranging from light body, pretty cherry taste to extraordinary complexity: captivating spice, berry and earth scents, silky texture, berries and plums flavor
Santenay		
Volnay		
Pommard		
Nuits-St.-Georges		
Vosne-Romanee		
Gevrey-Chambertin		
Clos de Vougeot, etc.		

  - ***Red Bordeaux***

  Merlot

Pomerol St. Emilion	Merlot, plus Cabernet Franc and Cabernet Sauvignon	Medium to full; oaky-vanilla scent, plum flavor

  Cabernet Sauvignon

Medoc	Cabernet Sauvignon, plus Merlot, Cabernet Franc, and Petit Verdot	Full; chunky-velvety texture; cedar-spice-toasty scent; dark berry flavor
Margaux		
Pauillac		
St-Estephe		

  - ***Rhone Red***

  Syrah, aka Shiraz

Cotes-du-Rhone	Mainly Grenache, Syrah, Cinsault, Mourvedre	Medium to full; juicy texture; spicy raspberry scent and taste
Cote-Rotie	Syrah, plus a splash of white Viognier	Full; brawny texture; peppery scent; plum and dark berry taste

| Hermitage | Syrah, plus a touch of the white grapes Marsanne and Roussane | Similar to Cote-Rotie |

| Chateauneuf-du-Pape | Mainly Syrah, Grenache, Cinsault, Mourvedre | Full; exotic leathery-spicy scent; spiced fig and berry compote taste |

(Red Zinfandel is here in the light-to-full body spectrum)

- **Spain**
  - *Rioja*

| Rioja Crianza, Reserva and Gran Reserva | Tempranillo, plus Garnacha, aka Grenache, and other local grapes | Ranging from soft and smooth, juicy strawberry character (Crianza); to full, caramel-leather scent, spicy-dried fruit taste (Reserva and Gran Reserva) |

  - *Ribera del Duero*

| | Mostly Tempranillo | Full; mouth-filling texture; toasty-spice scent; anise and plum taste |

  - *Priorat*

Sometimes Cabernet Sauvignon

| Priorat | Varied blends may include Cabernet Sauvignon, Garnacha, and other local grapes | Full; gripping texture; meaty-leathery-fig scent; superconcentrated plum and dark berry taste |

- **Italy**

  As you'll notice from the left column, Italy's classic regions mostly march to their own *bellissimo* beat.

  - *Veneto*

| Valpolicella | Corvina plus other local grapes | Light; mouthwatering, tangy cherry taste and scent |

| Amarone della Valpolicella | Corvina; same vineyards as Valpolicella | Full; rich, velvety texture; toasted almond/prune scent; intense dark raisin and dried fig taste (think Fig Newtons) |

- *Piedmont*

Dolcetto d'Alba (the best known of the Dolcettos, but others are good, too)	Dolcetto	Light; zesty, spicy, cranberry-sour cherry taste
Barbera d'Alba (look for Barbera d'Asti and others)	Barbera	Medium; licorice-spice-berry scent; earth and berry taste
Barolo Barbaresco	Nebbiolo	Full; "chewy" texture; exotic earth, licorice, tar scent; strawberry-spice taste

- *Tuscany*

Chianti/ Chianti Classico	Sangiovese	Ranges from light, easy, lip-smacking strawberry-spice character to intense, gripping texture; plum, licorice, and earth scent and taste
Vino Nobile di Monte-pulciano	Prugnolo (a type of Sangiovese)	Medium-to-full; velvety texture, earth-spice, stewed plum taste
Brunello di Montalcino	Brunello (a type of Sangiovese)	Very full; "chewy" in the mouth; powerful dark-fruit flavor

Sometimes Cabernet Sauvignon

"Super Tuscans"— not a region but an important category	Usually a blend of Sangiovese and Cabernet Sauvignon	Modeled to be a classy cross between French red Bordeaux and Italian Chianti; usually full, spicy, and intense, with deep plum and berry flavors

The bottom line on restaurant wine lists: In my opinion, it's not the size of the list that matters but rather the restaurant's effort to make enjoying wine as easy as possible for its guests. How? As always, it comes down to the basics:

Top Ten Tip-Offs You're in a Wine-Wise Restaurant

1. You're *never* made to feel you have to spend a lot to get something good.

2. Wine by the glass is taken as seriously as bottles, with a good range of styles and prices, listed prominently so you don't have to "hunt" to find them.

3. The wine list is presented automatically, so you don't have to ask for it (and wait while the waiter searches for a copy).

4. There are lots of quality bottle choices in the moderate price zone.

5. Wine service, whether glass or bottle, is helpful, speedy, and proficient.

6. Waiters draw your attention to "great values" rather than just the expensive stuff.

7. *Affordable* wine pairings are offered for the signature dishes—either on the menu or by servers.

8. You can ask for a taste before you choose a wine by the glass if you're not sure which you want.

9. It's no problem to split a glass, or get just a half-glass, of by-the-glass offerings. (Great for situations when you want only a little wine or want to try a range of different wines.)

10. There's no such thing as no-name "house white and red." (House-featured wines are fine, but they, and you, merit a name or grape and a region.)

BEST WINE BETS FOR EVERY OCCASION

Best "House" Wines for Every Day

(*House* means *your* house.) These are great go-to wines to keep around for every day and company, too, because they're tasty, *very* inexpensive, and go with everything from takeout to Sunday dinner. They're also wines that got high Kitchen Survivor™ grades, so you don't have to worry if you don't finish the bottle right away. (Selections are listed by body style—lightest to fullest.)

House Sparkling
Segura Viudas Aria Cava Brut Sparkling, Spain
Domaine Ste. Michelle Brut Sparkling, Washington

House Whites
Robert Mondavi Private Selection Riesling, California
Veramonte Sauvignon Blanc, Chile
McWilliam's Hanwood Chardonnay, Australia
Sebastiani Sonoma County Chardonnay, California

House Reds
Castle Rock Pinot Noir, California
Chapoutier Cotes-du-Rhone Belleruche, France
Borsao Tinto Garnacha/Tempranillo, Spain
Rosemount Diamond Label Shiraz/Cabernet, Australia
Columbia Crest Grand Estates Merlot, Washington
Falesco Vitiano Rosso, Italy

Impress the Date—Hip Wines
White
Pacific Rim Riesling, USA/Germany
Frog's Leap Sauvignon Blanc, California
Monkey Bay Sauvignon Blanc, New Zealand
Hirsch Gruner-Veltliner #1, Austria
Kali Hart Chardonnay, California

Red

Mark West Pinot Noir, Oregon

Joel Gott Zinfandel, California

Baron Philippe de Rothschild, Escudo Rojo Cabernet Blend, Chile

Catena Alta Malbec, Argentina

D'Arenberg The Footbolt Shiraz, Australia

Impress the Client—Blue Chip Wines

Sparkling/White

Taittinger Brut La Francaise Champagne, France

Matanzas Creek Sauvignon Blanc, California

Grgich Hills Chardonnay, California

Conundrum, California

Sonoma-Cutrer Russian River Ranches Chardonnay, California

Talbott (Robert) Sleepy Hollow Vineyard Chardonnay, California

Red

Etude Carneros Pinot Noir, California

Domaine Drouhin Willamette Valley Pinot Noir, Oregon

Duckhorn Napa Merlot, California

Ridge Geyserville (Zinfandel), California

BV Tapestry Reserve Cabernet blend, California

Heitz Cellars Napa Cabernet Sauvignon, California

You're Invited—Unimpeachable Bottles to Bring to Dinner

(You *do* still have to send a note the next day.)

Trimbach Riesling, Alsace, France

Robert Mondavi Napa Fume Blanc, California

Joseph Drouhin Pouilly-Fuisse, France

Chalk Hill Chardonnay, California

Calera Central Coast Pinot Noir, California

Ruffino Chianti Classico Riserva Ducale Gold Label, Italy

Penfolds Bin 389 Cabernet Sauvignon/Shiraz, Australia

St Clement Napa Cabernet Sauvignon, California

Mt. Veeder Napa Cabernet Sauvignon, California

Affordable Agers

Like many wine geeks, my husband John and I especially like wines with bottle age. For certain wines, a little bottle age or even a lot brings in flavors that simply can't exist in a young wine. For reds, that's often flavors of leather and mushrooms; for whites it's often a nutty-toasty, caramelized flavor. For both, the overall wine becomes more subtle and more complex at the same time. For me, there's nothing like a great wine with the right amount of bottle age.

Like many parents, we want to buy some wine to commemorate the birth year of our children, to hopefully share with them when they reach the legal age. The problem is that the best-known wines for reliable aging are often very expensive. So to help solve that problem, we have put together our list of "affordable agers." Of course, what is "affordable" depends on the person, and since there are so few wines that age well below $20, we have come up with three ager categories:

> Affordable agers - Wines under $50 that age gracefully
>
> Splurge-worthy agers - Wines between $50 and $150 that age well
>
> The Big Guns - Elite, classic wines over $150 that age well, and typically appreciate in value, with age (Chateau Latour, Romanee-Conti, Harlan Estate, etc.)

Below is a selection of the most broadly available bottles from this year's list. We taste aged wine as often as we can, and will update this section of the book every year. (The complete list, including The Big Guns and the latest updates, is on my Web site.)

Note that we have included some "agers" for medium-term cellaring, because we like to put bottles aside to mark annual milestones like anniversaries and birthdays. When appropriate I have indicated the number of years the wine will age gracefully if stored in reasonably cool cellar conditions.

Region	Affordable Agers*	Splurge-worthy Agers
Bordeaux red* Graves	Domaine de Chevalier, Cantemerle Cantenac-Brown	Smith-Haut-Lafitte
Margaux Pauillac St. Julien	Clerc-Milon Lagrange, Gruaud-Larose, Talbot	Palmer, d'Issan Lynch-Bages Leoville-Barton
Ste. Estephe St. Emilion	Simard Ormes de Pez	Calon Segur Figeac, Clos Fourtet La Lagune
Rhone red	Alain Graillot Crozes-Hermitage	Guigal Cote-Rotie Brune et Blonde, Chapoutier Hermitage
Burgundy Red (7-10 yr)	Sauzet Savigny-Les-Beaune, Faiveley Mercurey	LeClerc Gevrey-Chambertin, Engel Nuits St. Georges
Burgundy White (5-7 yr)	Chablis 1er Cru/ Grand Cru (Laroche, Louis Moreau)	Domaine Leflaive Puligny-Montrachet
California Cabernet Sauvignon	Mt. Veeder, Robert Mondavi Napa, St. Clement	Mondavi Reserve, Ridge Montebello, Grgich Hills Estate, Beringer Private Reserve, BV Georges de Latour
Pinot Noir (7-10 yr)	Etude, Lynmar	Williams-Selyem, Rochioli, Calera (single vineyards)
Chardonnay (6-8 yr)	Chalk Hill, Chalone, Franciscan Cuvee Sauvage	Kistler, Hanzell, Williams-Selyem
Oregon Pinot Noir (7-10 yr)	Cristom, Sokol-Blosser	Domaine Drouhin Oregon
Italy (8-12 yr)	Frescobaldi Chianti Rufina Riserva	Solengo, Badia a Coltibuono Sangioveto
Australia	Penfolds Bin 389 Cabernet-Shiraz, Penfolds St. Henri	Leeuwin Cabernet Sauvignon
Spain	La Rioja Alta Gran Reserva, Teofilo Reyes Ribera del Duero	Torre Muga Rioja, Lopez de Heredia Rioja

*The great chateaus of Bordeaux are an expensive category; as such we have defined "affordable" as under $100.

Cuisine Complements

Whether you're dining out, ordering in, or whipping it up yourself, the following wine recommendations will help you choose a wine to flatter the food in question. If your store doesn't carry that specific wine bottle, ask for a similar selection.

Thanksgiving Wines

More than any other meal, the traditional Thanksgiving lineup features a pretty far-flung range of flavors—from gooey-sweet yams to spicy stuffing to tangy cranberry sauce and everything in between. These wines are like a group hug for all the flavors at the table and the guests around it. My tip: choose a white and a red, put them on the table, and let the diners taste and help themselves to whichever they care to drink. (Selections are listed by body style—lightest to fullest.)

	White	Red
STEAL	Cavit Pinot Grigio, Italy	Louis Jadot Beaujolais-Villages, France
	Pacific Rim Riesling (USA/Germany)	Falesco Vitiano, Italy
	Kendall-Jackson Sauvignon Blanc, California	Castle Rock Pinot Noir, California
	Pierre Sparr Alsace-One, France	Chapoutier Cotes-du-Rhone, France
	Chateau Ste. Michelle Gewurztraminer, Washington	El Coto Rioja, Spain
	McWilliam's Hanwood Chardonnay, Australia	Cline Zinfandel, California
		Wolf Blass Yellow Label Shiraz, Australia
SPLURGE	Maso Canali Pinot Grigio, Italy	J Vineyards Russian River Pinot Noir, California
	Trimbach Riesling, France	Chateau de Beaucastel Chateauneuf-du-Pape, France
	Robert Mondavi To-Ka-Lon Reserve Fume Blanc, California	Penfolds Bin 389 Cabernet Sauvignon/Shiraz, Australia
	Avanthia Godello, Spain	Teofilo Reyes Ribera del Duero, Spain
	Mer Soleil Chardonnay, California	Catena Alta Malbec, Argentina

Barbecue

Bodegas Ochoa Rosado (rose), Spain
Dry Creek Fume Blanc, California
Jacob's Creek Shiraz/Cabernet, Australia
Hill of Content Grenache/Shiraz, Australia
Jaboulet Parallele 45 Cotes-du-Rhone, France
Ravenswood Old Vines Sonoma County Zinfandel,
  California

Chinese Food

Saint M Riesling, Germany
Jolivet Sancerre, France
Ca' del Solo Muscat, California
Hogue Gewurztraminer, Washington
Castle Rock Pinot Noir, California
Palacios Remondo La Vendimia Rioja, Spain
Ravenswood Vintner's Blend Zinfandel, California
Duboeuf (Georges) Beaujolais-Villages, France

Nuevo Latino (Cuban, Caribbean, South American)

Codorniu Cava Rose, Spain
Woodbridge Pinot Grigio, California
Burgans Albarino, Spain
Crios Torrontes, Argentina
Kaiken Ultra Malbec, Argentina
MontGras Carmenere Reserva, Chile
DeLoach Heritage Zinfandel, California

Picnics (all screw-caps)

Pierre Sparr Alsace-One, France
Tilia Torrontes, Argentina
Bonny Doon Vin Gris Pink Wine, California
Kim Crawford Chardonnay, New Zealand
La Vieille Ferme Cote de Ventoux red, France
A to Z Pinot Noir, Oregon

Sushi

Moët & Chandon White Star Champagne, France
Eroica Riesling, Washington
Martin Codax Albarino, Spain
Silverado Sauvignon Blanc, California
Schloss Gobelsburg Gruner-Veltliner, Austria
Joseph Drouhin La Foret Bourgogne, France
Calera Central Coast Pinot Noir, California

Clambake/Lobster Bake
Chalk Hill Sauvignon Blanc, California
Beringer Napa Chardonnay, California
Cambria Katherine's Vineyard Chardonnay, California
Miner Family Viognier, California
Duboeuf Moulin-a-Vent Beaujolais, France
Erath Pinot Noir, Oregon

Mexican Food
Pierre Sparr Alsace-One, France
Veramonte Sauvignon Blanc, Chile
Hugel Gewurztraminer, France
Beringer White Zinfandel, California
Miner Family Sangiovese, California
Cline Syrah, California
Wolf-Blass Yellow Label Shiraz, Australia

Pizza
Citra Montepulciano d'Abruzzo, Italy
Palacios Remondo La Vendimia Rioja, Spain
D'Arenberg The Footbolt Shiraz, Australia
Morgante Nero d'Avola, Italy
Woodbridge (Robert Mondavi) Zinfandel, California

The Cheese Course
Frescobaldi Nipozzano Chianti Rufina Riserva, Italy
Penfolds Bin 389 Cabernet Sauvignon/Shiraz, Australia
Chateau de Beaucastel Chateauneuf-du-Pape, France
Baron de Ley Rioja Gran Reserva, Spain
Taurino Salice Salentino Rosso Riserva, Italy
Pesquera Ribera del Duero, Spain
Rosemount GSM (Grenache-Shiraz-Mourvedre), Australia
Grgich Hills Napa Zinfandel, California
Mt. Veeder Napa Cabernet Sauvignon, California
Chateau Gruaud-Larose Bordeaux, France
Val di Suga Brunello di Montalcino, Italy

Steak
Chalk Hill Chardonnay, California
Leeuwin Art Series Chardonnay, Australia
J Vineyards Russian River Pinot Noir, California

Ruffino Chianti Classico Riserva Ducale Gold Label, Italy
Marchesi di Gresy Barbaresco, Italy
Shafer Merlot, California
BV Rutherford Cabernet Sauvignon, California
Beringer Knights Valley Cabernet Sauvignon, California
Robert Mondavi Cabernet Sauvignon Reserve, California
Groth Napa Cabernet Sauvignon, California
Frank Family Napa Cabernet Sauvignon, California
St. Clement Napa Cabernet Sauvignon, California
Louis Martini Gnarly Vines Zinfandel, California

Salad
Santa Cristina Orvieto, Italy
Hugel Pinot Blanc, France
Leitz Dragonstone Riesling, Germany
Louis Jadot Pouilly-Fuisse, France
Saintsbury Garnet Pinot Noir
Erath Pinot Noir, Oregon

Vegetarian
Gallo Family Vineyards Reserve Pinot Gris, California
Kim Crawford Chardonnay, New Zealand
Au Bon Climat Santa Barbara Pinot Noir, California
Castello di Gabbiano Chianti, Italy
Jaboulet Parallele 45 Cotes-du-Rhone, France
Val di Suga Rosso di Montalcino, Italy

ENTERTAINING WITH WINE

In my experience, people stress a lot about the wine aspect of entertaining—what to choose, how much to buy, and serving savvy. *Relax*, because the wine part is easy. There's no prep involved other than popping the cork, and wine can really make a gathering memorable. Here are my top ten tips for pulling it off with ease.

1. Set your budget to fit the occasion, and your comfort zone. At large or casual gatherings, any wine in this book with the crowd pleaser symbol ☺ will do you proud. For a dinner party with a special menu or a guest of honor, it's nice to trade up a little, and theme your choices to the dishes on the menu.

2. Serve one white and one red (at least). Even if your party menu is geared to a particular wine style (e.g., a burger bash & red wine), offer the other color, too, for those guests who strongly prefer it.

3. Offer a unique aperitif. Champagne is the classic aperitif (pre-dinner pour, usually with hors d'oeuvres), but you don't have to go with something expensive. Prosecco and Spanish cava are worthy budget bubblies. Rose wines and lighter whites like Riesling and Pinot Grigio also make great aperitifs.

4. Serve white before red, light before heavy, dry before sweet. For both wine and food, the fullest and sweetest flavors get served last, so they don't overpower the lighter dishes and wines.

5. Open the wines ahead of time. As long as you re-cork and keep them cool, the wines will taste great and you won't have last-minute stress.

6. An all-purpose glass is fine. Unless you are having a serious wine gathering, you don't need lots of different wine glasses. A good-quality glass with an ample bowl and thin rim will showcase most wines nicely.

7. Give guests a printout of the wines. A printed menu with the wine names is a nice touch, so guests can remember the names of the wines they enjoyed.

8. Don't fill glasses to the top. Pros leave plenty of head space in the glass for swirling the wine, which enhances the aromas. Many good wine glasses are designed so that a 5-6 ounce standard pour reaches the widest part of the bowl. At cocktail parties and wine tastings I go with smaller pours of 2-3 ounces, so guests have the opportunity to try different tastes, and then pour more of what they like best.

9. Calculate how much wine you will need. Each standard (750 ml) wine bottle contains about five 5-ounce glasses of wine. For a dinner party plan on consumption of about 2-3 glasses per guest. Multiply that times the number of guests, then divide by 5 to determine the number of bottles needed. For a cocktail party where you are only serving wine, estimate consumption of 1 1/2 per glasses per guest for the first hour, and 1 glass per guest for each hour after that. Divide the total number of glasses you think your guests will drink by five to determine the number of bottles needed. If a full bar is available at the cocktail party, figure that one-third of your guests will drink wine and then make the above calculations. A good rule of thumb is to assume guests will consume 60% white wine, and 40% red. Always have water and other nonalcoholic drinks available, too. For a bubbly toast, buy one bottle for every eight guests.

10. Host the easiest wine tasting cocktail party ever. Serve one selection from each of the Big Six grapes paired with a simple appetizer (e.g., Riesling & egg rolls, Sauvignon Blanc and goat cheese, Chardonnay and popcorn, Pinot Noir and stuffed mushrooms, Cab/Merlot and pesto bruschetta, Syrah/Shiraz and barbecued ribs. Arrange the paired wines and appetizers next to each other, buffet style. Give each guest a wine glass and menu/note sheet, and let them enjoy tasting their way through the different combos It's a blast!

FOOD & WINE PAIRING BASICS

Whether you are a wary wine novice or a certified wine geek, "What wine should I drink with...?" is a constant question. Why? I think it is simply that those of us who enjoy wine love food even more. And we intuitively sense the possibilities to enhance what we're eating by pairing it with wine.

 But a lot of people think that getting it "right" when it comes to pairing takes a big budget and a lot of wine knowledge. Far from it. Isn't it true that in Europe, the simplest of country lunches and bistro suppers, with wine, are often among the most memorable meals?

Back home, wine can transform your everyday dinners. Whether it's takeout, leftovers, or your best kitchen creation, you can just pour a glass of whatever wine you have handy and as long as it's one you like, you're bound to enjoy the match. That said, a well-chosen match can take the experience from nice, to knock-your-socks-off. To see for yourself, try some of my simple pairing pointers. They're a lot of fun and no hassle, so you won't need to wait for a special occasion to try them. In fact that's the whole point: everyday dinner *is* the occasion. Here's to making the most of it!

Pairing Basics

When I started as a sommelier, the pairing rule was "red wine with red meat, and white wine with fish." And in those days red wine meant Cabernet Sauvignon and Merlot, and white wine meant Chardonnay. "Meat" was beef, and fish was flounder or sole. Then along came...Malbec, and Shiraz, Pinot Noir, Riesling, Pinot Grigio...and a host of global grapes whose varied styles and flavors invited all kinds of new foods to the wine lover's table. Salmon and shrimp morphed from "special-occasion" to staple, pork and lamb gained new prominence, and exotic techniques and seasonings like stir frying, smoking, Asian accents, and southwestern salsas evolved into simply everyday fare. Since then I've had a ball playing matchmaker for all of these grapes and food flavors. And like any good couple, the best matches are based on either complement or contrast.

Complement simply means linking up common traits. For wine and food, that can mean matching body or flavors: if the wine and food are on a par, neither gets overpowered and the character of each can shine. For contrasting matches, pairing disparate flavors in the food and the wine can showcase the complexity of each. For example, a slightly sweet or tangy wine with a spicy-hot dish gives the palate a reprieve from the heat, priming your mouth for the next tasty forkful. A rich, creamy or buttery dish can find new balance and flavor complexity when paired with a crisp, tangy wine to cut through the heaviness and showcase the flavor layers. Here are some specific ways to put these ideas into practice.

Pairing Principles for White Wines...

When it comes to complementing matches, I focus on the body of the wine and the dish. Simply put, that means light-bodied whites with light-bodied dishes, and fuller-bodied whites with heavy or rich dishes. For example, the best wines for crisp salads are the light and crisp ones, particularly Pinot Grigio and Sauvignon Blanc. Richer salads such as Caesar or tuna fish call for a richer white like Chardonnay. In the same vein, lighter cheeses like goat and feta love a sparkling wine or Sauvignon Blanc. Heavier cheeses such as Parmigiano Reggiano or aged cheddar, match marvelously with a rich Chardonnay or Viognier. For seafood dishes think about the body of both the core fish or seafood, and the heaviness of the preparation. For example, lighter Asian stir-fry preparation I'd match a crisp white; with a cream sauce or buttery dish (like Shrimp Scampi), I'd go with a richer white. On that note, generally the tangy/gingery/sweet flavors of Asian-accented dishes are well-suited to white wines with vibrant acidity, and even a touch of sweetness (think Riesling, and Sauvignon Blancs from New Zealand). This point can illustrate either complement (tangy dish with tangy wine) or contrast (spicy-hot dish with sweet wine). And what about meat with whites? As a sommelier I've even served big Chardonnays to my guests ordering steak, pork and game. Remember, no matter what the pairing rule book says, the most important rule of all is: drink what you like.

...and for Red Wines

For red wines, again body is the basis for complementing matches. For example, a big Napa Valley Cab or Italian Super Tuscan red stands up to a big steak or a rich cheese like Parmigiano Reggiano or Camembert, but a delicate Pinot Noir or Beaujolais (based on the Gamay grape) is better suited to lighter grilled salmon, pork or chicken, and to goat cheeses. Beyond body, it's fun to also explore some complementing flavor matches for red wines. For example, the peppery spice of an Aussie Shiraz is the perfect flavor compliment to spicy dishes like barbecue or steak au poivre. Earthy wines such as Italian Chianti, Spanish Rioja, or Oregon or French Pinot Noir wines, are a great complement to earthy dishes based on mushrooms, grains such as barley and polenta, or legumes like lentils and chickpeas.

For contrasting matches, both tangy and tannic qualities in red wine can cut through richness in food. For example, tangy Chianti with cheesy tortellini, or tannic red Bordeaux with richly-marbled steak or prime rib, are great matches. Herbal flavors such as basil pesto, or a rosemary crust for lamb, make a fabulous contrast with the rich blackberry compote fruit flavors of Californian, Chilean and Washington Cabernets and Merlots. And finally, the ultimate contrasting match for me is a big, fruity red wine such as California Syrah, with dark chocolate.

When you put these opposites together, they bring out the best in each other. And that's really the whole point of pairing wine and food anyway.

ANDREA'S TOP
BUDGET WINES *

Best Whites and Reds
$15 and under

Name	Score	Price
Top 20 Budget Whites		
Saint M Riesling, Germany 2008	89	12
Sebastiani Chardonnay, Sonoma 2007	89	13
Beringer Dry Riesling, Napa 2008	89	14
Casa Lapostolle Cuvee Alexandre Chardonnay, Chile 2007	89	14
Kendall-Jackson Vintner's Reserve Chardonnay, California 2008	89	14
Crios Torrontes, Argentina 2008	89	14
Bastianich Tocai Friulano, Italy 20008	89	15
Veramonte Sauvignon Blanc, Chile 2008	88	12
J. Lohr Riverstone Chardonnay, California 2007	88	14
Pierre Sparr Riesling, Alsace 2007	87	9
Tilia Torrontes, Argentina 2008	87	10
Brancott Sauvignon Blanc, New Zealand 2008	87	11
Monkey Bay Sauvignon Blanc, New Zealand 2008	87	11
Haras Estate Sauvignon Blanc, Chile 2008	87	12
Kendall-Jackson Vintner's Reserve Sauvignon Blanc, California 2008	87	12
Murphy-Goode The Fume Sauvignon, Blanc, California 2008	87	12
McWilliam's Hanwood Chardonnay, Australia 2007	87	12
Oberon Sauvignon Blanc, Napa 2007	87	13
Flora Springs Pinot Grigio, California 2008	87	14
Walter Glatzer Gruner-Veltliner, Austria 2007	87	14

Name	Score	Price
Top 20 Budget Reds		
Deloach Heritage Zinfandel, California 2007	90	12
Falesco Vitiano, Umbria, Italy 2007	89	12
Chapoutier Cotes-du-Rhone Belleruche, Rhone, France 2007	89	13
Wolf-Blass Yellow Label Shiraz, Australia 2007	89	13
Abadia Retuerta Rivola, Spain 2006	89	14
Ravenswood Old Vine Zinfandel, Sonoma 2007	89	15
Taurino Salice Salentino Rosso Riserva, Italy 2007	88	12
Kaiken Ultra Malbec, Argentina 2007	88	12
Castle Rock Pinot Noir, Mendocino 2007	88	14
Chateau Ste. Michelle Merlot, Columbia Valley 2006	88	14
MontGras Carmenere Reserva, Chile 2007	88	14
El Coto de Imaz Rioja Reserva, Spain 2004	88	15
Jacob's Creek Shiraz-Cabernet, Australia	87	8
Rosemount Diamond Label Shiraz-Cabernet, Australia 2007	87	8
Sterling Vintners Collection Shiraz, California 2007	87	10
Wente Syrah, Livermore, California 2007	87	10
Robert Mondavi Private Selection Pinot Noir, California 2007	87	11
Jacob's Creek Reserve Cabernet Sauvignon, Australia 2007	87	12
Bogle Petite Sirah, California 2007	87	12
Navarro Correas Malbec, Argentina 2007	87	13

THE BENCHMARKS
OF WINE

These are the elite - the wines that "matter" to collectors, and to sommeliers in the finest restaurants. I believe they also matter "for everyone" because they are universally recognized as the quality and style leaders in their categories. While I included in my tasting notes a few favorites from this list that I had gotten the chance to try recently, for the most part even I can count the number of times I have tasted these wines on one hand. What makes them so special and expensive is typically a combination of both a like-no-other vineyard site, and a particularly skilled maker. As I said in the introduction, these are wines about which you can fantasize until your lottery ticket pays off. Or, do as some of my wine club members do: save up your money, and go in together with friends to split the cost of a rare bottle, and share the tasting experience.

Champagne/Sparkling—
  Krug Clos de Mesnil Champagne
  Salon Champagne
  Veuve Clicquot La Grande Dame Champagne

Riesling—
  Trimbach Clos Ste. Hune

Sauvignon Blanc—
  Dagueneau Pouilly-Fume
  Chateau Haut-Brion Blanc
  Chateau Laville Haut-Brion
  Chateau Smith-Haut-Lafitte
  Domaine de Chevalier Blanc
  Gaja Alteni di Brassica Sauvignon
  Sanct Valentin Sauvignon Blanc
  Tement Sauvignon Blanc
  Vie de Romans Sauvignon Blanc

Chardonnay—
  Coche-Dury Meursault
  Dauvissat Chablis
  Domaine de la Romanee-Conti Le Montrachet
  Domaine Leflaive Puligny-Montrachet Pucelles
  Gaja Gaia & Rey Chardonnay
  Henri Germain Meursault

Jermann Dreams
Joseph Drouhin Beaune Clos des Mouches &
    Montrachet Marquis de Laguiche
Kistler Chardonnay
Kongsgaard Chardonnay
Louis Latour Corton-Charlemagne
Marcassin Chardonnay
Patrick Javillier Meursault
Peter Michael Chardonnay
Ramey Chardonnay
Ramonet Le Montrachet & Meursault
Raveneau Chablis
Sauzet Batard-Montrachet
Staglin Family Vineyard Chardonnay

Other Whites—
Calera Mt. Harlan Viognier
Chateau Grillet (Viognier)
Clos de la Coulee de Serrant (Chenin Blanc)
Granges des Peres (Rhone varietals)
Guigal La Doriane Condrieu (Viognier)
Jermann Vintage Tunina (Italian blend)
Yves Cuilleron Condrieu (Viognier)

Pinot Noir—
Armand Rousseau red Burgundies (any)
Comte Armand Pommard
Comte de Vogue Musigny
Domaine de Courcel Pommard
Domaine de la Romanee-Conti red Burgundies (any)
Domaine Dujac Clos St. Denis & Bonnes-Mares
Domaine Roumier red Burgundies
Domaine Leroy red Burgundies (any)
Dugat Charmes-Chambertin
Faiveley Corton Clos des Corton
Joseph Roty Charmes-Chambertin
Kistler Pinot Noir
Kosta-Browne Pinot Noir
Marquis d'Angerville Volnays
Mongeard-Mugneret Clos de Vougeot
Ponsot Clos de la Roche
Roumier Bonnes Mares & Morey St. Denis
Williams-Selyem Pinot Noirs

Merlot/Cabernet Franc—
Castello di Ama L'Apparita
Chateau Ausone
Chateau Angelus
Chateau Canon
Chateau Cheval-Blanc
Chateau Clinet
Chateau Clos des Jacobins
Chateau Figeac
Chateau Gazin
Chateau La Conseillante

Chateau La Croix de Gay
Chateau La Fleur Petrus
Chateau Le Gay
Chateau L'Eglise-Clinet
Chateau Le Pin
Chateau L'Evangile
Chateau Pavie
Chateau Petrus
Chateau Troplong-Mondot
Chateau Trotanoy
Chateau Valandraud
Clos Fourtet
Falesco Montiano
Leonetti Cellar Merlot
Masseto
Pahlmeyer Merlot
Vieux Chateau Certan
Woodward Canyon Artist Series Merlot

Cabernet Sauvignon—
Abreu Madrona Ranch
Araujo Eisele Vineyard
Bond
Bryant Family
Chateau Beychevelle
Chateau Brane-Cantenac
Chateau Calon-Segur
Chateau Cantemerle
Chateau Cantenac-Brown
Chateau Ducru-Beaucaillou
Chateau Giscours
Chateau Haut-Brion
Chateau Lafite-Rothschild
Chateau La Mission-Haut-Brion
Chateau Latour
Chateau Leoville-Barton
Chateau Leoville-Las-Cases
Chateau Leoville-Poyferre
Chateau Montrose
Chateau Mouton-Rothschild
Chateau Palmer
Chateau Pichon-Longueville Comtesse de Lalande
Chateau Pichon-Longueville Baron
Chateau Pontet-Canet
Chateau Rausan-Segla
Chateau Talbot
Colgin Cellars
Clos Apalta
Dalla Valle
David Arthur
Delille Cellars
Gargiulo GMajor7
Grace Family Vineyard
Harlan Estate

Heitz Martha's Vineyard
Hestan
Hundred Acre
Joseph Phelps Insignia
Karl Lawrence
La Mondotte
Leeuwin Estate Art Series
Leonetti Cellar
Lokoya
Nicolas Catena Zapata
Nickel & Nickel
Ornellaia
Penfolds Bin 707
Ridge Montebello
Sassicaia
Screaming Eagle
Shafer Hillside Select
Staglin Family Vineyard
Stag's Leap Wine Cellars Cask 23, SLV & Fay
Viader
Woodward Canyon Artist Series

Syrah/Shiraz/Rhone-style—
Chapoutier L'Ermitage
Chateau Fortia
Chateau Rayas
Chave Hermitage
Clarendon Hills Astralis
D'Arenberg The Dead Arm
Grange des Peres
Guigal Cote-Roties (La Mouline, La Landonne, La
    Turque)
Henschke Hill of Grace
Jaboulet Hermitage La Chapelle
Jim Barry The Armagh
Penfolds Grange

Italian Reds—
Tuscany
Biondi-Santi Brunello di Montalcino
Ca' Marcanda Brunello di Montalcino
Guado al Tasso
Solaia
Solengo
Tenuta Sette Ponti Oreno
Tignanello
Piedmont
Aldo Conterno Barolos
Domenico Clerico Barolos
Elio Altare Barolos
Gaja Barbarescos
Giacosa Barbarescos
Sandrone Barolos
Scavino Barolos

Vietti Barolos
Other
Arnaldo Caprai Sagrantino di Montefalco
Dal Forno Romano Amarone
Giuseppe Quintarelli Veneto reds

Spanish Reds—
Amancio Rioja
Clos de L'Obac Priorat
Clos Erasmus Priorat
Clos Mogador Priorat
Finca Allende Calvario Rioja
Finca El Bosque Rioja (Sierra Cantabria)
Mas de Masos Priorat
Muga Aro Rioja
Numanthia Toro
Pesquera Janus Ribera del Duero
Teofilo Reyes Ribera del Duero
Torres Mas La Plana
Vega Sicilia Ribera del Duero

Other Reds—
Turley Zinfandels
Sine Qua Non reds

Dessert Wines—
Beringer Nightingale Botrytis Semillon
Chateau d'Yquem
Dolce by Far Niente
Fonseca Vintage Port
Quinta do Noval Nacional Port
Taylor-Fladgate Vintage Port

THE RISING STARS
OF WINE

Part of the job of a sommelier is the equivalent of a scout in sports - we are looking for the emerging talent in wine. I have listed here some of the wineries to watch - my opinion, of course, based on my early tastings and research. Some of the names are brand-new on the scene. Others may have been around awhile but are in my view newly noteworthy. My criterion for this is simply: in terms of quality, they have begun to stand out among their established, talented peers. They are well worth checking out because, like a farm club slugger on a hot streak, they stand with the big boys (of wine), but often for a much cheaper price. Watch this space: In future editions of the guide, I'll keep you up to speed on the wine world's newest noteworthy names.

Old World—Anywhere in Europe.

Bastianich, Italy—Stunning regional Italian whites & reds from Friuli, Tuscany and Piedmont

Inama, Veneto, Italy—Soave (honest!) and Sauv Blanc

Luigi Collavini, Friuli, Italy—Breathtaking whites

Remirez de Ganuza, Rioja, Spain—Stunning red and like-no-other white

New World—The rest.

Cliff Lede Cellars - Bordeaux-style blends and a like-no-other Sauvignon Blanc

Delille Cellars - Washington - Amazing Bordeaux-style whites and reds

DeSante, Napa, CA—As-good-as-the-cults Oakville Cabs and a really special Sauvignon Blanc

Detert Family Cellars, Napa, CA—Oakville Cabs

Furthermore Wines - Amazing Burgundian-style Pinots from the top PN zones in California

Gordon Brothers, Columbia Valley, WA—Cab blends.

J. Bookwalter, Washington - Outstanding Cabernet

Koehler Cellars, Santa Barbara, CA—Smokin' Viognier.

Pfendler, Sonoma Coast, CA—Estate Pinot & Chard.

Rocca Family, Napa, CA - Awesome Cabernet

Sequana, Russian River, CA—Single vineyard Pinots..

Thomas Winery, Oregon—Very Burgundian Pinot

Tres Sabores, Napa, CA—Fantastic, organically grown Zin & Cab blends from Napa muse Julie Johnson.

WINERY INDEX

Cuvee Alexandre Chardonnay   55
Cuvee Alexandre Merlot   110
Sauvignon Blanc   39

Castelgiocondo (Frescobaldi), Italy
Brunello di Montalcino   99

Castellare di Castellina, Italy
Chianti Classico   99
Chianti Classico Riserva   99

Castello Banfi, Italy
Brachetto d'Acqui   170
Brunello di Montalcino   100
Chianti Classico Riserva   100
Cum Laude Super Tuscan   100

Castello di Gabbiano, Italy
Alleanza   100
Chianti Classico   100
Chianti Classico Riserva   101
Pinot Grigio   26

Castello di Volpaia, Italy
Chianti Classico Riserva   101

Castle Rock, California
Pinot Noir Mendocino   86

Catena, Argentina
Alta Chardonnay   55
Alta Malbec   149

Cavit, Italy
Pinot Grigio   26

Caymus, California
Napa Cabernet Sauvignon   122

Ceretto, Italy
Arneis Blange   73
Asij Barbaresco   101
Zonchera Barolo   101

Chalk Hill, California
Estate Botrytis Semillon   170
Estate Cabernet Sauvignon   122
Estate Chardonnay   55
Estate Sauvignon Blanc   40

Chalone, California
Estate Chardonnay   55
Estate Pinot Noir   86
Estate Syrah   154
Monterey Chardonnay   56

Chambers, Australia
Rosewood Vineyards Rutherglen Muscadelle   170

Chateau Meyney, France
Bordeaux 125

Chateau Montelena, California
Chardonnay 56

Chateau Ste. Michelle, Washington
Canoe Ridge Estate Cabernet Sauvignon 125
Canoe Ridge Estate Merlot 110
Columbia Valley Cabernet Sauvignon 125
Columbia Valley Chardonnay 56
Columbia Valley Dry Riesling 32
Columbia Valley Gewurztraminer 73
Columbia Valley Merlot 110
Columbia Valley Sauvignon Blanc 40
Reserve Late Harvest Riesling 170

Chateau St. Jean, California
Cinq Cepages Cabernet Blend 126
Fume Blanc 40
Gewurztraminer 73
Robert Young Chardonnay 57
Sonoma Cabernet Sauvignon 126
Sonoma Chardonnay 57
Sonoma Merlot 110
Sonoma Pinot Noir 87

Chimney Rock, California
Fume Blanc 40

Citra, Italy
Montepulciano d'Abruzzo 101

Clean Slate, Germany
Riesling 32

Cline, California
Ancient Vines Mourvedre 150
Cashmere Grenache-Syrah-Mourvedre 150
Syrah 161
Zinfandel 158

Clos du Bois, California
Alexander Valley Reserve Cabernet Sauvignon 126
Marlstone 126
North Coast Chardonnay 57
North Coast Merlot 111
North Coast Pinot Noir 87
Pinot Grigio 26
Sonoma Cabernet Sauvignon 123
Sonoma Reserve Chardonnay 57

Clos du Val, California
Napa Cabernet Sauvignon 127

Cloudy Bay, New Zealand
Sauvignon Blanc 40

Cockburn's, Portugal
Fine Ruby Port 170

Deloach, California
Heritage Zinfandel	162
Russian River Valley Pinot Noir	87
Russian River Valley Zinfandel	162

Domaine Carneros, California
Brut	19
Le Reve	19
Pinot Noir	88

Domaine de Coyeaux, France
Muscat Beaumes de Venise	171

Domaine Drouhin, Oregon
Laurene Dundee Hills Pinot Noir	88
Willamette Valley Pinot Noir	88

Domaine Faiveley, Burgundy, France
Mercurey Clos des Myglands	88

Domaine Leflaive, Burgundy, France
Puligny-Montrachet	58

Domaine Ste. Michelle, Washington
Brut	20

Domaine Tempier, France
Bandol Rose	85

Dom Perignon, Champagne, France
Brut	20

Dr. Loosen, Germany
Blue Slate Riesling Kabinett Estate	33
"Dr. L." Riesling	32

Donnhoff, Germany
Riesling Estate	33

Dow's Colheita, Portugal
Tawny Port 1992	171

Dry Creek Vineyard, California
Chenin Blanc	74
Fume Blanc	41
Old Vine Zinfandel	163

Drylands, New Zealand
Sauvignon Blanc	41

Duboeuf (Georges), France
Beaujolais-Villages	83
Cotes-du-Rhone	155
Moulin-a-Vent	83

Duckhorn, California
Estate Grown Cabernet	128
Napa Merlot	111
Sauvignon Blanc	41
Patzimaro Estate Grown Cabernet	46

E & M Guigal, France
Cote-Rotie Brune et Blonde	151

King Estate, Oregon
Pinot Gris   28
Pinot Noir   90

Krug, France
Grande Cuvee Multivintage   21

Kunde Estate, California
Estate Viognier   76
Magnolia Lane Sauvignon Blanc   45

L'Ecole No. 41, Washington
Walla Walla Valley Merlot   113

La Crema, California
Russian River Valley Chardonnay   62
Sonoma Coast Pinot Noir   90

Ladera, California
Howell Mountain Cabernet Sauvignon   134

Landmark Vineyards, California
Overlook Chardonnay   63

Lang & Reed, California
Premier Etage Cabernet Franc   150

La Rioja Alta, Spain
Vina Ardanza Reserva   146

La Vieille Ferme, France
Cotes du Ventoux red   157

La Vite Lucente, Italy
Super Tuscan   103

Leacock's, Portugal
Rainwater Madeira   173

Leeuwin Estate, Australia
Art Series Chardonnay   63

Leitz, Germany
Dragonstone Riesling   35

Le Volte dell'Ornellaia, Italy
Super Tuscan   103

Leitz, Germany
Dragonstone Riesling   39

Liberty School, California
Cabernet Sauvignon   134

Lindemans, Australia
Bin 50 Shiraz   157
Bin 65 Chardonnay   63
Bin 99 Pinot Noir   90

Livio Felluga, Italy
Pinot Grigio   28

Long Boat, New Zealand
Sauvignon Blanc   45

Robert Sinskey, California
Los Carneros Pinot Noir 93

Rocca delle Macie, Italy
Chianti Classico 106
Occhio a Vento Vermentino 78

Rochioli, California
Russian River Valley Pinot Noir 93

Rodney Strong, California
Charlotte's Home Sauvignon Blanc 48
Knotty Vines Zinfandel 167
Sonoma Cabernet Sauvignon 138
Sonoma Chardonnay 65
Sonoma Merlot 115
Sonoma Zinfandel 166
Symmetry Meritage 138

Roederer Estate, California
Brut NV 24

Rosemount, Australia
Diamond Label Cabernet Sauvignon 138
Diamond Label Chardonnay 65
Diamond Label Pinot Noir 93
Diamond Label Shiraz 159
Diamond Label Shiraz/Cabernet Sauvignon 159
GSM (Grenache-Shiraz-Mourvedre) 159
Roxburgh Chardonnay 66

Rosenblum, California
Vintner's Cuvee Zinfandel 167

Royal Tokaji Wine Company, Hungary
Red Label Tokaji Aszu 174

Rubicon Estate, California
Red Blend 138

Ruffino, Italy
Aziano Chianti 106
Chianti Classico Riserva Ducale Gold Label 106
Lumina Pinot Grigio 29
Orvieto 78

Rust-en-Vrede, South Africa
Estate Red 138

Rutherford Hill, California
Merlot 115

St. Clement, California
Napa Cabernet Sauvignon 139
Napa Merlot 114

St. Francis, California
Old Vines Zinfandel 167
Sonoma Chardonnay 66

Tenuta Sette Ponti, Italy
  Crognolo Super Tuscan   107

Tignanello (Antinori), Italy
  Super Tuscan   107

Toasted Head, California
  Cabernet Sauvignon   137
  Chardonnay   69

Trefethen, California
  Estate Cabernet Sauvignon   142
  Estate Chardonnay   69
  Estate Dry Riesling   37

Trimbach, Alsace, France
  Pinot Gris Reserve   33
  Riesling   37

Twomey, California
  Merlot   117

Val di Suga, Italy
  Brunello di Montalcino   108
  Rosso di Montalcino   108

Val Llach, Spain
  Embruix Priorat   148

Veramonte, Chile
  Cabernet Sauvignon Reserva   143
  Primus   152
  Sauvignon Blanc   50

Viader, California
  Napa Valley Red Blend   143

Voss, California
  Sauvignon Blanc   50

Wairau River, New Zealand
  Sauvignon Blanc   50

Walter Glatzer, Austria
  Gruner-Veltliner Kabinett   79

Warre, Portugal
  10-Year-Old Otima Tawny Port   174

Wente, California
  Riva Ranch Chardonnay   70
  Syrah   160

Whitehaven, New Zealand
  Sauvignon Blanc   95

WillaKenzie, Oregon
  Pinot Gris   29
  Willamette Valley Pinot Noir   95

Willamette Valley Vineyards, Oregon
  Pinot Gris   29

Whole Cluster Pinot Noir	96
Reserve Pinot Noir	96

Williams-Selyem, California
Russian River Valley Pinot Noir	96

Willi Schaefer, Germany
Estate Riesling	37

Wolf Blass, Australia
Yellow Label Chardonnay	70
Yellow Label Shiraz	160

Woodbridge (Robert Mondavi), California
Chardonnay	70
Pinot Grigio	30
Sauvignon Blanc	50
Zinfandel	168

Yellowtail, Australia
Chardonnay	70
Shiraz	160

THANKS TO ...

My husband John Robinson, for his continued inspiration to refine this book to be the best, most helpful guide it can possibly be.

Lion Associates, Mark Lion and Troy Molander, for making this book, and the new Andreawine.com, look & work better than ever.

Publishers Group West, Perseus Books, and the major book retailers, for believing in this book.

DEDICATED TO ...

My husband, John and our amazing kids, Lucas, Jesse and Jack. Your love and laughter every day, are sweeter than the finest wine.

And in loving tribute to the memory of the missing from Windows on the World, where wine really was for everyone.

WHAT'S NEW...

I am excited to introduce my new stemware line, The One™ for whites and the The One™ for reds - the only glasses you will ever need to optimize all wines. They are beautiful, affordable ($49.95 per set of four), break-resistant and lead free. I spent about three years developing the prototype designs and then tasting and testing every style, grape, age and quality level of wine in these stems versus the benchmark glasses. They out-perform them all, even the grape-specific glasses when used with the grape or style of wine for which they are intended.

I have always looked for ways to simplify wine for people, and these glasses solve the problem of having to add a wing to your house, or spend a fortune, to have the right glass for making the most of your wine. I hope you will try them for yourself, and share our feedback. In the front of the book I have included a special promotion code for you to receive a discounted price when you order from International Wine Accessories (www.IWAwine.com). For a video about the glasses and more information, please visit me at www. andreawine.com. I hope that if you try the glasses, you will share your feedback with me. Specifically, I hope you will taste any wine you choose in your favorite glass, and then in my glass. I bet you will be amazed at the difference! I look forward to hearing from you!